THE SPELUNCEA

Making Jurisprudence Seriously Enjoyable

THE SPELUNCEAN CASE:

Making Jurisprudence Seriously Enjoyable

James Allan

Barry Rose Law Publishers Ltd
Chichester

ISBN 1 872328 72 5

Published by
Barry Rose Law Publishers Ltd.
Little London
Chichester
West Sussex

"For Cameron and Bronwyn"

Contents

Section Three

Introduction

Jurisprudence can be fun. Students and non-students alike can enjoy reading and thinking about law at an abstract level. Good theory need not come in the form of jargon-laden impenetrable prose, full of obscurities, ambiguities, rhetoric and all the many other obfuscating sins that plague so many writers today on legal philosophy (and indeed philosophy generally). One can be stimulated to think and wonder about issues fundamental to law, and to democracy and notions like the separation of powers, by texts which are lively, enjoyable and fun. Quite simply, wit and entertainment can go hand in hand with deep reflection on issues which lie at the heart of jurisprudence. These are claims, at any rate, which I hope this book proves to be true.

Lon Fuller's mythical hypothetical, about five cave explorers who become trapped after a landslide and ultimately kill and eat one of their own in order to survive long enough to be rescued, is the speluncean case to which this book's title refers. Fuller gives the reader five fictional judgments from the Supreme Court of a place he calls Newgarth. He sets the action and judgments far in the future in the year 4300 AD. Each judgment adopts a different perspective on the proper approach to statutory interpretation and on what it is and is not legitimate for judges to do in a democracy.

Students love to read this mythical hypothetical Fuller called "The Case of the Speluncean Explorers". The facts are riveting. The legal and moral considerations are distinct enough to raise all sorts of questions about the relation between law and morality. Readers often *want* to go back and read sections or judgments or the whole article again (which, when it comes to students, is a startling, or at least remarkable, accomplishment). And each new reading often leads the reader to change his or her mind about which judgment is most persuasive. Fuller's speluncean case article is simply a great introduction to the subject and study of jurisprudence (or legal theory as it is known to many non-Americans).

This book is prompted by Fuller's famous article. It gathers together the very best articles which that speluncean case hypothetical, written half a century ago, has inspired. Section One of the book starts with "The Case Of The Speluncean Explorers" itself. Then there are two other mythical hypotheticals which are based directly on the facts of Fuller's original. One is Anthony D'Amato's "The Speluncean Explorers — Further Proceedings" in which it is imagined that "right after the decision in the Speluncean Case was handed down, the Chief Executive of Newgarth constituted a Special Commission of three law professors at the University of Newgarth School of Law to present a recommendation on the question whether executive clemency should be extended to the convicted defendants."[1] D'Amato's goal is to see how Ronald Dworkin's rights thesis would apply to the speluncean case and so this second mythical hypothetical assumes a knowledge of Fuller's original.

James Allan's "A Post-Speluncean Dialogue" also assumes the reader is at least passingly familiar with the speluncean case. It is set in an academics' common room at Newgarth's oldest and most prestigious university, one year after the Supreme Court's decision in the case. Five legal theorists, or jurisprudential experts, sit down after dinner and over drinks debate the merits of the speluncean case. A variety of philosophies of law and of theories of interpretation and rights are presented through the mouths of the participants in the dialogue.

Section Two of the book leaves the mythical hypothetical format for the moment and provides an historical and analytical framework against which to understand the famous Fuller speluncean article. First William Twining, in an excerpt from a

---

1.   See p.37 below.

longer article on reading law, puts "The Case of the Speluncean Explorers" into its historical, analytical and applied contexts. Professor Twining, who says he starts all his courses on jurisprudence with Fuller's speluncean case, carefully takes the reader through the article's strengths and weaknesses. He finishes by noting what a bonus it is that the article "also suggests that studying [jurisprudence] can be fun."[2]

Secondly, William Eskridge Jr. argues that the five fictional judgments in Fuller's famous mythical hypothetical represent variously held historical schools of thought in America about statutory interpretation. "The Justices' opinions constitute a microcosm of this century's debates [in America] over the proper way to interpret statutes. A historical understanding of those debates reveals the breathtaking intellectual accomplishment of Fuller's article ..."[3] Eskridge then takes the reader through a history of American theories of statutory interpretation, relating those theories back to the five fictional judgments in Fuller's speluncean case.

The third and final section of this book returns to the mythical hypothetical format. In Section Three, however, the hypotheticals do *not* rely on the speluncean explorers' facts. Each of the three hypotheticals in this last section presents a completely new set of imaginary facts. Each is entertaining to read and yet each is thought-provoking and raises serious jurisprudential concerns. First there is another of Fuller's own mythical hypotheticals, this one called "The Case of the Contract signed on Book Day". The same five judges from the Supreme Court of Newgarth re-appear here and the reader will recognize each one's philosophical outlook and see it applied to the new fact situation.

Up second is Robert Seidman's "The Inarticulate Premiss", set fictitiously in some newly independent African country of the

2.   See p.73 below.
3.   See p.75 below.

early 1960s. Again, the interrelation of law and morality is explored through the opinions of judges in a difficult case. In Seidman's hypothetical an honest belief in witchcraft and in the victim's status as a witch is raised as a defence to murder. Mistake rather than necessity is the legal focus here.

The last contribution of all in this book is Allan Hutchinson's fictional judgment from the Supreme Court of Canengaustrus in the case of *Derek and Charles v. Ann and Martin*. Canengaustrus, as Hutchinson explains, is a small, little-known island in the mid-Atlantic. Something of a geographical enigma, its capital, Ottloncanwash, is equidistant from Ottawa, London, Canberra and Washington. Coincidentally, Hutchinson continues, the country is a common law jurisdiction and its law is a unique blend of Canadian, English, Australian and American sources. This last mythical hypothetical case forsakes the criminal law and considers a problem in the law of torts, this time through the judgments of justices Doctrin, Mill, Wright, Prudential and Lefft.

In all there are eight contributions to this book. Two are analyses of Fuller's speluncean hypothetical and the other six are what I have called mythical hypotheticals. Imaginary judgments, opinions and dialogues written in a lively and easy to read way is an equally apt description. All aim to make serious points and raise serious questions but to do so in an entertaining and enjoyable manner, taking advantage of the obvious appeal of this sort of presentation. As such, all these pieces together constitute an excellent introduction to the many aspects of the study of jurisprudence. They make jurisprudence seriously enjoyable.

A few short comments are necessary as regards the style and form of the papers. The authors are a multi-national lot and wrote their papers in the U.S., Canada, Ghana and New Zealand. Some therefore used British spellings and others American. As this book hopes to appeal to a multi-national audience I have basically left the spellings as they were when first written. I trust that little, if any, confusion will be caused by following this route.

In two or three of the contributions I have also pared down the number of footnotes and edited the text accordingly. My aim has been to end up with an enjoyable book and one prerequisite of that — in my view — is that it be easily readable. Those I have removed can be found by turning to the articles' place of original publication, listed in the preface above.

Finally, a brief explanation of the title of this book. My chosen title deliberately echoes Ronald Dworkin's well-known jurisprudential book *Taking Rights Seriously*. However we should or should not take rights, legal academics on the whole certainly need no encouragement to take themselves seriously. This tendency makes anything fun or enjoyable suspect. But I hope this book helps to show that attitude is unfortunate, that a little humour and enjoyment can aid in the understanding of difficult problems. Making jurisprudence seriously enjoyable makes it better understood. Enjoy.

Preface

This book grew out of a suggestion made to me by William Twining. I had just had a short article published which played upon Lon Fuller's famous article "The Case of the Speluncean Explorers". William Twining, after reading my paper, suggested there might now be enough good material drawing upon Fuller's Speluncean piece to make a book. I was intrigued and set about finding out just what there was. This book is the outcome of that search. It brings together in one place what I think might be described as the best of the Speluncean Explorers' tradition.

That tradition obviously started with Lon Fuller's work itself and so chapter one of this book is his "The Case of the Speluncean Explorers" and chapter six his "The Case of the Contract signed on Book Day". Both first appeared in *The Problems of Jurisprudence* published by Foundation Press. The former also appeared in the *Harvard Law Review* (volume 62, 1949).

Section One of this book has two further mythical hypotheticals building directly on Fuller's Speluncean facts. One is Anthony D'Amato's "The Speluncean Explorers - Further Proceedings", which first appeared in the *Stanford Law Review* (volume 32, 1979-80), and the other my "A Post Speluncean Dialogue" which first appeared in the *Journal of Legal Education* (volume 44, 1994).

Section Two of this book has an excerpt from William Twining's "Reading Law", which first appeared in the *Valparaiso University Law Review* (volume 31, 1989), and William Erskridge Jr's "*The Case of the Speluncean Explorers:* Twentieth-Century Statutory Interpretation in a Nutshell", which first appeared in the *George Washington University Law Review* (volume 61, 1993).

Section Three of this book has Lon Fuller's "Contract Signed on Book Day" hypothetical as well as two others. The first is Robert Seidman's "The Inarticulate Premiss", first published in the *Journal of Modern African Studies* (volume 3, 1965). The second is Allan Hutchinson's and Derek Morgan's *"Derek and Charles v. Anne and Martin"* which first appeared in the *Osgoode Hall Law Journal* (volume 20, 1982) a "The Canengusian Connection" and then was revised, retitled and appeared in Allan Hutchinson's book *Dwelling on the Threshold* (Carswell, Toronto).

All of the essays in this book appear with the permission of the authors (and in the case of Lon Fuller, his estate) and publishers. I am grateful to them all. Robert Seidman's paper is reprinted by permission of Cambridge University Press.

I am also grateful to my publishers Barry Rose Law Publishers for their courage in taking on this unusual project. In particular I would like to thank Mr. Barry Rose himself for his suggestions, help and wonderfully dry sense of humour.

William Twining inspired this book and gave me valuable advice along the way. To him, too, I owe a debt of gratitude. And of course there would be no book if Lon Fuller had not written such thought-provoking, yet entertaining, material to begin with.

Finally, as ever, I would like to thank my wife Heather. Her support and her marvellous sense of humour open many doors for me that would otherwise be closed.

James Allan
Dunedin, New Zealand
January 1998

SECTION ONE

The Case of the Speluncean Explorers in the Supreme Court of Newgarth, 4300
Lon Fuller

The defendants, having been indicted for the crime of murder, were convicted and sentenced to be hanged by the Court of General Instances of the County of Stowfield. They bring a petition of error before this Court. The facts sufficiently appear in the opinion of the Chief Justice.

TRUEPENNY, C.J.: The four defendants are members of the Speluncean Society, an organization of amateurs interested in the exploration of caves. Early in May of 4299 they, in the company of Roger Whetmore, then also a member of the Society, penetrated into the interior of a limestone cavern of the type found in the Central Plateau of this Commonwealth. While they were in a position remote from the entrance to the cave, a landslide occurred. Heavy boulders fell in such a manner as to block completely the only known opening to the cave. When the men discovered their predicament they settled themselves near the obstructed entrance to wait until a rescue party should remove the detritus that prevented them from leaving their underground prison. On the failure of Whetmore and the defendants to return to their homes, the Secretary of the Society was notified by their families. It appears that the explorers had left indications at the headquarters of the Society concerning the location of the cave they proposed to visit. A rescue party was promptly dispatched to the spot.

The task of rescue proved one of overwhelming

1

difficulty. It was necessary to supplement the forces of the original party by repeated increments of men and machines, which had to be conveyed at great expense to the remote and isolated region in which the cave was located. A huge temporary camp of workmen, engineers, geologists, and other experts was established. The work of removing the obstruction was several times frustrated by fresh landslides. In one of these, ten of the workmen engaged in clearing the entrance were killed. The treasury of the Speluncean Society was soon exhausted in the rescue effort, and the sum of eight hundred thousand frelars, raised partly by popular subscription and partly by legislative grant, was expended before the imprisoned men were rescued. Success was finally achieved on the thirty-second day after the men entered the cave.

Since it was known that the explorers had carried with them only scant provisions, and since it was also known that there was no animal or vegetable matter within the cave on which they might subsist, anxiety was early felt that they might meet death by starvation before access to them could be obtained. On the twentieth day of their imprisonment it was learned for the first time that they had taken with them into the cave a portable wireless machine capable of both sending and receiving messages. A similar machine was promptly installed in the rescue camp and oral communication established with the unfortunate men within the mountain. They asked to be informed how long a time would be required to release them. The engineers in charge of the project answered that at least ten days would be required even if no new landslides occurred. The explorers then asked if any physicians were present, and were placed in communication with a committee of medical experts. The imprisoned men described their condition and the rations they had taken with them, and asked for a medical opinion whether they would be likely to live without food for ten days longer. The chairman of the committee of physicians told them that there was little possibility of this. The wireless machine within the cave then remained silent for eight hours. When communication was re-established the men asked to speak again with the physicians. The chairman of the physicians' committee was placed before the apparatus, and Whetmore, speaking on behalf of himself and the defendants, asked whether they would be able to survive for ten days longer if they consumed the flesh of one of their number. The physicians' chairman reluctantly answered this question in the affirmative. Whetmore asked whether it would be advisable for them to cast lots to determine which of them should be eaten. None of the physicians present was willing to answer the question. Whetmore then asked if there were among the party a judge or other official of the government who would answer this question. None of those attached to the rescue camp was willing to assume the role of advisor in this matter. He then asked if any minister or priest would answer their question, and none was found who would do so. Thereafter no further messages were received from within the cave, and it was assumed (erroneously, it later appeared) that the electric batteries of the explorers' wireless machine had become exhausted. When the imprisoned men were finally released it was learned that on the twenty-third day after their entrance into the cave Whetmore had been killed and eaten by his companions.

From the testimony of the defendants, which was accepted by the jury, it appears that it was Whetmore who first proposed that they might find the nutriment without which survival was impossible in the flesh of one of their own number. It was also Whetmore who first proposed the use of some method of casting lots, calling the attention of the defendants to a pair of dice he happened to have with him. The defendants were at first reluctant to adopt so desperate a procedure, but after the conversations by wireless related above, they finally agreed on the plan proposed by Whetmore. After much discussion of the mathematical problems involved, agreement was finally reached on a method of determining the issue by the use of the dice.

Before the dice were cast, however, Whetmore declared that he withdrew from the arrangement, as he had decided on reflection to wait for another week before embracing an expedient so frightful and odious. The others charged him with a breach of faith and proceeded to cast the dice. When it came Whetmore's turn, the dice were cast for him by one of the defendants, and he was asked to declare any objections he might have to the fairness of the throw. He stated that he had no such objections. The throw went against him, and he was then put to death and eaten by his companions.

After the rescue of the defendants, and after they had completed a stay in a hospital where they underwent a course of treatment for malnutrition and shock, they were indicted for the murder of Roger Whetmore. At the trial, after the testimony had been concluded, the foreman of the jury (a lawyer by profession) inquired of the court whether the jury might not find a special verdict, leaving it to the court to say whether on the facts as found the defendants were guilty. After some discussion, both the Prosecutor and counsel for the defendants indicated their acceptance of this procedure, and it was adopted by the court. In a lengthy special verdict the jury found the facts as I have related them above, and found further that if on these facts the defendants were guilty of the crime charged against them, then they found the defendants guilty. On the basis of this verdict, the trial judge ruled that the defendants were guilty of murdering Roger Whetmore. The judge then sentenced them to be hanged, the law of our Commonwealth permitting him no discretion with respect to the penalty to be imposed. After the release of the jury, its members joined in a communication to the Chief Executive asking that the sentence be commuted to an imprisonment of six months. The trial judge addressed a similar communication to the Chief Executive. As yet no action with respect to these pleas has been taken, as the Chief Executive is apparently awaiting our disposition of this petition of error.

It seems to me that in dealing with this extraordinary case the jury and the trial judge followed a course that was not only fair and wise, but the only course that was open to them under the law. The language of our statute is well known: "Whoever shall willfully take the life of another shall be punished by death." N.C.S.A. (N.S.) § 12-A. This statute permits of no exception applicable to this case, however our sympathies may incline us to make allowance for the tragic situation in which these men found themselves.

In a case like this the principle of executive clemency seems admirably suited to mitigate the rigors of the law, and I propose to my colleagues that we follow the example of the jury and the trial judge by joining in the communications they have addressed to the Chief

Executive. There is every reason to believe that these requests for clemency will be heeded, coming as they do from those who have studied the case and had an opportunity to become thoroughly acquainted with all its circumstances. It is highly improbable that the Chief Executive would deny these requests unless he were himself to hold hearings at least as extensive as those involved in the trial below, which lasted for three months. The holding of such hearings (which would virtually amount to a retrial of the case) would scarcely be compatible with the functions of the Executive as it is usually conceived. I think we may therefore assume that some form of clemency will be extended to these defendants. If this is done, then justice will be accomplished without impairing either the letter or spirit of our statutes and without offering any encouragement for the disregard of law.

FOSTER, J.: I am shocked that the Chief Justice, in an effort to escape the embarrassments of this tragic case, should have adopted, and should have proposed to his colleagues, an expedient at once so sordid and so obvious. I believe something more is on trial in this case than the fate of these unfortunate explorers; that is the law of our Commonwealth. If this Court declares that under our law these men have committed a crime, then our law is itself convicted in the tribunal of common sense, no matter what happens to the individuals involved in this petition of error. For us to assert that the law we uphold and expound compels us to a conclusion we are ashamed of, and from which we can only escape by appealing to a dispensation resting within the personal whim of the Executive, seems to me to amount to an admission that the law of this Commonwealth no longer pretends to incorporate justice.

For myself, I do not believe that our law compels the monstrous conclusion that these men are murderers. I believe, on the contrary, that it declares them to be innocent of any crime. I rest this conclusion on two independent grounds, either of which is of itself sufficient to justify the acquittal of these defendants.

The first of these grounds rests on a premise that may arouse opposition until it has been examined candidly. I take the view that the enacted or positive law of this Commonwealth, including all of its statutes and precedents, is inapplicable to this case, and that the case is governed instead by what ancient writers in Europe and America called "the law of nature."

This conclusion rests on the proposition that our positive law is predicated on the possibility of men's coexistence in society. When a situation arises in which the coexistence of men becomes impossible, then a condition that underlies all of our precedents and statutes has ceased to exist. When that condition disappears, then it is my opinion that the force of our positive law disappears with it. We are not accustomed to applying the maxim *cessante ratione legis, cessat et ipsa lex* to the whole of our enacted law, but I believe that this is a case where the maxim should be so applied.

The proposition that all positive law is based on the possibility of men's coexistence has a strange sound, not because the truth it contains is strange, but simply because it is a truth so obvious and pervasive that we seldom have occasion to give words to it. Like the air we breathe, it so pervades our environment that we forget that it exists until we are suddenly deprived of it. Whatever particular objects may be sought by the various branches of our law, it is

7

apparent on reflection that all of them are directed toward facilitating and improving men's coexistence and regulating with fairness and equity the relations of their life in common. When the assumption that men may live together loses its truth, as it obviously did in this extraordinary situation where life only became possible by the taking of life, then the basic premises underlying our whole legal order have lost their meaning and force.

Had the tragic events of this case taken place a mile beyond the territorial limits of our Commonwealth, no one would pretend that our law was applicable to them. We recognize that jurisdiction rests on a territorial basis. The grounds of this principle are by no means obvious and are seldom examined. I take it that this principle is supported by an assumption that it is feasible to impose a single legal order upon a group of men only if they live together within the confines of a given area of the earth's surface. The premise that men shall coexist in a group underlies, then, the territorial principle, as it does all of law. Now I contend that a case may be removed morally from the force of a legal order, as well as geographically. If we look to the purposes of law and government, and to the premises underlying our positive law, these men when they made their fateful decision were as remote from our legal order as if they had been a thousand miles beyond our boundaries. Even in a physical sense, their underground prison was separated from our courts and writ-servers by a solid curtain of rock that could be removed only after the most extraordinary expenditures of time and effort.

I conclude, therefore, that at the time Roger Whetmore's life was ended by these defendants, they were, to use the quaint language of nineteenth-century writers, not in a "state of civil society" but in a "state of nature." This has the consequence that the law applicable to them is not the enacted and established law of this Commonwealth, but the law derived from those principles that were appropriate to their condition. I have no hesitancy in saying that under those principles they were guiltless of any crime.

What these men did was done in pursuance of an agreement accepted by all of them and first proposed by Whetmore himself. Since it was apparent that their extraordinary predicament made inapplicable the usual principles that regulate men's relations with one another, it was necessary for them to draw, as it were, a new charter of government appropriate to the situation in which they found themselves.

It has from antiquity been recognized that the most basic principle of law or government is to be found in the notion of contract or agreement. Ancient thinkers, especially during the period from 1600 to 1900 used to base government itself on a supposed original social compact. Skeptics pointed out that this theory contradicted the known facts of history, and that there was no scientific evidence to support the notion that any government was ever founded in the manner supposed by the theory. Moralists replied that, if the compact was a fiction from a historical point of view the notion of compact or agreement furnished the only ethical justification on which the powers of government, which include that of taking life, could be rested. The powers of government can only be justified morally on the ground that these are powers that reasonable men would agree upon and accept if they were faced with the necessity of constructing anew some order to make their life in common possible.

Fortunately, our Commonwealth is not bothered by the perplexities that beset the ancients. We know as a matter of historical truth that our government was founded upon a contract or free accord of men. The archeological proof is conclusive that in the first period following the Great Spiral the survivors of that holocaust voluntarily came together and drew up a charter of government. Sophistical writers have raised questions as to the power of those remote contractors to bind future generations, but the fact remains that our government traces itself back in an unbroken line to that original charter.

If, therefore, our hangmen have the power to end men's lives, if our sheriffs have the power to put delinquent tenants in the street, if our police have the power to incarcerate the inebriated reveler, these powers find their moral justification in that original compact of our forefathers. If we can find no higher source for our legal order, what higher source should we expect these starving unfortunates to find for the order they adopted for themselves?

I believe that the line of argument I have just expounded permits of no rational answer. I realize that it will probably be received with a certain discomfort by many who read this opinion, who will be inclined to suspect that some hidden sophistry must underlie a demonstration that leads to so many unfamiliar conclusions. The source of this discomfort is, however, easy to identify. The usual conditions of human existence incline us to think of human life as an absolute value, not to be sacrificed under any circumstances. There is much that is fictitious about this conception even when it is applied to the ordinary relations of society. We have an illustration of this truth in the very case before us. Ten workmen were killed in the process of removing the rocks from the opening to the cave. Did not the engineers and government officials who directed the rescue effort know that the operations they were undertaking were dangerous and involved a serious risk to the lives of the workmen executing them? If it was proper that these ten lives should be sacrificed to save the lives of five imprisoned explorers, why then are we told it was wrong for these explorers to carry out an arrangement which would save four lives at the cost of one?

Every highway, every tunnel, every building we project involves a risk to human life. Taking these projects in the aggregate, we can calculate with some precision how many deaths the construction of them will require; statisticians can tell you the average cost in human lives of a thousand miles of a four-lane concrete highway. Yet we deliberately and knowingly incur and pay this cost on the assumption that the values obtained for those who survive outweigh the loss. If these things can be said of a society functioning above ground in a normal and ordinary manner, what shall we say of the supposed absolute value of a human life in the desperate situation in which these defendants and their companion Whetmore found themselves?

This concludes the exposition of the first ground of my decision. My second ground proceeds by rejecting hypothetically all the premises on which I have so far proceeded. I concede for purposes of argument that I am wrong in saying that the situation of these men removed them from the effect of our positive law, and I assume that the Consolidated Statutes have the power to penetrate five hundred feet of rock and to impose themselves upon these starving men huddled in their underground prison.

Now it is, of course, perfectly clear that these men did an act that violates the literal wording of the statute which declares that he who "shall willfully take the life of another" is a murderer. But one of the most ancient bits of legal wisdom is the saying that a man may break the letter of the law without breaking the law itself. Every proposition of positive law, whether contained in a statute or a judicial precedent, is to be interpreted reasonably, in the light of its evident purpose. This is a truth so elementary that it is hardly necessary to expatiate on it. Illustrations of its application are numberless and are to be found in every branch of the law. In *Commonwealth v. Staymore* the defendant was convicted under a statute making it a crime to leave one's car parked in certain areas for a period longer than two hours. The defendant had attempted to remove his car, but was prevented from doing so because the streets were obstructed by a political demonstration in which he took no part and which he had no reason to anticipate. His conviction was set aside by this Court, although his case fell squarely within the wording of the statute. Again, in *Fehler v. Neegas* there was before this Court for construction a statute in which the word "not" had plainly been transposed from its intended position in the final and most crucial section of the act. This transposition was contained in all the successive drafts of the act, where it was apparently overlooked by the draftsmen and sponsors of the legislation. No one was able to prove how the error came about, yet it was apparent that, taking account of the contents of the statute as a whole, an error had been made, since a literal reading of the final clause rendered it inconsistent with everything that had gone before and with the object of the enactment as stated in its preamble. This

Court refused to accept a literal interpretation of the statute, and in effect rectified its language by reading the word "not" into the place where it was evidently intended to go.

The statute before us for interpretation has never been applied literally. Centuries ago it was established that a killing in self-defense is excused. There is nothing in the wording of the statute that suggests this exception. Various attempts have been made to reconcile the legal treatment of self-defense with the words of the statute, but in my opinion these are all merely ingenious sophistries. The truth is that the exception in favor of self-defense cannot be reconciled with the *words* of the statute, but only with its *purpose.*

The true reconciliation of the excuse of self-defense with the statute making it a crime to kill another is to be found in the following line of reasoning. One of the principal objects underlying any criminal legislation is that of deterring men from crime. Now it is apparent that if it were declared to be the law that a killing in self-defense is murder such a rule could not operate in a deterrent manner. A man whose life is threatened will repel his aggressor, whatever the law may say. Looking therefore to the broad purposes of criminal legislation, we may safely declare that this statute was not intended to apply to cases of self-defense.

When the rationale of the excuse of self-defense is thus explained, it becomes apparent that precisely the same reasoning is applicable to the case at bar. If in the future any group of men ever find themselves in the tragic predicament of these defendants, we may be sure that their decision whether to live or die will not be controlled by the contents of our criminal code. Accordingly, if we read this statute intelligently it is apparent that it does not apply to this case. The withdrawal of this situation from the effect of the statute is justified by precisely the same considerations that were applied by our predecessors in office centuries ago to the case of self-defense.

There are those who raise the cry of judicial usurpation whenever a court, after analyzing the purpose of a statute, gives to its words a meaning that is not at once apparent to the casual reader who has not studied the statute closely or examined the objectives it seeks to attain. Let me say emphatically that I accept without reservation the proposition that this Court is bound by the statutes of our Commonwealth and that it exercises its powers in subservience to the duly expressed will of the Chamber of Representatives. The line of reasoning I have applied above raises no question of fidelity to enacted law, though it may possibly raise a question of the distinction between intelligent and unintelligent fidelity. No superior wants a servant who lacks the capacity to read between the lines. The stupidest housemaid knows that when she is told "to peel the soup and skim the potatoes" her mistress does not mean what she says. She also knows that when her master tells her to "drop everything and come running" he has overlooked the possibility that she is at the moment in the act of rescuing the baby from the rain barrel. Surely we have a right to expect the same modicum of intelligence from the judiciary. The correction of obvious legislative errors or oversights is not to supplant the legislative will, but to make that will effective.

I therefore conclude that on any aspect under which this case may be viewed these defendants are innocent of the crime of murdering Roger Whetmore, and that the conviction should be set aside.

TATTING, J.: In the discharge of my duties as a justice of this Court, I am usually able to dissociate the emotional and intellectual sides of my reactions, and to decide the case before me entirely on the basis of the latter. In passing on this tragic case I find that my usual resources fail me. On the emotional side I find myself torn between sympathy for these men and a feeling of abhorrence and disgust at the monstrous act they committed. I had hoped that I would be able to put these contradictory emotions to one side as irrelevant, and to decide the case on the basis of a convincing and logical demonstration of the result demanded by our law. Unfortunately, this deliverance has not been vouchsafed me.

As I analyze the opinion just rendered by my brother Foster, I find that it is shot through with contradictions and fallacies. Let us begin with his first proposition: these men were not subject to our law because they were not in a "state of civil society" but in a "state of nature." I am not clear why this is so, whether it is because of the thickness of the rock that imprisoned them, or because they were hungry, or because they had set up a "new charter of government" by which the usual rules of law were to be supplanted by a throw of the dice. Other difficulties intrude themselves. If these men passed from the jurisdiction of our law to that of "the law of nature," at what moment did this occur? Was it when the entrance to the cave was blocked, or when the threat of starvation reached a certain undefined degree of intensity, or when the agreement for the throwing of the dice was made? These uncertainties in the doctrine proposed by my brother are capable of producing real difficulties. Suppose, for example, one of these men had had his twenty-first birthday while he was imprisoned within the mountain. On what date would we have to consider that he had attained his majority — when he reached the age of twenty-one, at which time he was, by hypothesis, removed from the effects of our law, or only when he was released from the cave and became again subject to what my brother calls our "positive law"? These difficulties may seem fanciful, yet they only serve to reveal the fanciful nature of the doctrine that is capable of giving rise to them.

But it is not necessary to explore these niceties further to demonstrate the absurdity of my brother's position. Mr. Justice Foster and I are the appointed judges of a court of the Commonwealth of Newgarth, sworn and empowered to administer the laws of that Commonwealth. By what authority do we resolve ourselves into a Court of Nature? If these men were indeed under the law of nature, whence comes our authority to expound and apply that law? Certainly *we* are not in a state of nature.

Let us look at the contents of this code of nature that my brother proposes we adopt as our own and apply to this case. What a topsy-turvy and odious code it is! It is a code in which the law of contracts is more fundamental than the law of murder. It is a code under which a man may make a valid agreement empowering his fellows to eat his own body. Under the provisions of this code, furthermore, such an agreement once made is irrevocable, and if one of the parties attempts to withdraw, the others may take the law into their own hands and enforce the contract by violence—for though my brother passes over in convenient silence the effect of Whetmore's withdrawal, this is the necessary implication of his argument.

The principles my brother expounds contain other

implications that cannot be tolerated. He argues that when the defendants set upon Whetmore and killed him (we know not how, perhaps by pounding him with stones) they were only exercising the rights conferred upon them by their bargain. Suppose, however, that Whetmore had had concealed upon his person a revolver, and that when he saw the defendants about to slaughter him he had shot them to death in order to save his own life. My brother's reasoning applied to these facts would make Whetmore out to be a murderer, since the excuse of self-defense would have to be denied to him. If his assailants were acting rightfully in seeking to bring about his death, then of course he could no more plead the excuse that he was defending his own life than could a condemned prisoner who struck down the executioner lawfully attempting to place the noose about his neck.

All of these considerations make it impossible for me to accept the first part of my brother's argument. I can neither accept his notion that these men were under a code of nature which this Court was bound to apply to them, nor can I accept the odious and perverted rules that he would read into that code. I come now to the second part of my brother's opinion, in which he seeks to show that the defendants did not violate the provisions of N.C.S.A. (N.S.) § 12-A. Here the way, instead of being clear, becomes for me misty and ambiguous, though my brother seems unaware of the difficulties that inhere in his demonstrations.

The gist of my brother's argument may be stated in the following terms: No statute, whatever its language, should be applied in a way that contradicts its purpose. One of the purposes of any criminal statute is to deter. The application of the statute making it a crime to kill another to the peculiar facts of this case would contradict this purpose, for it is impossible to believe that the contents of the criminal code could operate in a deterrent manner on men faced with the alternative of life or death. The reasoning by which this exception is read into the statute is, my brother observes, the same as that which is applied in order to provide the excuse of self-defense.

On the face of things this demonstration seems very convincing indeed. My brother's interpretation of the rationale of the excuse of self-defense is in fact supported by a decision of this court, *Commonwealth v. Parry*, a precedent I happened to encounter in my research on this case. Though *Commonwealth v. Parry* seems generally to have been overlooked in the texts and subsequent decisions, it supports unambiguously the interpretation my brother has put upon the excuse of self-defense.

Now let me outline briefly, however, the perplexities that assail me when I examine my brother's demonstration more closely. It is true that a statute should be applied in the light of its purpose, and that *one* of the purposes of criminal legislation is recognized to be deterrence. The difficulty is that other purposes are also ascribed to the law of crimes. It has been said that one of its objects is to provide an orderly outlet for the instinctive human demand for retribution. *Commonwealth v. Scape.* It has also been said that its object is the rehabilitation of the wrongdoer. *Commonwealth v. Makeover.* Other theories have been propounded. Assuming that we must interpret a statute in the light of its purpose, what are we to do when it has many purposes or when its purposes are disputed?

A similar difficulty is presented by the fact that although there is authority for my brother's interpretation of the

18

excuse of self-defense, there is other authority which assigns to that excuse a different rationale. Indeed, until I happened on *Commonwealth v. Parry* I had never heard of the explanation given by my brother. The taught doctrine of our law schools, memorized by generations of law students, runs in the following terms: The statute concerning murder requires a "willful" act. The man who acts to repel an aggressive threat to his own life does not act "willfully," but in response to an impulse deeply ingrained in human nature. I suspect that there is hardly a lawyer in this Commonwealth who is not familiar with this line of reasoning, especially since the point is a great favorite of the bar examiners.

Now the familiar explanation for the excuse of self-defense just expounded obviously cannot be applied by analogy to the facts of this case. These men acted not only "willfully" but with great deliberation and after hours of discussing what they should do. Again we encounter a forked path, with one line of reasoning leading us in one direction and another in a direction that is exactly the opposite. This perplexity is in this case compounded, as it were, for we have to set off one explanation, incorporated in a virtually unknown precedent of this Court, against another explanation, which forms a part of the taught legal tradition of our law schools; but which, so far as I know, has never been adopted in any judicial decision.

I recognize the relevance of the precedents cited by my brother concerning the displaced "not" and the defendant who parked overtime. But what are we to do with one of the landmarks of our jurisprudence, which again my brother passes over in silence? This is *Commonwealth v. Valjean.* Though the case is somewhat obscurely reported, it appears that the defendant was indicted for the larceny of a loaf of bread, and offered as a defense that he was in a condition approaching starvation. The court refused to accept this defense. If hunger cannot justify the theft of wholesome and natural food, how can it justify the killing and eating of a man? Again, if we look at the thing in terms of deterrence, is it likely that a man will starve to death to avoid a jail sentence for the theft of a loaf of bread? My brother's demonstrations would compel us to overrule *Commonwealth v. Valjean*, and many other precedents that have been built on that case.

Again, I have difficulty in saying that no deterrent effect whatever could be attributed to a decision that these men were guilty of murder. The stigma of the word "murderer" is such that it is quite likely, I believe, that if these men had known that their act was deemed by the law to be murder they would have waited for a few days at least before carrying out their plan. During that time some unexpected relief might have come. I realize that this observation only reduces the distinction to a matter of degree, and does not destroy it altogether. It is certainly true that the element of deterrence would be less in this case than is normally involved in the application of the criminal law.

There is still a further difficulty in my brother Foster's proposal to read an exception into the statute to favor this case, though again a difficulty not even intimated in his opinion. What shall be the scope of this exception? Here the men cast lots and the victim was himself originally a party to the agreement. What would we have to decide if Whetmore had refused from the beginning to participate in the plan? Would a majority be permitted to overrule him? Or, suppose that no plan were adopted at all and the others simply conspired to bring about Whetmore's death, justifying their act by saying that he was in the weakest condition. Or again, that a plan of selection was followed but one based on a different justification than the one adopted here, as if the others were atheists and insisted that Whetmore should die because he was the only one who believed in an afterlife. These illustrations could be multiplied, but enough have been suggested to reveal what a quagmire of hidden difficulties my brother's reasoning contains.

Of course I realize on reflection that I may be concerning myself with a problem that will never arise, since it is unlikely that any group of men will ever again be brought to commit the dread act that was involved here. Yet, on still further reflection, even if we are certain that no similar case will arise again, do not the illustrations I have given show the lack of any coherent and rational principle in the rule my brother proposes? Should not the soundness of a principle be tested by the conclusions it entails, without reference to the accidents of later litigational history? Still, if this is so, why is it that we of this Court so often discuss the question whether we are likely to have later occasion to apply a principle urged for the solution of the case before us? Is this a situation where a line of reasoning not originally proper has become sanctioned by precedent, so that we are permitted to apply it and may even be under an obligation to do so?

The more I examine this case and think about it, the more deeply I become involved. My mind becomes entangled in the meshes of the very nets I throw out for my own rescue. I find that almost every consideration that bears on the decision of the case is counterbalanced by an opposing consideration leading in the opposite direction. My brother Foster has not furnished to me, nor can I discover for myself, any formula capable of resolving the equivocations that beset me on all sides.

I have given this case the best thought of which I am capable. I have scarcely slept since it was argued before us. When I feel myself inclined to accept the view of my brother Foster, I am repelled by a feeling that his arguments are intellectually unsound and approach mere rationalization. On the other hand, when I incline toward upholding the conviction, I am struck by the absurdity of directing that these men be put to death when their lives have been saved at the cost of the lives of ten heroic workmen. It is to me a matter of regret that the Prosecutor saw fit to ask for an indictment for murder. If we had a provision in our statutes making it a crime to eat human flesh, that would have been a more appropriate charge. If no other charge suited to the facts of this case could be brought against the defendants, it would have been wiser, I think, not to have indicted them at all. Unfortunately, however, the men have been indicted and tried, and we have therefore been drawn into this unfortunate affair.

Since I have been wholly unable to resolve the doubts that beset me about the law of this case, I am with regret announcing a step that is, I believe, unprecedented in the history of this tribunal. I declare my withdrawal from the decision of this case.

KEEN, J.: I should like to begin by setting to one side two questions which are not before this Court.

The first of these is whether executive clemency should be extended to these defendants if the conviction is affirmed. Under our system of government, that is a question for the Chief Executive, not for us. I therefore disapprove of that passage in the opinion of the Chief Justice in which he in effect gives instructions to the Chief Executive as to what he should do in this case and suggests that some impropriety will attach if these instructions are not heeded. This is a confusion of governmental functions — a confusion of which the judiciary should be the last to be guilty. I wish to state that if I were the Chief Executive I would go farther in the direction of clemency than the pleas addressed to him propose. I would pardon these men altogether, since I believe that they have already suffered enough to pay for any offense they may have committed. I want it to be understood that this remark is made in my capacity as a private citizen who by the accident of his office happens to have acquired an intimate acquaintance with the facts of this case. In the discharge of my duties as judge, it is neither my function to address directions to the Chief Executive, nor to take into account what he may or may not do, in reaching my own decision, which must be controlled entirely by the law of this Commonwealth.

The second question that I wish to put to one side is that of deciding whether what these men did was "right" or "wrong," "wicked" or "good." That is also a question that is irrelevant to the discharge of my office as a judge sworn to apply, not my conceptions of morality, but the law of the land. In putting this question to one side I think I can also safely dismiss without comment the first and more poetic portion of my brother Foster's opinion. The element of fantasy contained in the arguments developed there has been sufficiently revealed in my brother Tatting's somewhat solemn attempt to take those arguments seriously.

The sole question before us for decision is whether these

defendants did, within the meaning of N.C.S.A. (N.S.) § 12-A, willfully take the life of Roger Whetmore. The exact language of the statute is as follows: "Whoever shall willfully take the life of another shall be punished by death." Now I should suppose that any candid observer, content to extract from these words their natural meaning, would concede at once that these defendants did "willfully take the life" of Roger Whetmore.

Whence arise all the difficulties of the case, then, and the necessity for so many pages of discussion about what ought to be so obvious? The difficulties, in whatever tortured form they may present themselves, all trace back to a single source, and that is a failure to distinguish the legal from the moral aspects of this case. To put it bluntly, my brothers do not like the fact that the written law requires the conviction of these defendants. Neither do I, but unlike my brothers I respect the obligations of an office that requires me to put my personal predilections out of my mind when I come to interpret and apply the law of this Commonwealth.

Now, of course, my brother Foster does not admit that he is actuated by a personal dislike of the written law. Instead he develops a familiar line of argument according to which the court may disregard the express language of a statute when something not contained in the statute itself, called its "purpose," can be employed to justify the result the court considers proper. Because this is an old issue between myself and my colleague, I should like, before discussing his particular application of the argument to the facts of this case, to say something about the historical background of this issue and its implications for law and government generally.

There was a time in this Commonwealth when judges did in fact legislate very freely, and all of us know that during that period some of our statutes were rather thoroughly made over by the judiciary. That was a time when the accepted principles of political science did not designate with any certainty the rank and function of the various arms of the state. We all know the tragic issue of that uncertainty in the brief civil war that arose out of the conflict between the judiciary, on the one hand, and the executive and the legislature, on the other. There is no need to recount here the factors that contributed to that unseemly struggle for power, though they included the unrepresentative character of the Chamber, resulting from a division of the country into election districts that no longer accorded with the actual distribution of the population, and the forceful personality and wide popular following of the then Chief Justice. It is enough to observe that those days are behind us, and that in place of the uncertainty that then reigned we now have a clear-cut principle, which is the supremacy of the legislative branch of our government. From that principle flows the obligation of the judiciary to enforce faithfully the written law, and to interpret that law in accordance with its plain meaning without reference to our personal desires or our individual conceptions of justice. I am not concerned with the question whether the principle that forbids the judicial revision of statutes is right or wrong, desirable or undesirable; I observe merely that this principle has become a tacit premise underlying the whole of the legal and governmental order I am sworn to administer.

Yet though the principle of the supremacy of the legislature has been accepted in theory for centuries, such is the tenacity of professional tradition and the force of fixed habits of thought that many of the judiciary have still not accommodated themselves to the restricted role which the new order imposes on them. My brother Foster is one of that group; his way of dealing with statutes is exactly that of a judge living in the 3900s.

We are all familiar with the process by which the judicial reform of disfavored legislative enactments is accomplished. Anyone who has followed the written opinions of Mr. Justice Foster will have had an opportunity to see it at work in every branch of the law. I am personally so familiar with the process that in the event of my brother's incapacity I am sure I could write a satisfactory opinion for him without any prompting whatever, beyond being informed whether he liked the effect of the terms of the statute as applied to the case before him.

The process of judicial reform requires three steps. The first of these is to divine some single "purpose" which the statute serves. This is done although not one statute in a hundred has any such single purpose, and although the objectives of nearly every statute are differently interpreted by the different classes of its sponsors. The second step is to discover that a mythical being called "the legislator," in the pursuit of this imagined "purpose," overlooked something or left some gap or imperfection in his work. Then comes the final and most refreshing part of the task, which is, of course, to fill in the blank thus created. *Quod erat faciendum.*

My brother Foster's penchant for finding holes in statutes reminds one of the story told by an ancient author about the man who ate a pair of shoes. Asked how he liked them, he replied that the part he liked best was the holes. That is the way my brother feels about statutes; the more holes they have in them the better he likes them. In short, he doesn't like statutes.

One could not wish for a better case to illustrate the specious nature of this gap-filling process than the one before us. My brother thinks he knows exactly what was sought when men made murder a crime, and that was something he calls "deterrence." My brother Tatting has already shown how much is passed over in that interpretation. But I think the trouble goes deeper. I doubt very much whether our statute making murder a crime really has a "purpose" in any ordinary sense of the term. Primarily, such a statute reflects a deeply-felt human conviction that murder is wrong and that something should be done to the man who commits it. If we were forced to be more articulate about the matter, we would probably take refuge in the more sophisticated theories of the criminologists, which, of course, were certainly not in the minds of those who drafted our statute. We might also observe that men will do their own work more effectively and live happier lives if they are protected against the threat of violent assault. Bearing in mind that the victims of murders are often unpleasant people, we might add some suggestion that the matter of disposing of undesirables is not a function suited to private enterprise, but should be a state monopoly. All of which reminds me of the attorney who once argued before us that a statute licensing physicians was a good thing because it would lead to lower life insurance rates by lifting the level of general health. There is such a thing as overexplaining the obvious.

If we do not know the purpose of § 12-A, how can we possibly say there is a "gap" in it? How can we know what

27

its draftsmen thought about the question of killing men in order to eat them? My brother Tatting has revealed an understandable, though perhaps slightly exaggerated revulsion to cannibalism. How do we know that his remote ancestors did not feel the same revulsion to an even higher degree? Anthropologists say that the dread felt for a forbidden act may be increased by the fact that the conditions of a tribe's life create special temptations toward it, as incest is most severely condemned among those whose village relations make it most likely to occur. Certainly the period following the Great Spiral was one that had implicit in it temptations to anthropophagy. Perhaps it was for that very reason that our ancestors expressed their prohibition in so broad and unqualified a form. All of this is conjecture, of course, but it remains abundantly clear that neither I nor my brother Foster knows what the "purpose" of § 12-A is.

Considerations similar to those I have just outlined are also applicable to the exception in favor of self-defense, which plays so large a role in the reasoning of my brothers Foster and Tatting. It is of course true that in *Commonwealth v. Parry* an obiter dictum justified this exception on the assumption that the purpose of criminal legislation is to deter. It may well also be true that generations of law students have been taught that the true explanation of the exception lies in the fact that a man who acts in self-defense does not act "willfully," and that the same students have passed their bar examinations by repeating what their professors told them. These last observations I could dismiss, of course, as irrelevant for the simple reason that professors and bar examiners have not as yet any commission to make our laws for us. But again the real trouble lies deeper. As in dealing with the statute, so in dealing with the exception, the question is not the conjectural *purpose* of the rule, but its *scope*. Now the scope of the exception in favor of self-defense as it has been applied by this Court is plain: it applies to cases of resisting an aggressive threat to the party's own life. It is therefore too clear for argument that this case does not fall within the scope of the exception, since it is plain that Whetmore made no threat against the lives of these defendants.

The essential shabbiness of my brother Foster's attempt to cloak his remaking of the written law with an air of legitimacy comes tragically to the surface in my brother Tatting's opinion. In that opinion Justice Tatting struggles manfully to combine his colleague's loose moralisms with his own sense of fidelity to the written law. The issue of this struggle could only be that which occurred, a complete default in the discharge of the judicial function. You simply cannot apply a statute as it is written and remake it to meet your own wishes at the same time.

Now I know that the line of reasoning I have developed in this opinion will not be acceptable to those who look only to the immediate effects of a decision and ignore the long-run implications of an assumption by the judiciary of a power of dispensation. A hard decision is never a popular decision. Judges have been celebrated in literature for their sly prowess in devising some quibble by which a litigant could be deprived of his rights where the public thought it was wrong for him to assert those rights. But I believe that judicial dispensation does more harm in the long run than hard decisions. Hard cases may even have a certain moral value by bringing home to the people their own responsibilities toward the law that is ultimately their creation, and by reminding them that there is no principle of personal grace that can relieve the mistakes of their representatives.

Indeed, I will go farther and say that not only are the principles I have been expounding those which are soundest for our present conditions, but that we would have inherited a better legal system from our forefathers if those principles had been observed from the beginning. For example, with respect to the excuse of self-defense, if our courts had stood steadfast on the language of the statute the result would undoubtedly have been a legislative revision of it. Such a revision would have drawn on the assistance of natural philosophers and psychologists, and the resulting regulation of the matter would have had an understandable and rational basis, instead of the hodgepodge of verbalisms and metaphysical distinctions that have emerged from the judicial and professorial treatment.

These concluding remarks are, of course, beyond any duties that I have to discharge with relation to this case, but I include them here because I feel deeply that my colleagues are insufficiently aware of the dangers implicit in the conceptions of the judicial office advocated by my brother Foster.

I conclude that the conviction should be affirmed.

HANDY, J.: I have listened with amazement to the tortured ratiocinations to which this simple case has given rise. I never cease to wonder at my colleagues' ability to throw an obscuring curtain of legalisms about every issue presented to them for decision. We have heard this afternoon learned disquisitions on the distinction between positive law and the law of nature, the language of the statute and the purpose of the statute, judicial functions and executive functions, judicial legislation and legislative legislation. My only disappointment was that someone did not raise the question of the legal nature of the bargain struck in the cave—whether it was unilateral or bilateral, and whether Whetmore could not be considered as having revoked an offer prior to action taken thereunder.

What have all these things to do with the case? The problem before us is what we, as officers of the government, ought to do with these defendants. That is a question of practical wisdom, to be exercised in a context, not of abstract theory, but of human realities. When the case is approached in this light, it becomes, I think, one of the easiest to decide that has ever been argued before this Court.

Before stating my own conclusions about the merits of the case, I should like to discuss briefly some of the more fundamental issues involved — issues on which my colleagues and I have been divided ever since I have been on the bench.

I have never been able to make my brothers see that government is a human affair, and that men are ruled, not by words on paper or by abstract theories, but by other men. They are ruled well when their rulers understand the feelings and conceptions of the masses. They are ruled badly when that understanding is lacking.

Of all branches of the government, the judiciary is the most likely to lose its contact with the common man. The reasons for this are, of course, fairly obvious. Where the masses react to a situation in terms of a few salient features, we pick into little pieces every situation presented to us. Lawyers are hired by both sides to analyze and dissect. Judges and attorneys vie with one another to see who can discover the greatest number of difficulties and distinctions in a single set of facts. Each side tries to find cases, real or imagined, that will embarrass the demonstrations of the other side. To escape this embarrassment, still further distinctions are invented and imported into the situation. When a set of facts has been subjected to this kind of treatment for a sufficient time, all the life and juice have gone out of it and we have left a handful of dust.

Now I realize that wherever you have rules and abstract principles lawyers are going to be able to make distinctions. To some extent the sort of thing I have been describing is a necessary evil attaching to any formal regulation of human affairs. But I think that the area which really stands in need of such regulation is greatly overestimated. There are, of course, a few fundamental rules of the game that must be accepted if the game is to go on at all. I would include among these the rules relating to the conduct of elections, the appointment of public officials, and the term during which an office is held. Here some restraint on discretion and dispensation, some adherence to form, some scruple for what does and what does not fall within the rule, is, I concede, essential. Perhaps the area of basic principle should be expanded to include certain other rules, such as those designed to preserve the free civilmoign system.

But outside of these fields I believe that all government officials, including judges, will do their jobs best if they treat forms and abstract concepts as instruments. We should take as our model, I think, the good administrator, who accommodates procedures and principles to the case at hand, selecting from among the available forms those most suited to reach the proper result.

The most obvious advantage of this method of government is that it permits us to go about our daily tasks with efficiency and common sense. My adherence to this philosophy has, however, deeper roots. I believe that it is only with the insight this philosophy gives that we can preserve the flexibility essential if we are to keep our actions in reasonable accord with the sentiments of those subject to our rule. More governments have been wrecked, and more human misery caused, by the lack of this accord between ruler and ruled than by any other factor that can be discerned in history. Once drive a sufficient wedge between the mass of people and those who direct their legal, political, and economic life, and our society is ruined. Then neither Foster's law of nature nor Keen's fidelity to written law will avail us anything.

Now when these conceptions are applied to the case before us, its decision becomes, as I have said, perfectly easy. In order to demonstrate this I shall have to introduce certain realities that my brothers in their coy decorum have seen fit to pass over in silence, although they are just as acutely aware of them as I am.

The first of these is that this case has aroused an enormous public interest, both here and abroad. Almost every newspaper and magazine has carried articles about it; columnists have shared with their readers confidential information as to the next governmental move; hundreds of letters-to-the-editor have been printed. One of the great newspaper chains made a poll of public opinion on the question, "What do you think the Supreme Court should do with the Speluncean explorers?" About ninety per cent expressed a belief that the defendants should be pardoned or let off with a kind of token punishment. It is perfectly clear, then, how the public feels about the case. We could have known this without the poll, of course, on the basis of common sense, or even by observing that on this Court there are apparently four-and-a-half men, or ninety per cent, who share the common opinion.

This makes it obvious, not only what we should do, but what we must do if we are to preserve between ourselves and public opinion a reasonable and decent accord. Declaring these men innocent need not involve us in any undignified quibble or trick. No principle of statutory construction is required that is not consistent with the past practices of this Court. Certainly no layman would think that in letting these men off we had stretched the statute any more than our ancestors did when they created the excuse of self-defense. If a more detailed demonstration of the method of reconciling our decision with the statute is required, I should be content to rest on the arguments developed in the second and less visionary part of my brother Foster's opinion.

Now I know that my brothers will be horrified by my suggestion that this Court should take account of public opinion. They will tell you that public opinion is emotional and capricious, that it is based on half-truths and listens to witnesses who are not subject to cross-examination. They will tell you that the law surrounds the trial of a case like this with elaborate safeguards, designed to insure that the truth will be known and that every rational consideration bearing on the issues of the case has been taken into account. They will warn you that all of these safeguards go for naught if a mass opinion formed outside this framework is allowed to have any influence on our decision.

But let us look candidly at some of the realities of the

administration of our criminal law. When a man is accused of crime, there are, speaking generally, four ways in which he may escape punishment. One of these is a determination by a judge that under the applicable law he has committed no crime. This is, of course, a determination that takes place in a rather formal and abstract atmosphere. But look at the other three ways in which he may escape punishment. These are: (1) a decision by the Prosecutor not to ask for an indictment; (2) an acquittal by the jury; (3) a pardon or commutation of sentence by the executive. Can anyone pretend that these decisions are held within a rigid and formal framework of rules that prevents factual error, excludes emotional and personal factors, and guarantees that all the forms of the law will be observed?

In the case of the jury we do, to be sure, attempt to cabin their deliberations within the area of the legally relevant, but there is no need to deceive ourselves into believing that this attempt is really successful. In the normal course of events the case now before us would have gone on all of its issues directly to the jury. Had this occurred we can be confident that there would have been an acquittal or at least a division that would have prevented a conviction. If the jury had been instructed that the men's hunger and their agreement were no defense to the charge of murder, their verdict would in all likelihood have ignored this instruction and would have involved a good deal more twisting of the letter of the law than any that is likely to tempt us. Of course the only reason that didn't occur in this case was the fortuitous circumstance that the foreman of the jury happened to be a lawyer. His learning enabled him to devise a form of words that would allow the jury to dodge its usual responsibilities.

My brother Tatting expresses annoyance that the Prosecutor did not, in effect, decide the case for him by not asking for an indictment. Strict as he is himself in complying with the demands of legal theory, he is quite content to have the fate of these men decided out of court by the Prosecutor on the basis of common sense. The Chief Justice, on the other hand, wants the application of common sense postponed to the very end, though like Tatting, he wants no personal part in it.

This brings me to the concluding portion of my remarks, which has to do with executive clemency. Before discussing that topic directly, I want to make a related observation about the poll of public opinion. As I have said, ninety per cent of the people wanted the Supreme Court to let the men off entirely or with a more or less nominal punishment. The ten per cent constituted a very oddly assorted group, with the most curious and divergent opinions. One of our university experts has made a study of this group and has found that its members fall into certain patterns. A substantial portion of them are subscribers to "crank" newspapers of limited circulation that gave their readers a distorted version of the facts of the case. Some thought that "Speluncean" means "cannibal" and that anthropophagy is a tenet of the Society. But the point I want to make, however, is this: although almost every conceivable variety and shade of opinion was represented in this group, there was, so far as I know, not one of them, nor a single member of the majority of ninety per cent, who said, "I think it would be a fine thing to have the courts sentence these men to be hanged, and then to have another branch of the government come along and pardon them." Yet this is a solution that has more or less dominated our discussions and which our Chief Justice proposes as a way by which we can avoid doing an injustice and at the same time preserve respect for law. He can be assured that if he is preserving anybody's morale, it is his own, and not the public's, which knows nothing of his distinctions. I mention this matter because I wish to emphasize once more the danger that we may get lost in the patterns of our own thought and forget that these patterns often cast not the slightest shadow on the outside world.

I come now to the most crucial fact in this case, a fact known to all of us on this Court, though one that my brothers have seen fit to keep under the cover of their judicial robes. This is the frightening likelihood that if the issue is left to him, the Chief Executive will refuse to pardon these men or commute their sentence. As we all know, our Chief Executive is a man now well advanced in years, of very stiff notions. Public clamor usually operates on him with the reverse of the effect intended. As I have told my brothers, it happens that my wife's niece is an intimate friend of his secretary. I have learned in this indirect, but, I think, wholly reliable way, that he is firmly determined not to commute the sentence if these men are found to have violated the law.

No one regrets more than I the necessity for relying in so important a matter on information that could be characterized as gossip. If I had my way this would not happen, for I would adopt the sensible course of sitting down with the Executive, going over the case with him, finding out what his views are, and perhaps working out with him a common program for handling the situation. But of course my brothers would never hear of such a thing.

Their scruple about acquiring accurate information

directly does not prevent them from being very perturbed about what they have learned indirectly. Their acquaintance with the facts I have just related explains why the Chief Justice, ordinarily a model of decorum, saw fit in his opinion to flap his judicial robes in the face of the Executive and threaten him with excommunication if he failed to commute the sentence. It explains, I suspect, my brother Foster's feat of levitation by which a whole library of law books was lifted from the shoulders of these defendants. It explains also why even my legalistic brother Keen emulated Pooh-Bah in the ancient comedy by stepping to the other side of the stage to address a few remarks to the Executive "in my capacity as a private citizen." (I may remark, incidentally, that the advice of Private Citizen Keen will appear in the reports of this court printed at taxpayers' expense.)

I must confess that as I grow older I become more and more perplexed at men's refusal to apply their common sense to problems of law and government, and this truly tragic case has deepened my sense of discouragement and dismay. I only wish that I could convince my brothers of the wisdom of the principles I have applied to the judicial office since I first assumed it. As a matter of fact, by a kind of sad rounding of the circle, I encountered issues like those involved here in the very first case I tried as Judge of the Court of General Instances in Fanleigh County.

A religious sect had unfrocked a minister who, they said, had gone over to the views and practices of a rival sect. The minister circulated a handbill making charges against the authorities who had expelled him. Certain lay members of the church announced a public meeting at which they proposed to explain the position of the church. The minister attended this meeting. Some said he slipped in unobserved in a disguise; his own testimony was that he had walked in openly as a member of the public. At any rate, when the speeches began he interrupted with certain questions about the affairs of the church and made some statements in defense of his own views. He was set upon by members of the audience and given a pretty thorough pommeling, receiving among other injuries a broken jaw. He brought a suit for damages against the association that sponsored the meeting and against ten named individuals who he alleged were his assailants.

When we came to the trial, the case at first seemed very complicated to me. The attorneys raised a host of legal issues. There were nice questions on the admissibility of evidence, and, in connection with the suit against the association, some difficult problems turning on the question whether the minister was a trespasser or a licensee. As a novice on the bench I was eager to apply my law school learning and I began studying these questions closely, reading all the authorities and preparing well-documented rulings. As I studied the case I became more and more involved in its legal intricacies and I began to get into a state approaching that of my brother Tatting in this case. Suddenly, however, it dawned on me that all these perplexing issues really had nothing to do with the case, and I began examining it in the light of common sense. The case at once gained a new perspective, and I saw that the only thing for me to do was to direct a verdict for the defendants for lack of evidence.

I was led to this conclusion by the following considerations. The mêlé in which the plaintiff was injured had been a very confused affair, with some people trying to get to the center of the disturbance, while others were trying to get away from it; some striking at the plaintiff, while others were apparently trying to protect him. It would have taken weeks to find out the truth of the matter. I decided that nobody's broken jaw was worth that much to the Commonwealth. (The minister's injuries, incidentally, had meanwhile healed without disfigurement and without any impairment of normal faculties.) Furthermore, I felt very strongly that the plaintiff had to a large extent brought the thing on himself. He knew how inflamed passions were about the affair, and could easily have found another forum for the expression of his views. My decision was widely approved by the press and public opinion, neither of which could tolerate the views and practices that the expelled minister was attempting to defend.

Now, thirty years later, thanks to an ambitious Prosecutor and a legalistic jury foreman, I am faced with a case that raises issues which are at bottom much like those involved in that case. The world does not seem to change much, except that this time it is not a question of a judgment for five or six hundred frelars, but of the life or death of four men who have already suffered more torment and humiliation than most of us would endure in a thousand years. I conclude that the defendants are innocent of the crime charged, and that the conviction and sentence should be set aside.

TATTING, J.: I have been asked by the Chief Justice whether, after listening to the two opinions just rendered, I desire to re-examine the position previously taken by me. I wish to state that after hearing these opinions I am greatly strengthened in my conviction that I ought not to participate in the decision of this case.

The Supreme Court being evenly divided, the conviction and sentence of the Court of General Instances is *affirmed*. It is ordered that the execution of the sentence shall occur at 6 a.m., Friday, April 2, 4300, at which time the Public Executioner is directed to proceed with all convenient dispatch to hang each of the defendants by the neck until he is dead.

POSTSCRIPT

Now that the court has spoken its judgment, the reader puzzled by the choice of date may wish to be reminded that the centuries which separate us from the year 4300 are roughly equal to those that have passed since the Age of Pericles. There is probably no need to observe that the *Speluncean Case* itself is intended neither as a work of satire nor as a prediction in any ordinary sense of the term. As for the judges who make up Chief Justice Truepenny's court, they are, of course, as mythical as the facts and precedents with which they deal. The reader who refuses to accept this view, and who seeks to trace out contemporary resemblances where none is intended or contemplated, should be warned that he is engaged in a frolic of his own, which may possibly lead him to miss whatever modest truths are contained in the opinions delivered by the Supreme Court of Newgarth. The case was constructed for the sole purpose of bringing into a common focus certain divergent philosophies of law and government. These philosophies presented men with live questions of choice in the days of Plato and Aristotle. Perhaps they will continue to do so when our era has had its say about them. If there is any element of prediction in the case, it does not go beyond a suggestion that the questions involved are among the permanent problems of the human race.

The Speluncean Explorers -
Further Proceedings
Anthony D'Amato

Lon Fuller's *The Case of the Speluncean Explorers is* a classic
in jurisprudence. Set in the Supreme Court of Newgarth in
the year 4300 the case presents five judicial opinions which
clash with each other and produce for the reader an
exhilarating excursion into fundamental theories of law and
the state and the role of courts vis-à-vis legislatures and
executives. Though the issues articulated by Professor Fuller
in 1949 are timeless, the past thirty years in jurisprudential
scholarship have produced at least one major new vantage
point — the "rights thesis" as advanced by Professor
Dworkin and others. Simply stated, the rights thesis holds
that there is a "right" answer, and only one right answer,
in every case. The litigants have a "right" to that and finally
— to add one more shade of meaning to the comprehensive
term "right" — the answer thus arrived at is dictated by
general requirements of justice. Since justice is a branch of
morality, the "right" answer is not only correct but also
right in a moral sense.

My purpose here is to examine how the rights thesis
would apply to the Speluncean Case, and to do so in the
spirit of my former teacher's presentation. Therefore, let us
imagine that, right after the decision in the Speluncean Case
was handed down, the Chief Executive of Newgarth
constituted a Special Commission of three law professors
at the University of Newgarth School of Law to present a
recommendation on the question whether executive

clemency should be extended to the convicted defendants.

OPINION OF PROFESSOR WUN

When I received news of the decision in this case, I was relieved that the Court had reached the only proper result. But later, as I read the opinions of the Justices, I realized how fragile the Court's decision really was. To recap the vote, Justices Handy and Foster voted for acquittal, Tatting withdrew from the case, and although Keen and Truepenny voted to affirm the findings of guilty they engaged in powerful pleas to the Chief Executive to extend clemency to the convicted defendants. Not one of them came even close to believing, as I do, that the defendants were clearly guilty of murder. Perhaps the most egregiously bankrupt opinion illustrating the Court's true feeling is that of Justice Keen, who found it necessary to resort to the old and discredited theory of positivism to prop up his conclusion. He insisted upon a separation between law and morality, holding that "the law" required a finding of guilty even though his own morality would lead to a different result. Without repeating familiar arguments against this positivistic stance, it may suffice to ask what morality compels Justice Keen to insist upon a separation between law and morality.

Since I believe that matters of right cannot be separated from matters of law, I might most efficiently begin by showing that what these defendants did is murder as a matter of morality, and only after that turn to the legal conclusion that murder was committed. As moral arguments are often best proved by analogies, let us consider four persons on the brink of death due to, respectively, a defective heart, diseased lungs, a destroyed liver, and a nonfunctioning kidney. Since their lives are at stake their "need" to have these organs replaced by healthy ones could not possibly be greater. We will assume that there are no replacement organs available. The four persons thereupon decide that they will kidnap a stranger who is in good health, take him to a medical office where they have several highly paid doctors waiting, kill the stranger, and have the doctors transplant his four healthy organs into the four conspirators. Four lives will thus be saved at the cost of only one, and the result can be said to have been objectively compelled by "necessity" and not by any personal malice toward the stranger or any wish to harm him.

I will assume that anyone would immediately conclude that these four persons would be morally guilty of murdering the stranger (and, consequently, that they should be prosecuted under the law for murder). But then, of course, we must ask whether there is any significant difference between the hypothetical and the speluncean explorers. Certainly not because the victim was a stranger whereas Whetmore was known to the explorers. For the case would not be morally improved if the four persons needing organ transplants had instead selected a victim who had been friendly with them. But, one might object, Whetmore was involved in the same enterprise as the other explorers; that surely makes a difference. Yet consider the following alteration: The four persons, partners in a research team, had their vital organs damaged because their machine had broken and emitted omicron rays. A fifth co-worker was also present, but miraculously she was not hurt. Are

44

the four damaged individuals thereby entitled to kill her and transplant her organs simply because she was involved in the same enterprise and at the same time as they?

What of another possible distinction: that Whetmore was going to die shortly of malnutrition anyway, whereas the stranger in the hypothetical case was in good health? Does that fact give the explorers a moral right to kill Whetmore? What if the persons needing transplants read in the papers that doctors had informed a certain individual that he had only six more months left to live? Would they be justified in kidnapping and killing that individual because his interest in living only six months is negligible in comparison with the four of them surviving for many years if they can have his organs? But even the six months can be questioned. The doctors might have been in error as to his good health; or the doctors may have been correct but a month later a cure could be discovered. Possibilities always exist, and they existed even for Whetmore. For the explorers trapped in the cave could not be *certain* that they would not be rescued the next day or even the next hour. Suppose the engineers had been wrong or that another entrance to the cave had been found and the defendants had been rescued two hours after they had killed and eaten Whetmore; would the Justices of our Supreme Court have been as sympathetic about the murder?

Let us look more deeply at estimating the possibility of survival for the four defendants trapped in the cave and the four persons needing organ transplants in the hypothetical case. Surely we cannot coerce *them* to be optimistic about the chance of rescue or of some dramatic medical breakthrough. They have the right to assess the odds for themselves. My contention is simply that they cannot force their version of the odds for survival upon Whetmore or upon the individual who was told he had six months to live.

But such a conclusion does not mean that we should give them a privilege of acting "out of necessity" to harm or kill someone else. At the very most they might decide upon a procedure to save most of their own lives at the expense of one or more of their own number. For example, since each of the four persons needing transplants needed a different organ, any three of them could survive with the healthy organs of the fourth. Suppose the four of them are in the medical office and they put on the table four identical-looking pills, three of which are placebos and the fourth an instantaneous deadly poison. If each selects a pill one would die and his or her organs could immediately be transplanted to the others. Such a procedure, incidentally, would not involve any of them actually killing any of the others; at worst they would each be guilty of attempted suicide and the victim would be guilty of actual suicide. But from a moral point of view, I tend to believe at the present time — unless someone persuades me that I have not refined my personal code of morality sufficiently and that further thought would lead to a different conclusion — that the four persons had a moral right to decide that three survivors would be better than no survivors and that such a procedure would thus be justifiable. Note that the decision to go ahead with the pill-taking was the result of the informed consent of all four persons, each of whom arrived independently at the conclusion that the odds of survival if no action was taken were negligible. The willingness to go ahead with this desperate procedure would prove the genuineness of each individual's decision as to the odds of survival.

Let us apply analogous reasoning to the explorers. Roger Whetmore, for his own reasons, which may have included optimism in a greater degree than any of the other explorers about the chances of an early rescue, did not want to participate in the cannibalism scheme. To be sure there are complicating elements: Whetmore first proposed such a scheme, he carried the dice used to cast lots, and he initially agreed to participate. Yet surely none of these points either in themselves or when taken together estops Whetmore to withdraw, or set up some sort of reliance by the others such that Whetmore could not fairly withdraw from the scheme. Their charging him with a "breach of faith" is outrageous. Such a charge might properly be levelled at one who attempted to withdraw from the scheme *after* being designated the victim, but it cannot be applied to a person who withdrew prior to the throw. Although the Justices of our Supreme Court have glossed over the significance of Whetmore's withdrawal, to me the point is of critical importance. By withdrawing, Whetmore both avoided the risk of being killed by the others and denied himself the chance to survive if the others went ahead with their plan. He chose to risk nothing and had nothing to gain. Certainly such an action cannot be labelled as unfair to others.

The others, however, *did have something to gain* by including Whetmore. To be sure, by including Whetmore, the others were taking a risk that Whetmore might end a winner. Curiously, however, when we examine the odds involved, the fact that Whetmore could be a winner is not as significant as the fact that he could be the loser. Consider the four men only. If one of them is to die so that the others will be saved, then each man's chance of dying is one in four, or 25%. If we include Whetmore, each man's chance of dying now becomes one in five, or 20%. In short, each of the four defendants in this case calculated — and they certainly did so calculate, for we know from the testimony that there was much discussion of the mathematical problems involved—that his own chance of survival *increased* by five percentage points from 75% to 80% if Whetmore was included. The forcible inclusion of Whetmore was distinctly in their self-interest. The motive for murder is clear.

Additionally we should not lose sight of the fact that the others had to *kill* Whetmore. A suicide procedure analogous to the pill-taking hypothetical might have been preferable in itself, but *such a procedure was not available to them.* We know Whetmore refused to throw the dice. Clearly he would have refused to take a pill. By his refusal to participate, Whetmore placed the burden of action upon the others. They had to kill him. In fact, they murdered him.

Although I believe that the preceding arguments establish the defendants' moral guilt, I recognize the possible objection that my position against the "necessity" excuse in criminal law proves too much. Surely there are situations where necessity is a legitimate excuse. What if Whetmore discovered on the twentieth day that his pickaxe, which he purchased with his own money, had a hollow handle filled with condensed food pills to be used in case of emergency. Assume that there are enough pills so that Whetmore and his companions could survive for another two weeks. Assume further that Whetmore had come to loathe his companions and offers only to sell them food pills at astronomical prices. When his companions *accept* his price, Whetmore decides that they could not be trusted to pay once they are freed from the cave, and so he asks for immediate payment in cash. At this point, would his companions have the moral right to take some of the pills away from Whetmore by force? I would say yes. But the distinguishing feature of this hypothetical is that a *property right* is being sacrificed to save one or more lives, whereas in the real case we are considering that a *life* can be sacrificed to save other lives. In short, property-for-life involves rights on a different level, whereas life-for-life involves rights on the same level. And when we operate on the same level, necessity is not a justification. Even in a property-for-property case, for example, a man facing bankruptcy cannot justifiably steal money from someone else so that he can save his own property.

At first blush my analysis may appear to be challenged by *Commonwealth v. Valjean,* a case cited by Justice Tatting, which refused to accept the excuse that the defendant stole a loaf of bread because he was starving. I suppose the court paused seriously over the trade between property and life in that case, but must have decided as it did because a decision in the defendant's favor would have had enormously disruptive consequences for society. For if the law were to allow the theft of property by a starving man, many people might soon put themselves into a condition approaching starvation (for example, by first squandering their money in a gambling parlor) and then use that condition as an excuse for stealing food or money without restraint. Thus the harshness of the result to the defendant in *Valjean* is dictated by the need to deter others from exploiting such an "excuse." In contrast, the facts of the speluncean explorers clearly preclude the possibility of general exploitation for the purpose of obtaining nutriment.

Suppose we alter my hypothetical so that Whetmore finds enough pills only to keep one person alive for two weeks. Then if the others force him to share the pills, each will be kept alive for two or three days, but not until the rescue team breaks in ten days later. In that case, Whetmore would be justified in keeping all the pills for himself. But then this is not a case of property winning over lives, it is still a life-for-life case. For if the others forcibly took away from Whetmore the pills he needed to survive, they would be killing him, even though they may have then redistributed to Whetmore a two or three-day supply equal to each of theirs. Thus even the *Valjean* case, upon further reflection, may be seen as a life-for-life case and thus explainable as directly analogous to the real case of the speluncean explorers. For if hungry people could steal loaves of bread, farmers would not grow as much wheat and bakers would not make loaves of bread for sale to others. The shortage of food would mean that all would starve, including the farmer, since starving men would take away all of his wheat. Allowing theft not only destroys the incentive to produce in order to sell to others, but also destroys the ability to grow wheat for one's own consumption, since as soon as it is grown it will be stolen by hordes of starving people. In brief, it may be very hard to find a true "necessity" case. And if my first pickaxe hypothetical example is such a case, it is different from that of the speluncean explorers.

Let us turn now to the legal analysis, which is coincident with the moral argument previously given. Clearly the statute under which the defendants were convicted covers the present case. Section 12-A of the Consolidated Statutes of Newgarth, N.C.S.A. (N.S.) § 12-A, provides: "Whoever

50

shall willfully take the life of another shall be punished by death." I do not have to explore the question whether this statute admits of exceptions, and I need not repeat the arguments of the Justices of our Supreme Court on the question whether self-defense is one such exception. Suffice it to say that if the statute does allow for exceptions, "necessity" is not one of them since it is a life-for-life and not a property-for-life case.

Nor am I troubled by Justice Foster's argument that the explorers, trapped in the cave, were removed from the jurisdiction of Newgarth and hence the law cannot be applied to them. For one thing, the explorers are nationals and citizens of Newgarth, and on that basis our criminal laws may be extended to them even if they were outside the territorial limits of Newgarth. (Of course they were not; they were in a cave within the Commonwealth.) Second, they killed a national of Newgarth and thereby harmed the Commonwealth itself; accordingly Newgarth has a right of vindication through its criminal law process. Third, the defendants expected to be rescued by citizens of Newgarth, and hence their "captors" — the first persons who would have jurisdiction over them — would be persons subject to our laws. Fourth, the taking of the life of another is the gravest possible violation of a human right enjoyed by everyone wherever located. Even if Judge Foster were correct that legislative power did not reach these explorers in their cave, our laws would provide a statutory and administrative basis for enforcing the universal prohibition against murder wherever perpetrated.

Finally, legal analysis requires us to consider the purpose of the statute. The purpose of the present or any other criminal statute is not primarily to punish someone for a past act but to deter the act from ever taking place. Such statutes institutionalize rights — the rights accorded to every person to *not* be the victim of criminal acts. The purpose of the statute in the present case, therefore, is to give to potential murder victims the protective power of the state. We might imagine Roger Whetmore saying something like the following to the four explorers as they advanced upon him: "What you are about to do is to commit murder. If you do so, and you survive and are rescued from this cave, the Commonwealth of Newgarth will try, convict, and execute you for murder. So do not attempt to kill me. I have not participated in your casting of lots, and you have no rights against me. Either try to hold out a while longer, as I have decided to do, or else do whatever you feel you must among the four of you alone. But do not include me; the law protects me against death at your hands."

Some such statement, I submit, is the only protection that the Whetmores of this Commonwealth may have when they are outnumbered and cannot protect themselves. As I have said earlier, the situation need not be so rare as explorers trapped in a cave; it includes my organ-transplant hypothetical, and any situation where a potential victim must rely on the law for protection. Our Supreme Court has upheld the law. Certainly as Chief Executive you should not undercut the sanction provided by the statute by commuting the sentence. What the defendants did in this case they did willfully. They acted out of self-interest, to increase the odds of their individual survival by forcibly including Whetmore. Now each defendant should pay fully for the murder he committed to advance his self-interest at the expense of the life of another.

OPINION OF PROFESSOR TIEU

As my colleague Professor Wun knows, I have always found it difficult to accept any conclusion he reaches. The present case is the clearest example so far. I believe that the four defendants are innocent of any crime. Since I disagree with Professor Wun's conclusion but not his logic, the difficulty must lie in his premises. His position rests upon a common, unstated, and usually unchallenged assumption that we are all discrete individuals and that the laws of murder provide an essentially nonrational zero-sum game rule for individual players competing with each other. I disagree with his implied definition of human life.

At the most fundamental level, the possibility of human life on earth rests upon the fate of the group, not the individual. The truism that "man is a social animal" tends to hide under a mask of triviality the ultimate fact that for the human species to survive, the individual must be subordinated to the welfare of the group. If, for example, a terrible disease destroyed all but a very few members of the human race, and left only a handful of these capable of reproduction, nothing would be more immoral than to sacrifice these fertile survivors before the others.

Because people have minds of their own, they tend to think that their own welfare has supreme value. Yet the desire for group preservation, over and above individual preservation, has stronger roots. To fully appreciate this point, we might profitably consider two kinds of behavior observed in other species: the warning behavior and the leadership phenomenon.

An impala will warn the rest of the herd if it spots a nearby lion; the repeated warning snorts enable the herd to run away, but the warner risks its life. A gazelle warns its fellows by leaping repeatedly stifflegged on all four feet. Yet this permits an approaching pack of predatory dogs to catch up with the gazelle that gives warning even though the rest of the herd escapes. What is noteworthy about these and other instances that have been reported of the "warning" function is that, under standard evolutionary theory, the warners should have been "selected out" eons ago. Clearly what is happening is that the *group* is being saved by an hereditary characteristic that causes the death of some of the members of the group. Species survival exceeds the survival of individuals, and it is not extinguished even though the individuals who give the warning are sacrificed.

As a further behavioral example, within a given territory or grouping of like animals, a particular animal is deferred to as the leader of the group. The leader is easy to identify; it is usually given the best food, choice of mate or mates, and the other animals respond to its movements as if they are commands. Should the leader be killed, the group will find an individual animal — who previously had only been a follower — to inherit the leadership mantle and assume that position. From an evolutionary point of view, the problem here is not the extinction of the leadership characteristic (as it was in the case of warners), but rather why the leadership trait has not become dominant. The leader of the group typically has the most offspring (due to choice of mates and other perquisites of leadership) and yet, over the centuries, the group's "follower" characteristic has not been extinguished. The answer, again, must be that leading and following are not individual characteristics but rather are functions of the group.

The "warning" and "leadership" behaviors have always been a part of human society. We have many words that indicate behaviors similar to the sacrificial warning behavior of animals: courage, heroism, martyrdom, nobility, gallantry, altruism, and so forth. When a group of people—or a nation — is endangered, these traits blossom forth in some individuals so that the group may be protected. Yet self-sacrifice is not selected out; courage and heroism never die. Similarly, leadership—not only political but also in the arts and sciences and in social groupings — is a commonplace event. We are in fact so accustomed to these behaviors that their importance has to be stressed here.

One could object at this point that I have only *described* behavior in some animals and some humans that points to the paramountcy of group survival, and that we cannot derive from this description a normative statement that would govern how all humans *ought* to behave. In other words, an "is" cannot produce an "ought." My reply is twofold. First, I deny that an "ought" does not follow from an "is." Our entire normative mode of reasoning rests upon our conviction that some things, as a consequence of their existence, should be maintained. For example, our life-supporting environment is a fact; from it we derive the proposition that we have a duty to maintain the environment not only for all humans in existence but for future generations as well. The very notion of a normative principle can have no meaning if it excludes the most fundamental imperative of all: that since human life exists, it ought to be maintained. If we cannot conclude from the fact that human life exists the proposition that it ought to continue to exist, then, I submit, we do not really know what is valuable, and without this, we cannot know the meaning of the term "ought" at all. In my previous examples, we saw that a group of animals could owe its continued existence to the genetic trait manifested in some of them who, at sacrificial cost, warned the rest of imminent danger. The only one who could conclude that the warning behavior was valueless would be one who denies that there is any value whatsoever in living. Such a person could not give any meaning to the term "morality," much less comment on whether morality can be derived from fact. Those who understand what "morality" means ultimately trace their understanding to observations of fact. Second, even if I must assume for the moment that "ought" cannot be derived from "is," my previous examples reduce to highly suggestive claims. Anyone looking dispassionately at the warning behavior in a social grouping of animals would have to concede that nature is trying to tell us something! And what nature is saying, rather unambiguously, is that "life" consists of the continued existence of the group rather than any of its members.

So far I have been somewhat abstract in defining the "life" of a group, and the definition should be made precise. Each particular animal is the manifestation of the blueprints of its genes, and the carrier of those genes. Bodies are in reality only the temporary supporters of the genes. The living genes are truly immortal, so long as the species which supports them continues to survive.

From this last observation I derive the ultimate moral imperative: that one may not destroy the possibility of reproduction. I think we have always perceived this fact even though it tends to go unnoticed in the routine of our lives. What are our laws but expressions of concern for group survival? From the lowliest traffic ordinance to the prohibition against genocide, the laws bespeak social preservation. If the perceptions of how society is best preserved change, the laws will surely change as well — even laws which seem clear and unchangeable. As an example, we might briefly reflect upon the history of abortion.

In the period following the Great Spiral, there was a perceived fear that human life might be snuffed out completely. Our numbers were small and the conditions of living were harsh. At that time a human fetus was considered a "life in being" and hence abortion was universally condemned as "murder" under the laws. But after several centuries of population growth and normal conditions, the laws against abortion were honored more in the breach than in the observance. Although religions continued to consider abortion a grave sin, hardly anyone was criminally prosecuted. Finally, in the modern era, overpopulation, and not underpopulation, is considered a grave threat to human survival. As the peril of overpopulation has become perceived and absorbed by the public and by the lawmakers, we have witnessed the total legalization of abortion. We have witnessed a historic change in the popular conception of a human fetus; it is no longer a "life," but rather, the mere possibility of one. Although religious institutions have been the slowest to react, we are also seeing changes in their doctrine. The very definition of "life" for the purpose of our laws against murder thus reflects a differential societal perception of the danger to human survival.

What of the more typical case of "murder"? Why does our statute provide that a human being who kills another shall forfeit his own life? If capital punishment is appropriate in our modern age of an overpopulated world, how could it ever have been appropriate in conditions of perceived underpopulation? Capital punishment was conceived for the purpose of deterrence. Even in an underpopulated society, the best way to ensure the minimum number of intentional killings is to threaten the killer with the loss of his own life. Unfortunately, in those few cases where the threat fails, society must exact capital punishment *not* because it has "promised" to do so or because vengeance is necessary, but rather — and only — to ensure the threat's credibility to future potential murderers. We have historical examples where, despite the statute, the penalty is not exacted. In time of war, when there have been severe shortages of military personnel, a convicted murderer will not be executed but will be sent into the front lines. Society does not want to "waste" even convicted murderers when, by being sent to the front fighting lines, they will contribute to its survival.

The foregoing considerations serve to indicate the narrowness of my colleague Professor Wun's individualistic approach to the present case. He views the law of murder as analogous to the rules of a game. He is afraid that the game will be impaired if the game rule is not applied to the four men who killed Whetmore. But why does he not inquire into the purpose of this game? Why do we have a law against murder? What values are at stake? These are the questions that go totally ignored in the one-dimensional approach of my colleague.

Under the view that I have outlined, we should consider the five explorers trapped in the cave as a total society. We do not have to do this in the same somewhat artificial sense expressed by Judge Foster. Rather, we can consider as a fact that the group existence of the five men would be terminated entirely unless they undertook strong action.

To survive, they had to kill and eat one of their number. We might draw an analogy to an individual who has to amputate a diseased limb that would otherwise threaten to destroy his body. (Similarly, the "body politic" in the cave had to kill one of its members to preserve the corpus.) As important as a leg or arm is to an individual, he or she should not hesitate to amputate it if that is the only way to preserve the life of the body. And, I might add, it is not essential to my analogy that the arm or leg be diseased. If one's limb were hopelessly trapped beneath a railroad tressle, amputation to avoid being killed by an oncoming train would be gruesome, but entirely rational. No religious prohibition of self-mutilation could make any sense in such a case. But then how can Professor Wun think that what the explorers did was in any sense immoral?

To the contrary, the most immoral act that we can conceive would be to terminate the life of the group. Conversely, one of the highest acts of morality is to preserve the life of a group. The explorers trapped in the cave must have sensed the force of this moral imperative. Despite all their previous training and all their previous social experiences and learned taboos, they had to reach the decision to engage in cannibalism in order to survive.

I could end my argument at this point, but perhaps it might be helpful for avoiding misunderstanding to spell out the acceptable procedures for implementing this moral imperative. Had one of the explorers been the "leader" in the cave, I would see nothing wrong with that leader *selecting* the victim whose flesh would provide the life-saving nutriment to the others. I would not second-guess the selection. Fairness in selection is as unimportant when the life of the group is at stake as it would be absurd, in my self-mutilation hypothetical, to have to be "fair" to all one's fingers if one of them has to be sacrificed. Thus the leader in the cave might base his selection of a victim on a ground as arbitrary as that suggested by Judge Tatting: Kill the one person who believes in afterlife, since the harm to him would be the least. Or it might be to kill the oldest, or the poorest, or the fattest. Or — to take care of Professor Wun's position — the decision might be to kill any individual who did not want to participate in the plan for group survival. Indeed, it would make no difference to me if the leader were to "reward" the person *who first proposed* the idea of cannibalism as a means of saving four out of five lives by selecting *him* as the victim.

Now, in fact, there was a "leadership" principle working in the cave, manifesting itself in the form of a democracy rather than an autocracy. The leadership was that of the group; its will became the ruling principle. It decided, in its wisdom, to give Roger Whetmore an even chance with the others in the throw of the dice. I do not consider that to have been a necessary part of the selection procedure, but the democratic nature of the proceedings in the cave certainly does not hurt my overall argument. Perhaps the "leadership" that emerged in the cave could only have emerged if it were grounded, as it was, upon conditions of fairness and equality. No matter. The fact is that four men survived. Had the leadership principle not emerged, the rescue party would have found in the cave five dead speluncean explorers. Would such a scene have been fair repayment for the tremendous efforts of the rescue party? Yet those who now want to execute the group for the crime of self-preservation would essentially recreate such a scene.

There has been no violation of N.C.S.A. (N.S.) § 12-A stating that "[w]hoever shall willfully take the life of another shall be punished by death," since we must construe "life" as the life of the group in the cave, as we would in a situation where the entire society's future existence is imperilled. It is with the greatest irony, then, that we must conclude that the only person in this case who could violate the statute would be the public executioner, if he is allowed to proceed to execute the four defendants. He *would* be "willfully taking the life of another." As Chief Executive, you need not be an instrumentality in the derivation of an immoral conclusion from absurd premises. I urge you to pardon the defendants.

OPINION OF PROFESSOR THRI

I recommend that you commute the sentence of the four defendants to several years' compulsory service in a hospital or similar place where they can help save the lives of others, for I believe that the defendants are neither guilty nor innocent of the crime of murder. Lest my position appear a compromise between those of my colleagues, I hasten to point out at the outset that no true compromise between their extreme positions appears possible. They present a thesis and an antithesis on what constitutes "life." Even so, I want to draw upon aspects of each of their separate opinions in constructing my own synthesis.

Let me start with Professor Tieu's argument that the

relevant unit in this case is the group and not the individual. As she well knows from our many discussions, I reject the metaphysics upon which she leans in fashioning a larger-than-life portrait of the group or the state. But metaphysics aside, I find her present argument nothing other than the old, and I should have thought discredited, philosophy of utilitarianism.

A classic objection to this form of utilitarianism is that in practice it becomes the tyranny of the majority. A society may, for example, enslave members of a different race, and then justify the continued system of slavery on the ground that the harm to a minority (the enslaved) is outweighed by the happiness and luxury afforded to the majority (the citizenry). There is a similar danger in Professor Tieu's espousal of the arbitrary grounds for selecting the explorers' victim. If Whetmore were selected arbitrarily, the procedure would be as morally unjustifiable as the perversion of utilitarianism that justifies slavery. I think Professor Tieu's argument would be improved if she *required* that each person in the cave be subjected to an equal chance of being killed. In that permutation we might see utilitarianism in its pure form.

But even with the proviso of fairness in the selection of the victim, her argument would still be vulnerable. Suppose a crime is committed which causes great public outrage, and many lives will be lost in riots if the killer is not apprehended and brought to justice quickly. If the police cannot find the killer, utilitarianism requires that the authorities select an innocent person as a scapegoat, manufacture evidence, and convict him. Many lives would be saved at the expense of one, although the law is perverted. Similarly, utilitarianism would condone Professor

Wun's organ-transplant hypotheticals, which save several lives at the expense of one. Since all these examples are logically required by utilitarianism, we can only conclude that the philosophy does not express a moral system.

But despite my criticisms of Professor Tieu's philosophical premises, I want now to derive an important argument from her insistence upon the group as the relevant unit. Her simplistic vision of the "group" usefully summarizes a complex set of mutual reliances. The explorers were in fact engaged in a co-operative enterprise. In general, when a person decides to join a society to go spelunking in the company of its members he knows by the very nature of its being a joint expedition that the others will support him if a common danger or emergency arises. Indeed, this is why explorers tend to work in groups. A solitary explorer would be taking enormous risks of being disabled and being unable to summon help. Even in a two-person exploring team, if one is hurt and needs continuous attention, there would be no third person to summon assistance. We can readily see that important safety increments may be added as each marginal person joins the group. We might well infer that in the absence of any other evidence, Whetmore's decision to go exploring with the others may have been critical in their decision to go exploring at all. They may have decided that safety considerations required five; and, impliedly, all five would have to undertake to pitch in to ensure group safety. In short, Professor Tieu is right in her criticism of Professor Wun's "zero-sum game" approach. Clearly the explorers were not engaged in a mutually antagonistic or competitive enterprise going into the cave or even when the landslide sealed off the passage.

It is in this sense that a coherent meaning can be given to the charge by the four defendants that Whetmore was guilty of a "breach of faith" when he withdrew from the lottery. Professor Wun assumes the charge was based solely upon Whetmore's withdrawing from the lottery after having suggested it was the right thing to do. But a more reasonable explanation of their charge is that Whetmore had no right not to contribute to the solution of the emergency that threatened all of them, just as he would have had no right to refuse to take his turn at chopping through the wall of the cave if that had been a feasible means of escape. When he joined the group, Whetmore knew that he was committing himself to *full participation* in the event of emergency. If Whetmore at the outset of the exploration had declared that if he was not in the mood when an emergency arose he would feel no obligation to do his share in helping to meet it, we can be quite certain that the others would not have accepted him as part of their group.

If Whetmore had no right to withdraw from the group's attempt to meet the emergency, does it follow that the defendants had a right to include him in their lottery and to kill him when he emerged the loser? If I could answer this question affirmatively, I would reach the same result as Professor Tieu and conclude that the defendants are innocent of any crime. However, the argument stops short of fully convincing me because of the following objection.

In joining the group Whetmore implicitly agreed to do his share of the work and to participate in the handling of emergency situations. Thus if the combined effort of five men could have moved the boulders that sealed the cave, he would have had no right to refuse to participate. But there are two limits, each decisive, to the inferred agreement to participate in an emergency. First, joint exploration does not require that any person be required to risk his *life* to save the others. Such an act of moral altruism is rare in any circumstance and certainly has never been a part of normal expected behavior. A mountain climber, for example, might slip and be placed in mortal danger; the others in the group must do everything to help her save herself, but they are not expected to risk their lives to save hers. (Of course, I am talking of a meaningful risk of life, and not a negligible one which might indeed be present in any exploring venture; in fact, I am talking about a 20% risk of life, which was the chance in the lottery in the present case.) Second, even if we concede that the explorers agreed to risk their lives to save another in an emergency, the situation in the cave was entirely beyond their agreement. In the normal case a risk is undertaken in which all might be saved. Rescuer and rescued combine to overcome a situation so that both will survive. But in the cave the explorers had passed that point. The boulders were unmovable. Nature had already won. Indeed, the exploring enterprise was over, for no amount of effort, no degree of risk against nature could make any difference. It was inconsistent with the idea of a lottery that everyone could survive. Therefore such a situation was not at all contemplated in the agreement to go exploring. Whetmore had not lost the right to choose not to be a part of a pact that would result in certain death "by inference" when he originally agreed to go exploring. It is clear that unless another argument is made on behalf of the defendants, the "group" argument is insufficient to exonerate them.

But such an argument can be made, I believe, if we examine closely the reasoning relating to the defense of "necessity" in Professor Wun's opinion. Professor Wun disclaims total opposition to the "necessity" argument. Clearly his own hypothetical example of Whetmore finding food pills in the pickaxe handle is a compelling case for allowing such a defense. This Commonwealth certainly recognizes that each human being has a privilege, if survival is at stake, to appropriate the property of another. It is a property-for-life case, and the defendants in the pickaxe hypothetical would have a legal right to take the pills by force, so long as they left Whetmore enough pills so that *he* could survive.

The problem that I have with my colleague's reasoning is his easy assumption that the speluncean explorers is a life-for-life case. My colleague argues that when Whetmore tells the others that he has withdrawn from the scheme, they could have excluded Whetmore and proceeded to work out a suicide pact among themselves. Accordingly, one of the four would lose and would have killed himself. The three would be entitled to eat his dead flesh, and Whetmore, having excluded himself from the total arrangement, would not be so entitled. But here is the flaw in my colleague's reasoning. At that point Whetmore *would* be entitled to eat the nutriment, since it is no longer a "life" but is merely the "property" of the other three explorers. The fact that his withdrawal from the lottery was conditioned upon his subsequent disentitlement to partake of the nutriment is nothing other than a statement that the other three explorers have a property interest in the dead body. Yet this interest can legally be overcome when a life (Whetmore's) is at stake, just as in the pickaxe example a property interest in the pills can be overcome when survival is at stake.

We can well imagine what would happen a day or two after one of the four explorers died and the others are surviving on his dead flesh. Whetmore might beg for food, he might repent his "ill-advised" decision not to participate in the lottery, and he would surely point out that there is ample food for all to survive for ten more days, and that their insistence upon excluding him now would mean that he would die when he could otherwise survive at no cost to them. An argument exists for Whetmore to the effect that the others will be guilty of murder if they deprive him of the nutriment. For if he has a legal right to the nutriment — a right based upon the property-for-life argument from "necessity" — then they have no right to deprive him of it. Such a deprivation would in fact amount to murder.

Thus we arrive at the conclusion that there was no way legally for the others to exclude Whetmore from surviving on the dead flesh of one of their number. Or to put it differently, at the moment Whetmore withdrew from the lottery, he was in effect, if not consciously, trying to ensure his own survival at no risk to himself. Clearly the law cannot single out one person for special treatment, requiring the others to risk their own lives to save Whetmore. Conversely, the others were legally justified in forcibly including him in their lottery.

We now have the argument in behalf of the defendants. First, the "group" argument operates to show that they had a right *to some extent* to rely upon Whetmore's participation. Second, the "necessity" argument indicates that there was no reasonable nor fair alternative to their forcibly including Whetmore in the lottery. But while these two arguments distinguish the present case from Professor Wun's organ-transplant hypotheticals, the defendants are not completely innocent. They took a life, and they profited from it; technically, they violated the statute. Yet if it ever made sense to have a pardoning power, it makes sense to have it in a case of technical violation of a statute where a substantial justification can be advanced for the violation. And the pardoning power is not an all-or-nothing tool. The defendants' sentences can be commuted to *lesser* penalties. I would urge that the defendants be sentenced to three or four years' compulsory service in a hospital or similar institution where they may be in a position to save the lives of people who need help. In that fashion, I believe, exact justice will have been achieved.

A Post-Speluncean Dialogue

The year is 4301 in Newgarth, one year since the Supreme Court's infamous decision was handed down in "The Case of the Speluncean Explorers". In an academics' common room of Newgarth's most venerable and prestigious university five legal theorists are sitting down for an after-dinner drink.

Thomas Devine: I heard that the Chief Executive this afternoon overturned the guilty verdicts of the four speluncean explorers. Will their families receive any compensation?

Lawrence Leg: I don't know. The Chief Executive's rationale was typically circumspect though. Besides, do you know the legislature still hasn't moved to change the law to allow for a defence of necessity?

Hercule Droit: That's because there's no need to Lawrence. The best answer in the Speluncean Case was always 'not guilty.' The judges, or at least Justice Keen and the Chief Justice, simply got it wrong.

Here, let's take the second-half of Foster's judgment as a starting point, for Foster there comes the closest of any of the five justices to a correct approach to judicial interpretation. He says, more or less, that we must interpret law in light of its purpose and where a strict application of a statute defeats its purpose then the courts must prefer an interpretation which is intelligent and fulfils the purpose. Now that's not quite the way to put it. What judges should do is to hold statutes up against their own conceptions of the community's larger political beliefs and morality and interpret in such a way that the statute best meshes with that morality and those beliefs. The problem with the way Foster puts it is that talk of purpose is ambiguous. The purposive approach can also suggest that the intentions of the law-making body are determinative. Yet seeking legislative intentions is not only foolish but impossible. Attributing some sole original intent to one person would be precarious. Doing so to an assemblage of individuals representing diverse and frequently conflicting interests is almost disingenuous.

Stan Readdi: We agree on that much, Hercule.

Lawrence Leg:
(after a pause)   But Hercule, your approach is open to the same sort of criticism as Tatting hints at when he says to Foster that more than

one purpose can be ascribed to a law. As a matter of evident fact, different judges will hold different views about what is the best community morality.

Stan Readdi: And no doubt those views will depend on the judges' socio-economic background. Any observed uniformity will be due more to the shared privileged backgrounds of most judges and their past experiences as highly paid lawyers than to any 'correct' type of reasoning.

Hercule Droit: Now wait a minute. I nowhere deny that different judges will come to different answers. That's obvious. It's also true that different judges will have different views of what constitutes the society's best political morality. But that does not mean there is more than one right view. Look at it this way. If Lawrence, Stan and I were watching Mandy play the shell game and, with very quick deftness of hand, she hid a ball under one of the three shells, it might be that all three of us thought the ball was under a different shell, although none of us was absolutely sure. Each of us would hold an honest belief about the location of the ball. However, only one of us would be right. When it comes to judicial interpretation there can also be right answers. It's just

71

that one cannot simply lift shells to see who is right. One has to argue, give reasons, become a participant. Start with Newgarth's clear-cut statutes, authoritative cases and settled constitutional provisions and then construct a scheme which best justifies all of them. One scheme, one shell if you will, will do this better than any other. And in the Speluncean Case the best answer was 'not guilty'.

Lawrence Leg: You're a very clever man Hercule and it's a very clever theory of interpretation. Unfortunately you make assumptions, implicit assumptions, which may not be easily accepted were they made explicit. For one thing, you compare and equate the shell game to constructing a best political morality. But the former is about the external world where, at least in theory, there are right answers. We all know, for instance, that this pen in my hand will fall if I let go of it and not even Stan, I suspect, would want to argue that whether the pen falls or not is a question of context, of frameworks, or of hierarchies. There are things about the external world which we can know. Yet I'm not sure questions of right and wrong, of best and worst, of what is Newgarth's best or right political morality, fall into the same category. I'm not sure moral standards and principles, rights if you will, have the objective foundations you require.

Sometimes there are no clear answers when judges are interpreting statutes. And then judges simply make law; they legislate. And yes it is retrospective. But that's better than not resolving the conflict at all.

Thomas Devine: I've never been much inspired by games, not even the shell-game. But at the same time it does strike me that occasionally you're not hard-headed enough Lawrence. Of course you're right that judges make law - does anyone honestly doubt that in the year 4301? - but you don't carry through the analysis. What makes the Speluncean Case so fascinating is that all five judges, deep down, don't think that the four spelunkers who killed and ate Whetmore really did anything morally wrong in the circumstances. The language of the statute itself is as clear as possible: "Whoever shall wilfully take the life of another shall be punished by death." The five justices were not in doubt about the meaning of this rule. The problem was not one of indeterminacy of meaning, the problem was more fundamental. The consequences of applying this murder statute, this legal rule, conflicted with the judges' moral or normative senses. Now this situation is very unusual in Newgarth; in most instances our legal rules can be seen as crystallizations of broadly shared, if amorphous, values. The legal rule is the result of a choice if you will, not a deduction or discovery, falling somewhere within a moral consensus. But in the Speluncean Case none of the five judges treats the legal rule as producing a moral result. And so really what you see in the Speluncean Case are five differing judicial responses to a conflict between law and morality. Handy follows his own sense of justice which he equates with that of the majority of the population. Foster is much more sophisticated but ultimately insists on law being filtered through a moral strainer. The Chief Justice, on the other hand, quietly abdicates moral evaluations to the Chief Executive. Keen, not so quietly, does so to the legislature. For him, law is the only proper realm for the judge, however distasteful the result. And as for Tatting, well he just loses himself in a sea of conflicting duties.

Lawrence Leg: But Thomas, opting to enforce the legal rules, even when the judge feels them to be wrong, is itself a moral position. Keen's decision is as much a 'moral' one as Foster's. Keen simply thinks the best long-term consequences, the 'right' thing to do in your terminology, flow from letting the elected legislature, not the unelected judiciary, make the ultimate social policy decisions.

Stan Readdi: You tend to be a bit too analytical, Lawrence. Sometimes you miss the forest for the trees. What is interesting about law is explaining the moral consensus, in fact lack of consensus, that supports it. The legal order arbitrarily and indefensibly favours certain outcomes that are no more objective or mandated or justified than their opposites. Hence individualism is privileged over communitarianism, rules over non-rule standards, and this takes place in a way such that any other preference or privileging is categorized as irrational and incoherent at worst or immoral and illegitimate at best. You've been quiet Mandy. Don't you agree?

Mandy Arkal:
(*having been
inattentive
for a while*):   Actually, I get a bit bored with this all. You men seem to think that fundamental

difficulty in the way of understanding law is the absence of a fully descriptive, or perhaps prescriptive, theory of judicial interpretation.

Stand Readdi
and Lawrence Leg
(*in unison*):   That's not true. Other aspects of legal philosophy are much more important.

Mandy Arkal: Let me finish, please. The constant focus on appeal court reasoning - a focus which pervades this university's and all Newgarth's law schools, not just in jurisprudence - obscures much that needs to be seen about law in society. Who made the legal rules and who do they benefit? What are the society's power hierarchies and relationships? How can law be used to undermine, rather than support, those relationships and hierarchies? It's all very well examining the sorts of judicial reasoning in the Speluncean Case but such speculations don't have much relevance to my concerns about law.

Stan Readdi: I couldn't have said it better myself, Mandy. The sociological structures and determining modes of material relations, de-contextualized from their current teleological and privileged foundations, and reconstituted for a just, egalitarian, non-hierarchical society, must focus law's study.

Thomas Devine
(*after a lenghty pause*):

Yes, well, perhaps. But then, we're all *legal* academics aren't we? What training or expertise do any of us have in sociology, economics, indeed philosophy? All these demands for 'law and society' courses might more aptly be presented as 'sociology, economics and whatever else you want to know by unqualified lawyers' courses.

Stan Readdi
(*reddening*):

I may not be a sociologist Thomas but at least I keep my eyes trained on this world, not on some ethereal realm of intuited right conduct. Your whole frame of reference presupposes the most unbelievable ...

Thomas Devine
(*interrupting*):

Do you ever have anything positive, anything not solely destructive, to add? What little you do say that's 'programmatic' - is that the term? - is far more utopian than anything I'd venture.

Hercule Droit:

Come, come. There's no reason to let the

conversation degenerate into name-calling. Lawrence, pass the port over to Thomas and Stan. There, that's better.

At least you and I can agree, I take it Thomas, that there are right answers to questions of interpretation.

Thomas Devine: Well in this case there was. But I think 'guilty' was the right answer.

Hercule Droit: Surely not Thomas. The spelunkers were clearly 'not guilty'. The statute does not apply here and the principle, drawn from the best synthesis of Newgarth's political morality, that 'No wrong occurs where only a prophet could act otherwise' is determinative.

Thomas Devine: No. What the four defendants did in killing Whetmore was wrong, morally wrong. These four men wilfully took a life not threatening their own. That was self-evidently evil and bad. Justice demanded that they be punished for that act, for breaking the categorical moral imperative. Whatever synthesis you might manufacture Hercule out of the body of Newgarth's statutes and cases cannot change that. No one can sympathise with the defendants' awful plight more than I, but following one's duty is not always easy. Indeed that is its attraction. Of course this is not to say I approve of capital punishment. I do not. It is no more just for the state to take life than it is for the individual.

Mandy Arkal
(*winking at Lawrence*): But why do you think there are right answers to all questions of judicial interpretation, Thomas?

Thomas Devine: I never said that. I said there are answers, true, right answers, to what conduct or action is or is not moral. To that extent I agree with Hercule, although it seems to me that you, Hercule, are embarrassed to come out of the closet and publicly support my position on this point. You want to say there are best, right answers to what is the community's true political morality - against which all interpretation is to be done - but you refuse to say that this true morality is objective, timeless and categorical. In what sense can a political morality be right or true if moral standards are not externally validated or reasoned to? You can't have it both ways here Hercule, reaping the certainties of my moral objectivism without having to defend its corresponding world-view against the likes of Lawrence and Stan.

(turning to Mandy)

I'm not sure where to put you on this question, Mandy?

Mandy Arkal: As an interested bystander I think, Thomas.

Hercule Droit: I think I've made myself clear on this point, Thomas. Unlike you I limit my sense of 'right' or 'best' to a particular society, say Newgarth last year. Now it may be that other societies and cultures have differing values, differing right answers, from Newgarth's. But for Newgarth in 4300 the settled statutes, cases and constitutional provisions will provide a best answer to all questions of principle. There will be disagreement but one answer, perhaps one not yet advanced, will have more reasons in its favour than any of the others.

Mandy Arkal: But can't I simply say, nonetheless, that the existing statutes, cases and the rest won't constrain my decision? I mean even were it possible, definitively, to 'find' the original intent of the legislature I don't see why a judge need always be bound by it. And your best fit is no different. Why is *it* always binding?

Lawrence Leg: I'm afraid you don't convince me either Hercule. However there is definitely an attraction to what you say. It partly comes from this, I think. In a society with a more or less 'benevolent' political structure it is easy, indeed it seems quite natural, to see legal statutes and rules as aligning with some broad political morality somehow drawn from or related to those settled rules. By limiting ourselves to 'benevolent' societies we have ruled out in advance, after all, any deep and sustained conflict between legal rules and moral norms of a certain sort. So when in doubt about legal rules what is less conspicuous than for a judge to turn to this political morality for an answer? Hence your advocacy of looking to a best political morality for an answer is certainly attractive, although I say again that no one answer is right or best when it comes to morality even for a particular 'benevolent' polis. But such an intermingling of legal rules and political moral norms is much less attractive if one finds herself living in a 'wicked' legal system. Put your theory to work in the context of the Darthic States during its cultural revolution or during Newgarth's own slave-owning period and it's quite clear that the best, or some most favourable, framework which explains all the settled statutes, cases and constitutional provisions is still pretty horrific, or would be judged so by large chunks of the population. Why interpret legal rules against such a best fit in those circumstances? Is the judge still bound to follow the best fit interpretation in a 'wicked' system? If not, who decides - I detect circularity here - if the system's 'wicked'? In all these instances of a 'wicked' system don't you really rely on, and assume to exist, the same sort of over-arching, objective moral norms as Thomas?

Stan Readdi: Perhaps, Hercule, you might adopt one of my lines of thought here and say to Lawrence that 'wicked' legal systems collapse into 'benevolent' ones if one changes her vantage.

Thomas Devine: Hercule's not that much of an apostate yet, Stan.

Hercule Droit: Nor do I need to be.

Mandy Arkal: I hope we're not about to open that can of worms about a judge's duty in an evil political system. Nothing is ever resolved. Thomas says the good judge should resign; Lawrence says the good judge should stay on and do what can be done to alleviate the law's grosser injustices; Hercule, surprisingly, says the good judge may have to lie and follow morality over the dictates of evil laws; Stan, meanwhile, seems much less moved by horribly wicked regimes than by the far slighter injustices closer to home. Really, I do hope we're not going to discuss this issue again because...

(breaking off as she notices an assortment of cheeses and fruits being served)

Shall we take a break?

— 10 minutes later—

Stan Readdi: That was delicious.

Thomas Devine: In the context of an interactive non-discoursing, non-disgorging, non-disengaging encounter between animate and animately-challenged you mean?

Lawrence Leg
(quickly inter-jecting): Getting back to the Speluncean Case, I am prepared to defend the view that when the rules aren't clear judges should look at consequences - good consequences. Stripping away the self-assuredness this is one way to read

Handy's judgment and, with caveats, it's the one I too would adopt.

Stan Readdi: But Handy effectively says that he knows what's right and just and to hell with the rules. I'm surprised that appeals to you Lawrence.

Lawrence Leg: Well of course the claim to have authoritative access to rightness or truth is preposterous.

Thomas Devine: It is in *this* instance.

Hercule Droit: I agree.

Lawrence Leg: But there are two points to be raised in Handy's defence. Firstly, he's more honest, at least, than the judge who also favours a particular outcome as the most 'just' but who never reveals this, preferring to reach her desired outcome in traditional garb and through familiar methods.

(*Turning to Hercule*)

You may say this never happens.

Stan Readdi
(*jumping in*): But it does, and one could ask why truth is more desirable than right outcome or

good consequences.

Lawrence Leg: I'll make a consequentialist or utilitarian of you yet, Stan. Certainly there is no *necessary* connection between truth and good consequences. The pessimistic utilitarian will say truth and good consequences do not always align and opt for the latter when he thinks they conflict. The optimist, like me, will say that there is never anything to fear from the truth. At least in the long-term, Handy's ingenuousness will lead to better consequences than a paternalistic concealment.

Mandy Arkal: But there's no way to know that for sure is there?

Lawrence Leg: Utilitarianism gives no sure answers Mandy, only a sure approach — look to consequences! You see you and I may differ both about likely consequences *and* about preferred outcomes and yet we may both be utilitarians. It is not an approach that provides certainty; it is an approach that limits uncertainty in a radically subjective moral world. Agree to count individuals' welfare equally and agree on who is to count (and these, after all, are also mere subjective preferences) and then the only variables utilitarianism throws up are likely consequences and varying preferences. And there *are* right answers to the former, albeit not the latter.

Thomas Devine: Of course one might always object that right and wrong, true morality, do *not* depend upon the particular evaluator and are not radically subjective.

Lawrence Leg: Yes, *if* persuasive that contention would lessen the attraction of consequentialism.

Thomas Devine: Because in that case the dictates of consequentialism might well conflict with right morality.

Hercule Droit: Look, the flaw in this utilitarian approach is more basic than that Thomas. The flaw is in giving any weight at all to an individual's preferences about others' outcomes.

Mandy Arkal: Why? If Lawrence is right about a radically subjective moral world then not counting such external preferences is merely your own subjective preference Hercule. If there is something intrinsically wrong with such counting aren't you agreeing with Thomas?

Stan Readdi
(*breaking in*):   I want to go back and hear what
                     Lawrence has to say is the second thing
                     that can be said in defence of Handy's
                     approach. I frankly thought it was a
                     terrible judgment. One part sage and one
                     part populist, it reeked of 'trust-me-I'm-a-
                     judge'.

Mandy Arkal: To answer you my guess is that
                     Lawrence might ask you to take a more
                     dispassionate   perspective.   Distance
                     yourself from this particular case and try
                     to see the workings of the legal system as
                     a whole. Take the vantage not of the
                     participating litigant but of the observer,
                     of the uninvolved visiting Martian?

Hercule Droit
(*grumbling*):   That's not possible.

Mandy Arkal
(*ignoring Hercule
and continuing*):   From the spectator's point of view a legal
                     system may well be healthier and more
                     vibrant when there's a variety of different
                     approaches to judicial interpretation.
                     Were all judges to follow Keen's lead
                     there'd certainly be certainty but at great
                     cost in flexibility and adaptability to
                     changing circumstances. But a court full
                     of Fosters would be no improvement
                     either for then social policy-making

would rightly be seen to have shifted largely to an unrepresentative elite and predictability would require a sound knowledge of the size of the particular judge's foot. From the disinterested observer's vantage a mixture of approaches is perhaps best.

Hercule Droit
(quietly to himself):
The losing litigant won't be much condoled by prescriptions to take a more Olympian point of view.

Lawrence Leg:
Yes, exactly Mandy, and in that context even the odd renegade like Handy who thinks he knows what's right and just and will bend heaven, earth, statutes or case-law to get there may be beneficial, provided that there are institutional constraints to ensure there aren't too many Handys and that all but the most clever of them are overturned on appeal.

Stan Readdi:
But to accept the desirability of diverging approaches doesn't one first have to be prepared to concede that there are no 'right' answers to interpretation?

Thomas Devine:
I don't think one need go that far. One could, presumably, hold to the view that there are right answers in theory but that

88

finding those answers, even as regards best interpretive approaches, is often or sometimes beyond the power of mere human beings. And having conceded that fallibility the safest course may well be to ensure there are a multiplicity of outlooks and approaches, not just a variety of socio-economic, cultural and personal backgrounds as Stan and Mandy might like.

Leanne O'Tea
(*who has entered
and been listening
quietly and now
comments*):
I haven't heard anyone do more than gloss over the nature of rules. Both Lawrence and Hercule have talked of rules but not to my satisfaction. Thomas's talk of crystallizations of values is no less vague.

Lawrence Leg:
Leanne, rules must be seen from two vantages. For the Martian observer rules result in regular social behaviour. Cars can be seen regularly to stop before red lights say. But rules must also be seen from the vantage of her who is subject to them; she feels an obligation to follow them whether she ultimately does so or not. And *legal* rules are simply those social rules that have been created or

89

evolved in accordance with a way that is politically accepted. In other words legal rules are formally created or recognized prescripts which produce regular behaviour and felt obligations.

Hercule Droit: Perhaps, but that is only half the story. Rules are only intelligible when set against the background of a whole set of shared, or largely shared, values and principles. Rules are *not* disembodied givens; they further some general scheme of values, of life.

Thomas Devine: Actually, as I've already hinted, rules are lines drawn somewhere within the spectrum of moral consensus, a crystallization in the spirit of people's moral sense.

Stan Readdi: Ha! There's more conflict than consensus in society, Thomas. These indefinite references to higher moralities implicit in law are nothing more than one set of preferences - yours - together with a few obvious efficiencies like clarity of formulation, possibility of performance or non-retroactivity. But even these efficiencies are breached regularly. Laws are often unclear, widely unknown and occasionally retrospective.

Mandy Arkal
(*impatiently*):   This is all a little off topic isn't it?

Leanne O'Tea: I don't think so. How can one understand
                  interpretation without first understanding
                  rules?

Hercule Droit
(*rising to leave*):   Sorry, I've got to go. I'm late for a game
                  of bridge. By the way Thomas, what
                  grounds did the Chief Executive give for
                  overturning the guilty verdicts?

Thomas Devine: She said that it was wrong to hang an
                  accused where the Supreme Court was
                  evenly divided. For capital punishment
                  to be appropriate an actual majority was
                  needed in that court. She had some quite
                  scathing things to say about Tatting and
                  his refusal to decide one way or the
                  other. I can't recall exactly but I think she
                  hinted that he'd breached his judicial
                  duties and that an inquiry would be set
                  up to look into the question.

Mandy Arkal: Her rationale though, in plain words, was
                  that the normal rule in the event of a
                  divided court did not apply in capital
                  cases? She's just another lawyer turned
                  politician relying on her previously
                  acquired skills.

Stan Readdi:	That's a bit harsh. She's only been in office for six months. She has no personal stake in this.
Hercule Droit:	I don't believe there's any precedent on the issue of whether an evenly divided appellate court must be taken, in a capital case, to be upholding the lower court's decision. I wonder. My first thought is that the Chief Executive got the principle spot on. Well, I'm off.
Lawrence Leg (*rising*):	I'd better get going too. It's a long bike ride home. Next week at eight o'clock? (*the others nod*) Good-night.

POSTSCRIPT

There is probably no need to observe to the reader that the legal theorists who have spoken here are as imaginary as the judges and facts in Lon Fuller's original article cited above. The author does not speak through the mouth of any one of them but rather seeks to present, in a lively form, diverging philosophies of law. It is for the reader to form his or her own opinion about the lasting questions of law and morality, of which issues of interpretation form a part.

SECTION TWO

SECTION TWO

Cannibalism and
The Case of the Speluncean Explorers
(an excerpt from "Reading Law")
William Twining

For my next example, I want to turn to a classic of Jurisprudence. The text is Lon Fuller's *The Case of the Speluncean Explorers*. The fact that I intend to subject it to quite stringent criticism should be taken as a compliment: normally, only classics deserve such attention.

Before describing and criticizing the text from a particular perspective, let me briefly state my own view of legal theory.[1] Jurisprudence is the theoretical part of law as a discipline. A theoretical question is a question posed at a relatively high level of generality; a philosophical question is one posed at a very high level of abstraction. "What constitutes valid reasoning?" is a philosophical question. "What constitutes valid reasoning about questions of law?" is a question of legal philosophy. "What constitutes valid reasoning in American state appellate courts?" or "in the English Court of Appeal?" are still sufficiently general to be regarded as questions belonging to legal theory, but they are not purely philosophical questions, because answering them also requires some familiarity with

---

1. See William Twining, *Legal Theory and Common Law* (Oxford, 1986) chs.4, 13; *Rethinking Evidence* (1990), ch.11.

particular institutional contexts.[2] Jurisprudence is thus equivalent to legal theory, but is wider than legal philosophy. Since generality is a relative matter, theory cannot be sharply separated from particular fields of study. Theory knows no boundaries. Since there is no necessary correlation between generality and utility or uselessness, the idea that all theory is useful or useless is a fallacy, just as contrasting theory and practice involves a false dichotomy.

Teachers of Jurisprudence generally fall into one of two categories — those who teach *about* Jurisprudence and those who ask their students to *do* it. In most countries Jurisprudence is seen as a vast heritage of classic or near-classic texts, from which a very few are selected for study; so one reads bits of the work of Hart or Fuller or Aristotle or Aquinas or Dworkin; one learns about their ideas; and one interprets and criticizes them. In the other approach, theorizing is seen as an *activity* involving posing, refining, answering, and arguing about important general questions relating to law, ideally to stimulate students to work out their own positions in a coherent and relatively informed way. The range of significant questions is not as vast as the heritage of attempted answers, but nevertheless selection is still necessary in almost any Jurisprudence course. So even in the activity courses, attention tends to be focused on a few questions from one sphere of legal

---

2. For example, philosophers who contribute to discussions of "legal reasoning" tend to assume that the distinction between questions of fact and questions of law can be treated as unproblematic in judicial contexts and that "legal reasoning" is the only or the main or the most distinctive kind of reasoning engaged in by lawyers, judges, and other participants in legal processes.

theory, such as ethical or epistemological questions or questions about reasoning about disputed issues of law. I am a late convert to the idea of treating theorizing as an activity rather than a subject. I still use selected texts as the main means for raising questions and getting students to develop their own answers through dialogue with the text. The difference is one of emphasis, but it is significant: we study questions raised by Bentham or Dworkin and their attempted answers as a means to clarifying our own views on the significance of the questions and the validity of our own answers. We are not studying Bentham or Dworkin as such.

My conception of legal theory and legal theorizing is relevant here because I start my courses on Jurisprudence with *The Case of the Speluncean Explorers*. I use it, first, to present and discuss different conceptions of Jurisprudence, and, second, to suggest a particular method of reading juristic texts as a vehicle for stimulating students to clarify their own ideas.

Given that the objective of reading juristic texts is to enter into intelligent dialogue with them, and given that the texts are selected because they raise important questions and suggest answers, reasons, and perspectives bearing on those questions, what might be a reasonably systematic way of reading such texts for this purpose? Over the years I have developed a quite simple and flexible method. I ask students to approach any juristic text at three levels: the historical, the analytical, and the applied.

The extent to which the historical context of a work is important in interpreting and evaluating it has been a matter of central concern to theologians, intellectual historians, literary theorists, and jurists, among others. Here one can by-pass some of those controversies, because our reading is for a specific ahistorical purpose: the text is being used as a means to clarifying one's own views on significant questions *today*. Why, then, bother about history at all? A brief answer is that at the very least setting the text in its historical context can help one to identify the central concerns of the author and hence enter into an intelligent dialogue with the text in a way that avoids some of the cruder caricatures that contaminate much secondary writing about Jurisprudence. It also can have other uses, as I shall illustrate with reference to the Speluncean Explorers. Usually it is quite sufficient for this particular purpose to learn enough about the background of the text and its author to establish the general nature of his enterprise and its underlying concerns. In short: What was biting him? (Most classic jurists are, alas, still male.)

Translating concerns into questions marks the transition from the historical to the analytical mode of reading. And as Professor Hart has shown, some articulated questions are very poor expressions of their underlying concerns.[3] If one is puzzled about the meaning of a familiar abstract word, such as "law" or "right" or "justice," a question expressed in the form of a dictionary definition is unlikely to be helpful. If one interprets Oliver Wendell Holmes' 'The Path of the Law'[4] as an expression of concern about legal education at Harvard becoming out of touch with the realities of everyday legal practice, then it is strange to read

---

3. H.L.A. Hart, "Definition and Theory in Jurisprudence", 70 *Law Quarterly Review* 37 (1953).
4. O.W. Holmes, "The Path of the Law" 10 *Harvard Law Review* 457 (1897).

it as a text centrally concerned with the question 'What is law?' and intended to launch a general theory of law. Identifying, clarifying, and, if necessary, reposing questions involves interpretation and is often not a straightforward matter.

The most basic kind of analytical reading can be designated as "reading for plot." What questions does this text address? What answers does it propose? What are the alleged justifications for the answers? Elementary reading for plot provides the basis for the next step in dialectical reading: Do I agree with the questions? Do I agree with the answers? Do I agree with the reasons? This process of dialogue can be extended in many directions almost indefinitely, again depending on one's purposes and the value of reading this text for those purposes. In my experience, Holmes' 'The Path of the Law', like *Hamlet*, yields fresh interpretations, insights, and puzzles at each reading — perhaps the highest compliment one can pay to any text. Of the analysis of texts there is no end, but in this context, the suggested method provides an economical and disciplined basis for entering into worthwhile dialogues without getting bogged down unnecessarily.

The third level, rather uncomfortably designated as "the applied," involves exploring particular implications and applications of the questions, answers, and reasons attributed to the text and alternatives developed in the course of the dialogue. Theorizing involves considering particulars in relation to general ideas. To put the matter briefly and crudely: In studying Bentham's classic exposition of the principle of utility in *An Introduction to the Principles of Morals and Legislation,*[5] we begin by clarifying Bentham's concerns. What seems to be a plausible interpretation of this version of his utilitarianism developed in that text? Is this the least vulnerable interpretation of utilitarianism in the view of the reader (this may involve looking at other texts)? The purpose is to stimulate each student to develop an answer to the question: Am I a utilitarian? Moving to the applied level is a means of testing out a position provisionally adopted at the general level: Does utilitarianism necessarily commit you both to vegetarianism and to justifying torture and punishment of the innocent in extreme circumstances? If so, are you sure you are a utilitarian? And so on.

This, in outline form, is a simple recommended intellectual procedure for a systematic approach to the reading of juristic texts for a given purpose. Let us apply it briefly to *The Case of the Speluncean Explorers* by way of illustration.

Historical

The Case of the Speluncean Explorers was written in about 1948. It was the first of a series of hypothetical examples in a course on Jurisprudence at Harvard Law School. At the time Fuller was in his mid-forties. Ten years later he was to come into prominence as the first and one of the most important critics of the positivism of H.L.A. Hart and as a

---

5.   Jeremy Bentham, *An Introduction to the Principles of Morals and Legislation* (eds. Burns & Hart, Clarendon, 1970).

leading exponent of the idea that no sharp distinction can be made between legal and moral reasoning in debating questions of law. Fuller wrote *The Case of the Speluncean Explorers* before the appearance of Hart, Dworkin, Nozick, and Rawls. Marxism, Critical Legal Studies, and Economic Analysis of Law had not yet made themselves felt in American law schools. So it is hardly surprising that none of these feature in what can reasonably be interpreted as an attempt to provide a conspectus of rival approaches to legal argument (and, more broadly, competing visions of law). So perhaps we can impute the following objective to Fuller: to introduce Harvard students to the subject in the late 1940s by raising a range of central and perennial questions in Legal Philosophy and by presenting a conspectus of different approaches and positions on those questions.

Analysis — Plot First

The Case of the Speluncean Explorers is based on two leading cases involving cannibalism and the defence of necessity in criminal law—the English case of *Regina v. Dudley and Stephens*[6] and the earlier American case of *U.S. v Holmes*.[7] Brian Simpson's recent book[8] reveals that Fuller had intelligently researched the background. Fuller's version takes the form of five opinions of the Supreme Court of

---

6.   [1884] 14 Q.B.D. 273, *affirmed* [1885] 14 Q.B.D. 560.
7.   26 F. Cas. 360 (E.D. Pa. 1842) (No.15, 383).
8.   A.W.B. Simpson, *Cannibalism and the Common Law* (Clarendon, 1984).

Newgarth in the year 4300 (a time roughly equidistant from 1950 as 1950 was from the Age of Pericles). Four members of the Speluncean Society had been trapped in an underground cave. Stupendous efforts were made to rescue them, at the cost of ten lives and a great deal of money. By the twentieth day the unfortunate explorers decided that they could only avoid death by starvation before they could be rescued if they killed and ate one of their number. One of them, Whetmore, suggested that they should decide who should be the victim by casting dice. The others agreed only after much hesitation, whereupon Whetmore declared that he withdrew from the arrangement. The others decided to go ahead and one of them cast the dice on Whetmore's behalf. The throw went against Whetmore and he was killed and eaten. In due course the survivors were rescued and charged with murder. The report contains five individual judgments, each of which adopts a seemingly different approach.

Fuller's standpoint in this context was that of a Socratic teacher, and this was not intended as a coherent statement of his own views. However, his views can to some extent be inferred from the opinion of Foster, J., and, indirectly, from the element of caricature in his treatment of some of the other judges. His perennial concern with problems of value is revealed by the single question he appended to the case in his collection of materials entitled *The Problems of Jurisprudence:*

> It is fairly clear that the root difficulty in the case of the Speluncean Explorers lies in the fact that values ordinarily protected by law have come into irreconcilable conflict, so that one must be sacrificed if

the other is to be preserved. In the case as it is put the values in conflict are human lives. Would it be possible to construct a similar case in which one property value was pitted irreconcilably against another? If it is more difficult to construct such a case, why is this so?[9]

The standard way of reading the case is to identify the issues and the competing positions taken on each of them. It is widely regarded as an excellent way of starting a Jurisprudence course. However, in the present context, let us look at it in terms of Fuller's conception of Jurisprudence: What did he consider to be central questions and what did he consider to be the most important competing approaches or theories?

We can restate the main issues in the case in non-Fullerian language as follows:

1. Is it ever morally:

    (a) justifiable
    (b) excusable to kill and eat a fellow human being?

2. Whether or not it is morally justifiable or excusable, is it legally justifiable to kill and eat a fellow human being in order to save one's own life? Alternatively, is necessity a defense to a charge of murder?

3. What is the connection, if any, between questions I and 2?

---

9. Lon Fuller, *The Problems of Jurisprudence* (temp. ed. 1949), p.645.

4. What is the proper role of an appellate judge in deciding a hard case on a question of law? How does this differ from other officials?

5. What kinds of reasons are admissible, valid, and cogent in:

    (a) reaching

    (b) justifying a judicial decision in a hard case?

    What is the relationship between (a) and (b)? In particular, should public opinion be taken into account in reaching and justifying such decisions?

6. Do (a) citizens (b) judges owe an indefeasible duty of fidelity to law?

The five judges take a variety of positions on each of these issues. Three of them think that the killing was excusable to some degree, allowing for mitigation. Keen, J., implies that it may be completely justifiable, and Tatting, J., seems unsure of the morality of the action. Truepenny and Keen consider that the accused were nonetheless guilty of murder; Handy and Foster, J.J., would quash the conviction; Tatting, J., considers the case too hard and withdraws, with the result that, the court being equally divided, the conviction is affirmed. In justifying their decisions, Truepenny and Keen concentrate on the wording of the statute, which they consider to be clear; Tatting relies on precedent and analogy; Foster appeals to purpose, which he considers to be in conflict with and to override the wording; and Handy decides on "common sense" backed by articulated public opinion. Each of the judges expresses his views on the role of judges in hard cases and their relationship to other officials (in this case the prosecutor, the Chief Executive, and the Legislature).

Analysis — Critique Second

The Case of the Speluncean Explorers raises a rich range of issues and arguments. It is splendid pedagogical material; it is readable, profound, and calculated to engage the interest and concern of all but the most closed-minded students. It forces students to clarify their own positions on a number of questions and to see how those views relate to different intellectual traditions. Subliminally, it communicates two important messages: Jurisprudence can be enjoyable and "relevant." When, like many teachers, I use it in class, we address the substantive issues it raises, and I ask students to note with which judge they have instinctively identified to start with and to review this at the end of the course. It is not a bad touchstone of self-definition.

Here, I want to consider the text as an indication of Fuller's picture of the world of Jurisprudence. In a Postscript Fuller claims that "the case was constructed for the sole purpose of bringing into common focus certain divergent philosophies of law and government ... [which] presented men with live questions of choice in the days of Plato and Aristotle and which are among the permanent problems of the human race."[10]

---

10. Fuller, *The Case of the Speluncean Explorers*, p.46 in this book.

How far is the last claim sustained from the perspective of today? *The Case of the Speluncean Explorers* brings together a number of standard issues in Legal Theory and illustrates their inter-connectedness: positive law and the law of nature; the relationship between law and morals; different modes of interpreting statutes and reasoning about questions of law; the proper role of judges and its relationship to the roles of the legislator and various executive roles; the relationship between law and public opinion; and the ultimate basis of government and the nature of fidelity to law.

Single cases or case-studies are useful as dramatizing and concretizing devices, but they have limitations as vehicles for presenting comprehensive or systematic overviews. In 1948 one might have been able to suggest a number of improvements; for example, instead of presenting a near-consensus on the morality of the action, one judge could have been a moral absolutist maintaining an indefeasible right to life, another a moral nihilist or skeptic, maintaining that moral judgments are nonsensical or purely subjective expressions of opinion, a third a utilitarian and so on. Similarly, more than one different kind of purposive interpretation could have been illustrated (for example, principled, consequentialist, or the Golden Rule) and a wider range of philosophies of government. One could also suggest that standard kinds of Legal Positivism (as represented by Austin and Kelsen) could have been presented more starkly and that Handy, J., is a rather unsympathetic caricature of a Realist.

These are by no means fatal flaws. Indeed, a good discussion can bring out most of the points. Similarly, it is not difficult to update Fuller's version. It is quite possible, as an example of working at the applied level, to set an exercise of writing a judgment in the case from some point of view not canvassed by Fuller, especially approaches that have come into prominence since his day. This works well with approaches, such as that of Ronald Dworkin or Economic Analysis of Law or some versions of Critical Legal Studies, that share Fuller's concern with the nature of appellate judging. It also works quite well with actual judges, such as Lord Denning, Lord Simmonds, or Judge Posner. It does not work so well with approaches that are less court-centered or are concerned with other issues, such as Marxism, Anarchism, Feminism, or macro-sociological theories. The central questions addressed by such theories tend to be rather different. Thus, one student purporting to write a feminist judgment in the case concluded that it raised no difficult issues at all since the person eaten was a man. Whether or not one finds that amusing, it trivializes the concerns of feminism precisely because those concerns are not central to the text. Similarly, while it is possible to subject the case to a Marxist analysis, this does not work, firstly, because the situation does not bear intimately on central Marxist concerns about power, class, *etc.* and, secondly, because both the author and the reader are invited to adopt the standpoint of appellate judges *within* a legal system, some of the ideological and institutional aspects of that system are taken for granted in ways that Marxists are concerned to attack or at least to question.

For me, it is highly significant that *The Case of the Speluncean Explorers* works quite well in regard to some of our stock of theories of and about law, but does not work so well for others. To put it bluntly, for the sake of succinctness, Fuller's case-study, and theories that fit it well, exhibit the classic symptoms of what Jerome Frank called "appellate court-itis," in this case treating a hard case on a question of law as paradigmatic of legal theorizing. It is revealing that some central ideas of Fuller, Dworkin, and critical scholars (and their critics) who debate about legal interpretation, and even some brands of Economic Analysis of Law fit the case quite easily. These have at least some shared concerns and issue is joined.

On the other hand, the positivisms of Hart and Kelsen and even Holmes sit less easily precisely because the root concerns of positivism are not about how appellate judges and their satellite functionaries should reason or choose. I would also argue that American Legal Realism is caricatured by Fuller for similar reasons. In my view, it is a common fallacy to interpret the Realists as being solely or even primarily concerned with appellate court judging. One move away is to broaden our concerns to include disputed questions of fact, as Frank suggested, or to extend this to all important decisions in litigation, as has been done by those who view litigation as a complex total process in which contested trials and appellate decisions are in practice exceptional events. But if one's view of law extends beyond appellate courts to trial courts, and beyond trial courts to pre-trial and post-trial events, and beyond litigation to dispute prevention and resolution and perhaps even beyond these, then a conspectus of legal theories that uses a case study set in the peculiar institutional context of a common law appellate court will not do. It is too narrowly focused, too unrepresentative, and too culture-bound to provide a basis for capturing a balanced overview of the range of general questions that need to be asked and tackled as part of a general understanding of the subject-matter of the discipline of law.

It is just because *The Case of the Speluncean Explorers* illustrates a view of Jurisprudence that I am concerned to attack that I continue to use it in teaching the subject. The fact that it also suggests that studying the subject can be fun is a bonus.

The Case of the Speluncean Explorers: Twentieth-Century Statutory Interpretation in a Nutshell
William N. Eskridge, Jr.

Roger Whetmore is cannibalized by his cave-exploring colleagues in Lon Fuller's hypothetical case of the Speluncean Explorers.[1] The survivors are convicted of violating a law making it a crime that one "willfully take the life of another,"[2] notwithstanding their defense of necessity. The explorers were trapped in a cave and would have died but for the sustenance of Roger Whetmore.[3] An evenly divided Supreme Court of Newgarth affirms the convictions. Voting to affirm, Justice Keen follows the plain meaning of the statute and refuses to consider the equitable defense of necessity,[4] while Chief Justice Truepenny urges the Chief Executive to grant clemency based upon the defense.[5] Voting to reverse, Justice Foster argues that neither the understandings of common society nor the

---

1. For excellent introductions to Fuller and his philosophy, see Robert Summers, *Lon L. Fuller* (Stanford University Press, 1984) and Martin Golding, "Jurisprudence and Legal Philosophy in Twentieth-Century America: Major Themes and Developments" 36 *Journal of Legal Education* 441 at pp.473-480 (1986).
2. The "Case of the Speluncean Explorers" (pp.1-46 above; hereinafter "Fuller"), p.5 (opinion of Truepenny, C.J.).
3. Fuller, p.4 (opinion of Truepenny, C.J.).
4. Fuller, pp.24-33 (opinion of Keen, J.).
5. Fuller, pp.1-6 (opinion of Truepenny, C.J.).

purpose of the statute is served by conviction,[6] while Justice Handy votes to reverse as well, relying on virtual consensus in popular opinion.[7] Anguished Justice Tatting — the potential tiebreaker — recuses himself because he cannot choose among the various arguments.[8]

The Justices' opinions constitute a microcosm of this century's debates over the proper way to interpret statutes. A historical understanding of those debates reveals the breathtaking intellectual accomplishment of Fuller's article, which closes one period of American statutory law (legislative positivism), announces its successor (the legal process school), and anticipates the arguments that will bedevil the successor in its turn.

I. The Pre-History of the Speluncean Explorers: The Positivism Natural Law Debate in Statutory Interpretation, 1890-1940

One way to situate the case of the Speluncean Explorers is to view it as a moment in the Anglo-American debate over the role of equity and natural law in statutory interpretation. Justice Keen's plain-meaning opinion conceptualizes the enterprise as nothing more than implementing the positive law enacted by the legislature. That view, separating law from politics and morals, is challenged in the opinions of Justices Handy (who argues

---

6. Fuller, pp.6-16 (opinion of Foster, J.).
7. Fuller, pp.33-45 (opinion of Handy, J.).
8. Fuller, pp.16-24 (opinion of Tatting, J.).

that law *is* politics) and Foster (who argues that law implicates morality). The debate between positivism and natural law was a prominent theme of statutory interpretation debates in the first half of the century, and Fuller's article is an accessible time capsule of that debate.

Before the 1890s, American theories of statutory interpretation largely tracked English theory: Follow the plain meaning of the statute, except in the rare case in which the plain meaning is absurd. Thus, American theory was in the main positivist, demanding that courts follow the rules enacted by the legislature. It contained a safety valve—the exception for absurd results—that was jurisprudentially ambiguous, however. A meaning leading to an absurd result should not be imputed to the legislature *either* because the result was probably not the legislature's intent (the positivist argument) *or* because it was not right, just, or fair (the natural-law argument). This ambiguity is illustrated by the Supreme Court's most celebrated statutory case of the *Lochner* era.

In 1892, the Supreme Court decided *Church of the Holy Trinity v. United States.*[9] The church had hired an English clergyman to be its rector and provided for his transportation to the United States.[10] The latter action appeared to violate a federal immigration statute making it "unlawful for any person ... in any manner whatsoever, to prepay the transportation, or in any way assist or encourage the importation or migration of any alien or aliens, any foreigner or foreigners, into the United States ...

---

9.   143 U.S. 457 (1892).
10.   *Ibid.*, pp.457-458.

to perform labor or service of any kind in the United States."[11] Although the prohibition against employment contracts facilitating immigration was broad and filled with loophole-plugging language,[12] the Supreme Court refused to interpret the statute to exclude the rector from entering the United States. The Court held "that a thing may be within the letter of the statute and yet not within the statute, because not within its spirit, nor within the intention of its makers."[13] To determine the statute's "spirit," the Court first relied on positive evidence, mainly the statute's legislative history, which suggested that the words "'labor and service'" really should have read "'manual labor' or 'manual service'" and assuredly were not meant to cover "brain toilers."[14] The Court's opinion, however, then proceeded to a natural-law appeal, arguing that our history as a "Christian nation" should remove all doubt that the statute might intend to obstruct efforts to

---

11. Act of February 26, 1885, ch.164, 23 Stat. 332, *repealed* by Act of June 27, 1952, ch.477, § 403(a)(2), 66 Stat. 166, 273.
12. Elsewhere, for example, the statute listed specific occupations excluded from the prohibition, and clergy were not mentioned. *Ibid.*, § 5, 23 Stat. at 333 (exception from the statute professional actors, artists, lecturers, and singers, among others).
13. *Holy Trinity Church,* 143 U.S. at p.459.
14. *Ibid.*, p.464. It appears from the case that the committee was operating under end-of-session pressure and did not believe it necessary to vote an amendment to the statute. The Supreme Court also relied on the statute's title and the circumstances of its adoption to hold it inapplicable to "brain toilers". *Ibid.*, p.465.

bring religious leaders into the country.[15]

Holy Trinity Church was a prolegomenon to the *Lochner* era, in which the Court expressed a constitutional hostility to socio-economic regulatory statutes that displaced old common-law rules.[16] The judicial philosophy of the *Lochner* era, scorned by Professor Roscoe Pound as "mechanical jurisprudence,"[17] was one nostalgic for the economic, libertarian values of the common law, which judges felt were under assault from new regulatory statutes. The conservatives of the bench and bar in that period expressed their arcadian philosophy through statutory as well as constitutional interpretation. The common law had long been a natural-law surrogate in statutory interpretation, and a nostalgic Supreme Court pursued that theme episodically for two generations, from 1892 to 1938.

The rallying cry of anti-Court progressives during this period was distinctly positivist: They contended that the common law was no longer sufficient to the needs of a complex, strife-ridden society, that the legislature was in a better position to gather facts and make judgments necessary for such a society, and that the role of courts lay in following these progressive commands of the legislature

---

15. *Ibid.*, p.471. See too p.465 ("[N]o purpose or action against religion can be imputed to any legislation, state or national, because this is a religious people"). The author of the opinion, Justice David Brewer, was the evangelical son of Christian missionaries.
16. The standard citation is *Lochner v. New York*, 198 U.S. 45 (1905), in which Justice Brewer and his allies struck down a statute setting maximum work hours for bakers in New York.
17. Roscoe Pound, "Mechanical Jurisprudence" 8 *Columbia Law Review* 605 at pp.615-616 (1908).

and abandoning their *Lochnerian* obduracy. Pound argued, for example, that the importation by judges of their libertarian values into statutes was "spurious" statutory interpretation and inconsistent with the proper role of courts in a democracy.[18] According to Pound, the proper method of statutory interpretation was an "imaginative reconstruction" of the legislature's specific intent.[19] That view had many adherents among progressive jurists[20] but was not so jurisprudentially sophisticated as the progressive theory of Justice Oliver Wendell Holmes, Jr.

Justice Holmes believed that statutory interpretation was usually just an exercise in determining the statute's ordinary meaning.[21] Like Pound, Holmes was a positivist who astringently believed in the separation of law and morals. Like Pound, he rejected as spurious a judge's effort to read his own values into statutes and believed the judge ought to bow to legislation expressing authentic social forces, such as the labor movement and nosey social regulations. Unlike Pound, however, Holmes emphasized the importance of plain meaning, not only for reasons of democratic theory,

---

18. Roscoe Pound, "Spurious Interpretation" 7 *Columbia Law Review* 379 at p.382 (1907).
19. For Pound, the role of the judges should be to discover "what the law-maker meant by assuming his position, in the surroundings in which he acted, and endeavouring to gather from the mischiefs he had to meet and the remedy by which he sought to meet them, his intention with respect to the particular point in controversy". *Ibid.*, p.381.
20. Judge Learned Hand was perhaps the most notable of these.
21. "We do not inquire what the legislature meant; we ask only what the statute means." Oliver Wendell Holmes, "The Theory of Legal Interpretation", 12 *Harvard Law Review* 417 at p.419 (1899).

but also for rule-of-law reasons. According to Holmes, our polity could not be a government of laws and not men unless legal standards were external to the decisionmaker. For the same reasons that Holmes favored a "reasonable man" standard in torts cases, he advocated a "normal speaker" theory of plain meaning.[22]

The legislature-grounded positivism of Holmes's plain-meaning theory is similar to Justice Keen's opinion in *The Case of the Speluncean Explorers*. Keen makes quite a show of segregating his own moral view—that the defendants should not be punished—from his responsibility as a judge:

> [A] question that I wish to put to one side is that of deciding whether what these men did was "right" or "wrong," "wicked" or "good." That is ... a question that is irrelevant to the discharge of my office as a judge sworn to apply, not my conceptions of morality, but the law of the land. ...
>
> ...
>
> Whence arise all the difficulties of the case ... ? The difficulties, in whatever tortured form they may present

---

22. See Holmes, *ibid.*, pp.417-418:
    "[W]e ask, not what this man meant, but what those words would mean in the mouth of a normal speaker of English, using them in the circumstances in which they were used ... [T]he normal speaker of English is merely a special variety, a literary form, so to speak, of our old friend the prudent man. He is external to the particular writer, and a reference to him as the criterion is simply another instance of the externality of the law."

themselves, all trace back to a single source, and that is a failure to distinguish the legal from the moral aspects of this case. To put it bluntly, my brothers do not like the fact that the written law requires the conviction of these defendants. Neither do I, but unlike my brothers I respect the obligations of an office that requires me to put my personal predilections out of my mind when I come to interpret and apply the law of this Commonwealth.[23]

In a representative democracy, the *law* *is* the statutes enacted by the elected representatives in the legislature, which is supreme in lawmaking. "From that principle [of legislative supremacy] flows the obligation of the judiciary to enforce faithfully the written law, and to interpret that law in accordance with its plain meaning without reference to our personal desires or our individual conceptions of justice."[24] For Keen, as for Holmes, bending the statute to accommodate the members of the Speluncean Society would be a sacrifice of law's objectivity and hence of both its democratic legitimacy and its usefulness.

Although Keen's approach to statutory interpretation was (when Holmes was writing) a progressive approach, it was one that had been undermined by the time Fuller wrote *The Case of the Speluncean Explorers*. The realists in the 1920s and 1930s had debunked the possibility of objectivity in statutory or any other kind of interpretation, arguing that judges had an enormous lawmaking discretion that was little confined by statutory plain meaning or imaginative

---

23. Fuller, pp.25-26 (opinion of Keen, J.).
24. Fuller, pp.27-28 (opinion of Keen, J.).

reconstruction. The realists unsettled the statutory interpretation debate. Although the realists had no use for *Lochner*-style conservatives or natural law, neither were they simple legislative supremacists, as Pound and Holmes were. The realists viewed the sovereign's rules as the results of the judicial and not the legislative process (i.e., because there is no law until the statute has been interpreted) and also tended to accept the tenets of ethical positivism.[25] Moreover, because they believed that judges have great leeway in reading their own policy preferences into statutes, the realists emphasized the importance of instrumental, policy-driven considerations.

In *The Case of the Speluncean Explorers*, Justice Handy reflects the realists' disdain for the "obscuring curtain of legalisms" and "abstract theory."[26] and their endorsement of doctrinal solutions that reflect "efficiency and common sense."[27] Handy is Keen's doppelgänger: Keen emphasizes the stability and externality of law, and Handy emphasizes its mobility and contingency.[28] Keen rigidly separates legal interpretation from politics, and Handy responds by making

---

25. By "ethical positivism", I mean the view that law is the command of the sovereign and that the goodness of law (the "ought") is a matter separate from what the law actually requires (the "is").
26. Fuller, pp.33 and 34 (opinion of Handy, J.).
27. Fuller, p.36 (opinion of Handy, J.).
28. I believe theirs is an uneven match however. I read Keen's opinion as a serious intellectual statement reflecting the respect that Holmes still engendered at the Harvard Law School in the 1940s. I read Handy's opinion as more of a caricature of realism, reflecting both Fuller's ambivalence about realism and the Harvard Law School's tendency to consider the realist project as having presented nothing particularly new or productive.

legal interpretation an exercise in practical politics (stressing, for example, the role of popular opinion in his vote to acquit) Keen is serious and pompous while Handy winks at the reader, deflates the pretensions of his colleagues, and treats the case like a game.

If *The Case of the Speluncean Explorers* had been written in the early 1930s, when realism was overtaking the philosophies of Pound and Holmes, a debate between Keen's law/formalism and Handy's politics/functionalism might have been the centerpiece of the case. Instead, the centerpiece is Justice Foster's opinion,[29] which specifically reflects intellectual developments from the end of the 1930s. The New Deal ensured the complete defeat of mechanical jurisprudence and offered the prospect of a very attractive positive law regime in which smart young judges and administrators (many of whom were prominent realists) were making policy. Yet at the very moment of progressive positivism's electoral triumph over *Lochner*-based natural law, positivism found itself intellectually vulnerable. As American intellectuals learned about European fascism in the 1930s, the more restive they became with a positivist separation of law and morals. Were Nazi decrees "law" in the same way that New Deal statutes were? Were decrees that basically attacked an entire segment of the body politic

---

29. Foster's is the opinion that best resonates with Fuller's own work, see Lon Fuller, *The Law in Quest of Itself* (The Foundation Press, 1940). It is the second opinion in the case (following the Chief Justice's, which simply states the facts and then rests its legal analysis on a fatuous appeal to executive clemency that no one else takes seriously), and it is the primary focus of the critical responses in the opinions of Justices Tatting, Keen and Handy.

entitled to obedience?

Like others on the eve of America's entry into World War II, Fuller himself invoked these quandaries as an occasion to question ethical positivism in law. In his 1940 Rosenthal Lectures, Fuller suggested, first, that decrees such as those of the Nazis were not binding law, because the conditions of human coexistence ceased to exist for most of the citizenry.[30] Second, he argued that there is no sharp distinction between the "is" and "ought" in law.[31] Both suggestions show up nine years later in the opinion of Justice Foster.

Accordingly, one reason that Foster gives for acquitting the defendants is that the positive law ceased to apply to them when they were thrust back into a "state of nature" by their entrapment in the cave:

> Whatever particular objects may be sought by the various branches of our law, it is apparent on reflection that all of them are directed toward facilitating and improving men's coexistence and regulating with fairness and equity the relations of their life in common. When the assumption that men may live together loses its truth, as it obviously did in this extraordinary situation where life only became possible by the taking of life, then the basic premises underlying our whole legal order have lost their meaning and force.[32]

---

30. *Ibid.*, pp.122-125.
31. *Ibid.*, pp.4-15.
32. Fuller, p.8 (opinion of Foster, J.).

Under pure natural law, Foster asserts, the defendants acted out of necessity and were "guiltless of any crime" as a result.[33]

Foster asserts a second and independent reason for voting to acquit, one more subtly echoing natural-law influences. Even conceding that the explorers' conduct "violates the literal wording of the statute," he argued that one "may break the letter of the law without breaking the law itself" and that a law must "be interpreted reasonably, in the light of its evident purpose."[34] To a reader of the 1920s and 1930s, Foster's statement would have been an uncomfortable echo of the natural law in *Holy Trinity*, with Foster's rejection of the law's "letter" for the law's "purpose" (a seeming euphemism for *Holy Trinity's* "spirit"). Could the invocation of a "Christian nation" be far behind? By the late 1940s, readers would have been more comfortable with Foster's second argument, whose intellectual background and relationship to his first argument I shall now explore in detail.

II. *After the Positivism/Natural Law Debate:* **The Case of the Speluncean Explorers** *and the Legal Process Synthesis, 1940-1958*

American law faced an intellectual crisis on the eve of World War II. Formalist theories of law, like those of

---

33. Fuller, p.9 (opinion of Foster, J.).
34. Fuller, p.12. To support his interpretation of the law's purpose, Justice Foster invokes the exception to murder statutes for self-defense.

Newgarth's Justice Keen, were vulnerable to realist attacks concerning their objectivity. On the other hand, realist theories, like the view of Justice Handy that judges are nothing more than another set of political actors, seemed inconsistent with traditional theories of democracy or the rule of law. The shortcomings of both formalism and realism gave rise to a demand for a theory of statutory interpretation that tied law to reason as well as to democracy and rules. Judges and academics grappled with this conundrum, and a tentative answer emerged in the period from 1939 to 1942: Statutory interpretation must be informed by the purposive role of state actors. Although earlier scholars had acknowledged the idea that legislative purpose was important to statutory interpretation, and the Supreme Court had occasionally invoked purpose-based reasoning,[35] this idea did not become central until 1939-1942, after the New Deal had been politically consolidated, just as the New Deal majority was forming on the Supreme Court, and right before the United States entered World War II.

The new generation of scholars and judges accepted the realist argument that unelected officials *do* engage in lawmaking, but they suggested that such lawmaking had some direction from democratic sources. "Legislation has an aim," asserted Justice Felix Frankfurter. "[I]t seeks to obviate some mischief, to supply an inadequacy, to effect

---

35. See *United States v. Whitridge*, 197 U.S. 135, 143 (1905) (Holmes, J., for the Court) ("[W]e cannot forget that ... the general purpose is a more important aid to the meaning than any rule which grammar or formal logic may lay down").

a change of policy, to formulate a plan of government."[36] Hence, added Professor Harry Willmer Jones, '[t]he 'law' of a statute is not complete when the legislative stamp has been put upon it; subsequent judicial decisions add meaning and effect to the statutory direction."[37] Such subsequent lawmaking would be guided by "the principle that in determining the effect of statutes in doubtful cases judges should decide in such a way as to advance the objectives which, in their judgment, the legislature sought to attain by enactment of the legislation."[38] By tying statutory interpretation to legislative purpose, these thinkers established a link to democratic theory. They argued further that this link contributed to the rule of law, because ascertaining legislative purpose could be determined easily by examining the statute's legislative history.

Remarkably, at the same time that the academic consensus was forming against the plain-meaning rule and in favor of interpreting statutes to fulfill their purposes, the New Deal Court was filling the U.S. Reports with the fruits of that consensus. Writing for the Court in 1940, Justice Stanley Reed (who had been Solicitor General during the early New Deal era) explained in *United States v. American Trucking Associations, Inc.*[39]

---

36. Felix Frankfurter, "Some Reflections on the Reading of Statutes" 47 *Columbia Law Review* 527 at pp.538-539 (1947).
37. Harry Jones, "Extrinsic Aids in the Federal Courts" 25 *Iowa Law Review* 737 at p.761 (1940).
38. *Ibid.*, p.757.
39. 310 U.S. 534, 543-44 (1940) (footnotes omitted).

There is, of course, no more persuasive evidence of the purpose of a statute than the words by which the legislature undertook to give expression to its wishes ... In such cases we have followed their plain meaning. When that meaning has led to absurd or futile results, however, this Court has looked beyond the words to the purpose of the act. Frequently, however, even when the plain meaning did not produce absurd results but merely an unreasonable one "plainly at variance with the policy of the legislation as a whole" this Court has followed that purpose, rather than the literal words. When aid to construction of the meaning of words, as used in the statute, is available, there certainly can be no "rule of law" which forbids its use, however clear the words may appear on "superficial examination."

The purposive spirit of Justice Reed's opinion in *American Trucking* was followed for a generation by the Supreme Court.

Justice Foster's opinion in *The Case of the Speluncean Explorers* deploys the purpose-of-the-statute theory in several interesting and important ways. Foster introduces the purpose rule with a neat rhetorical appeal to history and tradition:

Now it is, of course, perfectly clear that these men did an act that violates the literal wording of the statute which declares that he who "shall wilfully take the life of another" is a murderer. *But one of the most ancient bits of legal wisdom is the saying that a man may break the letter of the law without breaking the law itself.* Every proposition of positive law, whether contained in a statute or a judicial precedent, is to be interpreted reasonably, in the light of its evident purpose. *This is a truth so elementary that it is hardly necessary to expatiate on it.*[40]

For this "truth so elementary," Foster cites (fictional) cases in which the court followed such an antiliteralist approach, and readers in 1949 could have substituted *American Trucking* and other chestnuts that had been publicized by academics in the 1930s.[41] Most tellingly, Foster invokes the established exception for self-defense: No matter how broadly a murder statute is phrased, wouldn't a court infer a self-defense exception? Such an exception is lawful and not merely equitable, he argues, because it is the interpretation supported by the deterrent purpose of a criminal statute.

Foster is aware of the then-familiar charge of *Lochner*ism, for Keen specifically maintains that Foster's purposivist interpretation is nothing more than judicial "revision" of a statute and a "specious" approach to statutes, both of which are inconsistent with legislative supremacy and its corollary "obligation of the judiciary to enforce faithfully the written law."[42] Not only does Foster deny the charge, but he responds that his approach, not Keen's, best reflects "fidelity to enacted law" and the role of the judiciary as agents of the legislature:

---

40. Fuller, pp.12-13 (opinion of Foster, J.) (emphasis added).
41. The main cite was *Heydon's Case*, 76 Eng. Rep. 637, 638 (Ex. 1584), which urged courts to interpret statutes in a way "as shall suppress the mischief, and advance the remedy" sought by the statute.
42. Fuller, pp.27-28 (opinion of Keen, J.).

No superior wants a servant who lacks the capacity to read between the lines. The stupidest housemaid knows that when she is told "to peel the soup and skim the potatoes" her mistress does not mean what she says. She also knows that when her master tells her to "drop everything and come running" he has overlooked the possibility that she is at the moment in the act of rescuing the baby from the rain barrel. Surely we have a right to expect the same modicum of intelligence from the judiciary. The correction of obvious legislative errors or oversights is not to supplant the legislative will, but to make that will effective.[43]

The most important contribution of Foster's opinion extends beyond these specific arguments and responses in the interplay of his two grounds for decision. Foster asserts that the second ground for decision (interpret the law to fulfill its rational purpose) is independent of the first (the rule of law lapsed when the explorers became trapped in the cave), but the two are related insofar as they share a common theory of state legitimacy. Just as the second ground insists that laws be interpreted with reference to statutory purpose, the first ground insists that law is purposive generally. Recall Foster's observation that law is "directed toward facilitating and improving men's coexistence and regulating with fairness and equity the relations of their life in common."[44] Foster makes the point more clearly two pages later: "The powers of government can only be justified

---

43. Fuller, p.15, (opinion of Foster, J.).
44. Fuller, p.8 (opinion of Foster, J.).

morally on the ground that these are powers that reasonable men would agree upon and accept if they were faced with the necessity of constructing anew some order to make their life in common possible."[45] It is this view of the state as an organism of cooperation in Foster's first ground for decision that validates the normative assertion in the second ground that statutes must be interpreted in accord with their purposes.

This normative insight in Foster's opinion provided scholars in the emerging legal process school with a political theory by which to rethink statutory interpretation. In the 1950s, Fuller's colleagues at the Harvard Law School, Professors Henry Hart and Albert Sacks, dilated the theoretical structure of Foster's opinion into more than 1,400 pages of materials on what they called "The Legal Process."[46] Following the views of Foster's opinion, Hart and Sacks' intellectual starting point was the interconnectedness of human beings and the utility of law in helping us coexist together peacefully. "Law is a doing of something, a purposive activity, a continuous striving to solve the basic problems of social living," they asserted.[47] Because the legitimacy of law rests upon its purposiveness and not upon abstract social contract principles, Hart and Sacks further maintained that "[e]very statute must be conclusively presumed to be a purposive act. The idea of a statute without an intelligible purpose is foreign to the

---

45. Fuller, p.10 (opinion of Foster, J.).
46. Henry Hart and Albert Sacks, *The Legal Process: Basic Problems in the Making and Application of Law* (tend. ed. 1958).
47. *Ibid.*, p.217.

idea of law and inadmissible."[48]

Hart and Sacks emphasized that the process of lawmaking hardly ends with the enactment of a statute and that law is a process of reasoned elaboration of purposive statutes by courts and agencies. Following not only Foster's opinion but also the leading statutory scholars of the 1940s, Hart and Sacks reasoned that, because "every statute . . . has some kind of purpose or objective,"[49] ambiguities can be intelligently resolved, first, by identifying that purpose and the policy or principle it embodies, and then by deducing the result most consonant with that principle or policy. Hart and Sacks not only rejected the plain-meaning rule in favor of a rule of reasonable interpretation but rejected imaginative reconstruction as well.

The legal process theory of purposive statutory interpretation was an intellectually robust legacy of the New Deal and World War II. Under such a theory, statutory interpretation could be both dynamic and legitimate, equitable as well as lawlike. Although Fuller's precise influence on Hart and Sacks (his faculty colleagues after 1940) is unknowable to us today, it is clear that the primary analytical devices in legal process's theory of interpretation were precisely anticipated by Justice Foster's opinion in *The Case of the Speluncean Explorers*. For this reason alone, Fuller's fictional exercise must be counted as one of the important jurisprudential documents in this century.

---

48. *Ibid.*, p.1156.
49. *Ibid.*, p.166.

III. The Case of the Speluncean Explorers *and Problems with the Legal Process Synthesis, 1958-Present*

As the creator of Speluncean Justice Foster, Lon Fuller was a parent of legal process theory. What may be even more interesting, however, is the way in which Fuller was also legal process's most perceptive critic, nine years before the Hart and Sacks materials assumed their final form and decades before serious attacks on the theory were launched by the next generation of scholars. Recall that no one in *The Case of the Speluncean Explorers* joins Foster's opinion and that the explorers' conviction is affirmed. More significantly, all the other opinions attack the aspirational vision in Foster's work. True to his academic integrity, Fuller made sure that the attacks have bite, so much so that they generally anticipated the next generation's criticisms of purposive theory. Consider the main lines of attack on Foster's approach.

1. *Because Purpose Is Fictional, Interpretation Becomes Judicial Lawmaking*

No one else on the Newgarth Supreme Court accepts Justice Foster's argument that purposive interpretation is not judicial lawmaking, and Justices Tatting and Keen appear to refute it altogether. Tatting (the Justice too conflicted to cast a vote) finds Foster's purpose-of-the-statute argument appealing but ultimately unpersuasive, in part because the criminal law has several purposes other than to deter wrongdoing.[50] These other purposes include retribution

---

50. Fuller, p.20 (opinion of Tatting, J.).

and rehabilitation, both of which would be served by punishing cannibals, even cannibals acting under conditions of necessity. Tatting further wonders whether deterrence is really a serious purpose of criminal laws, when so many of their sanctions seem unrelated to any plausible deterrence.[51] "Assuming that we must interpret a statute in the light of its purpose, what are we to do when it has many purposes or when its purposes are disputed?"[52] Finally, Tatting questions whether even the deterrent purpose of the criminal law would not be subserved by convicting the explorers. "The stigma of the word 'murderer' is such that it is quite likely, I believe, that if these men had known that their act was deemed by the law to be murder they would have waited for a few days at least before carrying out their plan."[53] Tatting might have observed that the explorers could have cannibalized the first of their numbers to have died, and that they might have chosen that strategy had they better internalized society's prohibition of murder. In some circumstances, waiting a few days could mean the difference between life and death.

Tatting's opinion suggests that purposivist statutory interpretation is no more determinate or objective than the approaches (plain meaning and imaginative reconstruction)

---

51. Fuller, pp.21-22. Tatting cites *Commonwealth v. Valjean*, in which the hypothetical Court upheld the conviction of a man for stealing a loaf of bread for his family. In today's America, the willingness of the state to execute convicted criminals, notwithstanding unimpressive evidence of deterrent effects, is testimony to this point.
52. Fuller, p.20 (opinion of Tatting, J.).
53. Fuller, p.22 (opinion of Tatting, J.).

criticized by the legal realists. Although one advantage of grounding statutory interpretation on legislative purpose is that general purpose is more easily determinable than specific intent, a corresponding disadvantage is that purpose is *too* easy to determine, yielding a plethora of purposes, cross-cutting purposes, and purposes set at such a general level that they could support several different interpretations. Purposive statutory interpretation, therefore, might be even less determinate than more traditional approaches. This has been a standard criticism of legal process interpretation.

Justice Keen presses this criticism more deeply when he observes that "not one statute in a hundred has any such single purpose, and ... the objectives of nearly every statute are differently interpreted by the different classes of its sponsors."[54] Although Keen does not develop this criticism in detail, subsequent legal scholars and judges have done so, based upon theories of the political process such as public choice theory. The criticism suggests that legislators often support statutes for nothing more than self-serving political pressures and that statutes might have no overall public-regarding purpose at all. Even if *legislators* had purposes, the *legislature* probably does not, and the process of statutory enactment undermines any coherent purpose the proposed statute might at one point have had. The process by which statutes are enacted is one of coalition-building, compromise, and sometimes deceit. Different groups and interests supporting enactment of a statute might have very different ideas about what the statute is

---

54.   Fuller, p.29 (opinion of Keen, J.).

attempting to do, and this heterogeneity might be encouraged by the sponsors themselves. In short, inquiries based upon legislative purpose may be worse than indeterminate; they may be incoherent or analytically impossible.

If that is so, Foster's theory of interpreting statutes to carry out their purposes is judicial lawmaking, a concession discreetly made by Hart and Sacks.[55] Lawmaking by unelected officials requires justification under traditional theories of democracy. Neither Foster nor his intellectual heirs, Hart and Sacks, provided such justification. This theoretical gap has left legal process theory vulnerable to critique from both the left and the right. Both wings of the critique are anticipated by opinions in *The Case of the Speluncean Explorers*.

2. *Judicial Lawmaking Is Questionable for Reasons of Democratic Theory and Institutional Competence*

Justice Keen's opinion in *The Case of the Speluncean Explorers* lays out the primary objection to judicial revision of statutes: It is inconsistent with "the supremacy of the legislative branch of our government."[56] Subsequent legal process work has built on this "counter-majoritarian

---

55. Hart and Sacks speak of "what purpose ought to be attributed to a statute". See fn.46, *supra*, p.1157. In attributing purpose, they suggest that a court "should not do this in the mood of a cynical political observer, taking account of ... short-run currents of political expedience that swirl around any legislative session." *Ibid.*, p.1414.

56. Fuller, p.27 (opinion of Keen, J.).

difficulty"[57] as the key problem with activist statutory interpretations by courts. Indeed, the issue of legislative supremacy is a primary litmus test that divides "liberal" process thinkers from more "conservative" ones. The former are more likely than the latter to update statutes to reflect changed circumstances, to interpret a statute to effectuate a reasonable purpose notwithstanding a contrary plain meaning, and to read a statute to avoid inequities and not just absurd results.

Justice Keen invokes both rule-of-law and democratic values in defending the primacy of legislative supremacy. His initial defense emphasizes rule-of-law values and tradition:

> I am not concerned with the question whether the principle that forbids the judicial revision of statutes is right or wrong, desirable or undesirable; I observe merely that this principle has become a tacit premise underlying the whole of the legal and governmental order I am sworn to administer.[58]

Yet he also hints that a polity's failure to follow a "clear-cut principle"[59] of governmental ordering can have calamitous consequences:

> There was a time in this Commonwealth when judges did in fact legislate very freely, and all of us know that

---

57. The term is taken from Alexander Bickel, *The Least Dangerous Branch: The Supreme Court at the Bar of Politics.*
58. Fuller, p.28 (opinion of Keen, J.).
59. Fuller, p.27 (opinion of Keen, J.).

during that period some of our statutes were rather thoroughly made over by the judiciary. That was a time when the accepted principles of political science did not designate with any certainty the rank and function of various arms of the state. We all know the tragic issue of that uncertainty in the brief civil war that arose out of the conflict between the judiciary, on the one hand, and the executive and the legislature, on the other.[60]

Although no one (these days) asserts that the republic will end if judges revise statutes, a Keen-like formalism grounded upon the concept of legislative supremacy has proven to be an enduring theme of conservative legal process attacks on purposive or creative statutory interpretations as politically illegitimate.

At the end of his opinion, Justice Keen provides a functional, democratic justification for text-centred statutory interpretation that ignores the equities:

"Now I know that the line of reasoning I have developed in this opinion will not be acceptable to those who look only to the immediate effects of a decision and ignore the long-run implications of an assumption by the judiciary of a power of dispensation. A hard decision is never a popular decision ... But I believe that judicial dispensation does more harm in the long run than hard decisions. Hard cases may even have a certain moral value by bringing home to the people their own responsibilities toward the law that is ultimately their creation, and by

---

60. Fuller, p.27 (opinion of Keen, J.).

reminding them that there is no principle of personal grace that can relieve the mistakes of their representatives.

Indeed, I will go farther and say that not only are the principles I have been expounding those which are soundest for our present conditions, but that we would have inherited a better legal system from our forefathers if those principles had been observed from the beginning. For example, with respect to the excuse of self-defense, if our courts had stood steadfast on the language of the statute the result would undoubtedly have been a legislative revision of it. Such a revision would have drawn on the assistance of natural philosophers and psychologists, and the resulting regulation of the matter would have had an understandable and rational basis, instead of the hodgepodge of verbalisms and metaphysical distinctions that have emerged from the judicial and professorial treatment.[61]

Keen's analysis rests upon a theory of comparative institutional competence in a democracy: Courts are not institutionally as competent as legislatures to create whole new policy regimes. If courts insist on performing that gap-filling function, they will discourage the legislature from doing so, which is not only undemocratic but is also bad policy.

This line of argument has been a recurring theme of conservative process theory and has been of particular

---

61. Fuller, pp.32-33 (opinion of Keen, J.).

interest to Justice Scalia on the current US Supreme Court. Like Keen, Scalia invokes both formalist and functional reasons for a plain-meaning approach to statutory interpretation. Thus, Scalia and his legal process allies invoke tradition and constitutional structures to insist upon a textualist approach to reading statutes. They argue, moreover, that statutory interpretation should not aspire to reach results that are good ex post but should instead subserve ex ante goals, such as providing Congress with "clear interpretive rules" so that it can know the effect of language it adopts. This approach, they argue, stimulates Congress and not the courts to make important policy decisions. "I think we have an obligation to conduct our exegesis in a fashion which fosters th[e] democratic process" embedded in the Constitution, Scalia has said.[62] Though there is much to be said for his insistence that elected representatives and not unelected judges update statutes, Scalia's argument is subject to the response that the democratic process can foster itself, and that the democratic process has delegated the lawmaking responsibilities to courts and agencies—and the duty to do justice ex post—when it enacts broad statutes.

A final line of conservative legal process thought is anticipated by the opinion of Chief Justice Truepenny. After stating the facts, the Chief Justice announces that he will follow the plain meaning of the statute and vote to affirm the convictions.[63] He accommodates the equitable concerns in the case somewhat differently than Justice Keen does. At

---

62. *United States v. Taylor*, 487 U.S. 326 at 346 (1988).
63. Fuller, pp.5 and 6 (opinion of Truepenny, C.J.).

the end of his opinion, the Chief Justice invokes "the principle of executive clemency" as the most legitimate way "to mitigate the rigors of the law" and urges the Chief Executive to ameliorate the defendants' punishment.[64]

The Chief Justice's opinion is something of a lark in Fuller's exercise, but it does have a serious point that has become a pillar of conservative process theory: the principle of institutional settlement. Hart and Sacks made this principle a centerpiece of their legal process materials. Because law must be dynamic and adaptive and because the exact direction of the change is unpredictable, it is more important for a polity to agree on the procedures and institutional roles for making such changes than it is for the polity to map out the substantive rules themselves.[65] Exactly what these institutional roles ought to be has become an important battleground in process theory. Echoing Truepenny and Keen, conservative process theorists and judges argue for very little law-updating by the judiciary and for law-changing by organs more connected

---

64. Fuller, pp.5 and 6 (opinion of Truepenny, C.J.). This recommendation is bitterly denounced by Justice Keen, who believes that the defendants should be pardoned but does not think it appropriate for the Court to instruct the Chief Executive. Justice Handy reveals secret evidence that the Chief Executive is not inclined to grant clemency and then shows how all the Justices are bending their judicial roles in transparent efforts to sway the Executive.

65. See Hart and Sacks, fn.46, *supra*, pp.3-4. ("[I]nstitutionalized procedures ... are obviously more fundamental than the substantive arrangements in the structure of a society ... since they are at once the source of the substantive arrangements and the indispensable means of making them work effectively").

with the political process (particularly the Executive Branch). Echoing Foster and Handy, liberal process theorists and judges argue for more law-updating by the judiciary and against excessive reliance on legislative and executive organs.

3. *Judicial Lawmaking Is Questionable on Grounds of Elitism*

Although Keen's opinion is a rather complete statement of conservative objections to purposivist interpretation, Handy's opinion suggests just an outline of subsequent progressive objections to purposivist interpretation. Handy's main objection, made against both Keen and Foster, is that their opinions rest upon legalisms and abstractions, both of which deflect attention from the "human realities" of the case.[66] His philosophy is stated at the outset:

> [G]overnment is a human affair, and ... men are ruled, not by words on paper or by abstract theories, but by other men. They are ruled well when their rulers understand the feelings and conceptions of the masses. They are ruled badly when that understanding is lacking.
>
> Of all branches of government, the judiciary is the most likely to lose its contact with the common man.[67]

Handy's charge is elitism. The legitimacy of government rests upon how well it serves "We the People." A danger of any kind of judge-made legalism is that it is alienated

---

66. Fuller, p.34 (opinion of Handy, J.).
67. Fuller, p.34 (opinion of Handy, J.).

from popular needs. Handy's theme has surfaced in the work of progressive republican scholars who urge popular, political engagement rather than judicial surrogacy as the aspiration for progressive legal work.

Handy's charge can be broadened and even turned against its author, who is after all a judge who must by his own admission be "most likely to lose ... contact with the common man."[68] Although he lamely tries to escape the charge by appealing to public sentiment in his opinion,[69] Handy is just as unelected and unaccountable as his brethren *and* more arrogant in asserting the rightness of his own views. Indeed, Handy's willingness to rest private rights on public opinion reveals him to be a less sympathetic figure in that respect. This willingness reveals an ironic and final line of progressive critique of legal-process statutory interpretation.

The image of the Commonwealth of Newgarth that emerges from the five opinions, including Handy's, is one of a false homogeneity. The world of *The Case of the Speluncean Explorers* and of its Justices—and Lon Fuller's world—presents itself as a world in which the only actors who matter are male, white, affluent, and heterosexual. Unless Newgarth is vastly different from America of 1949, that image is false, for half the real people are women, a majority are not affluent, and many are not white or heterosexual. These people (a majority) are not only ignored

---

68. Fuller, p.34 (opinion of Handy, J.).
69. I say "lamely", because Handy is interpreting a "text", just as Keen and Foster are. His text is "a poll of public opinion", which is just as subject to interpretation and manipulation as statutory text and purpose.

(as in the opinions) but are also segregated—confined to the kitchen, the other side of the tracks, the closet—in ways that Handy's "popular opinion" approves. The same public opinion that supported Handy's willingness to overturn the convictions of the Speluncean Explorers would, in 1949, have supported racial apartheid, unequal job opportunities for women, and aversion therapy for lesbians, gay men, and bisexuals.

A similar criticism can be made of purpose-based statutory interpretation. Notwithstanding Handy's own elitism, his suggestion that legal process's purposive interpretation threatens to alienate government from the people and obscure their underlying problems is a criticism that has gained force over time, especially from progressive communities. Focusing on solving the problems arising out of people's coexistence in the melting pot of the 1950s, legal-process theory seems to assume a cultural homogeneity that was more apparent in the 1940s and 1950s than it is today, in an era of emerging multiculturalism. Multicultural approaches to statutory interpretation would depart from legal-process theory in a number of ways.

Feminist theory is critical of the distance placed by the original Justices between the case's social context and the Justices' reasoning and grand theorizing. This critique affects one's approach to the case in several ways. One is that feminist theorists tend to be more interested in the "effect of [the Justices'] decisions on distributions of power among groups in our society," especially gender-based distributions. Such theorists might explore various cross-cutting implications for battered women who kill their batterers, abusive male lovers, and future Spelunceans. Relatedly, feminist theory tends to be empathetic, viewing the situation at least in part from the perspective of the people being judged. This approach seems likely to "resist the question" insisted upon by the original Justices and to view the case from an angle different from the original Justices. For instance, it could lead to a remand for a more complete development of the facts of the case, or to a remand for a jury trial, or even to an outright reversal because the explorers acted only after the authorities refused to advise them on how to cope with their dilemma.

Critical race theory could prove in this case to be more sharply critical, even angry. Like feminism, race theory is aware of patterns of subordination that pervaded Lon Fuller's America. Unlike most theories of feminism, however, critical race theory directly attacks the assumed legitimacy of American democracy and could form the basis of an extended indictment of the racist foundations of American culture and an attack on the unwarranted sympathy shown to the "privileged" defendants in this case, in stark contrast to the unsympathetic treatment accorded defendant Valjean for stealing bread to feed his family. The broader gist of this sort of critique is that race and poverty differences are not only pervasive in America, but that elite legal culture enforces these differences in draconian practice while ignoring the differences doctrinally.

I believe that *The Case of the Speluncean Explorers* is most valuable, not just as classic jurisprudential text by Lon Fuller, or as a vehicle to rehash Hart and Sacks and their critics, but as a challenge to feminist and critical race theorists to apply their experiences and insights to statutory interpretation, and not just to issues of jurisprudence or constitutional law.

SECTION THREE

The Case of the Contract Signed On Book Day
In the Supreme Court of Newgarth, 4305
Lon Fuller

Action for breach of contract brought in the Court of General Instances in Pinwright County. Judgment for the defendant. Affirmed. The facts sufficiently appear in the opinion of the Chief Justice.

TRUEPENNY, C.J. The bare facts of this case are relatively simple; the legal background of those facts considerably more complex. I shall accordingly begin with a brief recital of the essential facts, including the action of the court below.

In April, 4304, the defendant, a resident and citizen of this Commonwealth, entered into a contract to sell ten barrels of pickled squids to the plaintiff, an importer having his principal place of business in Outerclime. A written contract was drawn up and signed. This contract bore the date of April 15, 4304, the day on which it was in fact concluded and signed. It contained a provision that its interpretation and effect should be determined by the law of Outerclime. The defendant failed to perform the agreement, and the plaintiff brought suit for damages. In the court below judgment was entered for the defendant on the ground that a contract concluded on April 15 is, by the law of Outerclime, unenforceable and void.

In both of the nations involved in this litigation, the fifteenth of April is the chief secular holiday. Known popularly as "Book Day," its official title is "The Day of the

140

Recovery of the Books." It commemorates the date when, many centuries ago, Newgarth and Outerclime being still one nation, our common ancestors succeeded in devising a means of penetrating into the centers of ancient civilization for the purpose of removing the books contained in their libraries — books that had since the Great Spiral lain for generations unused and unread, but preserved from decay and the ravages of insects by the same malignant forces that prevented our forefathers from obtaining access to them.

There is every reason why we should celebrate as the most glorious in our history the date on which our ancestors initiated the great undertaking known as the Recovery of the Books. That date marks the dawn of modern civilization. Every art and science that gives comfort to our existence, or depth and meaning to our lives, takes its origin from that time. The Recovery of the Books is also associated in our minds with the greatest feat of collective heroism in our history. For at least a century after the Recovery began the procedures for removing the books remained highly hazardous and the slightest misstep brought a hideous death to those engaged in the undertaking. This circumstance placed our ancestors in a dread dilemma such as no other people has ever confronted. It was essential that the most important and useful books should be removed first. The rude physical conditions under which our forefathers lived made precious every treatise on chemistry or physics that could assist in the conquest of their hostile environment. The recurring social disorders and disruptions of the times made men eager to draw on the wisdom of the ancients in devising principles for the organization of society that would promote justice and order. Which of the buried books could contribute most directly toward these ends was a question that only the best intellects of the time were capable of judging. It was necessary, therefore, to send into the enveloped cities the most gifted and learned men then living, so that they might select from the libraries the books most needed. Nearly four fifths of those who so engaged themselves perished in the undertaking.

About a century after the Recovery began, there was enacted a statute entitled "An Act to Commemorate the Recovery of the Books." In addition to providing for the erection of certain statues and the holding of public celebrations, the Act contained the following language: "The fifteenth day of April shall henceforth be known as the Day of the Recovery of the Books, and shall forever be held sacred by the citizens of this Commonwealth. On that day, no man shall engage in any trivial pursuit, nor in any mechanical or useful occupation, nor shall any business be transacted or any contract between one man and another be signed or concluded."

We are confronted in this case with the question whether a contract executed on Book Day is legally enforceable. This is a question that has not often arisen in the past, nor is it one likely to arise frequently in the future. Such is the spirit in which Book Day is held that very little business is in fact transacted on that day, even in modern times. There is furthermore an almost universal folk belief that a contract signed on that day is unenforceable. This view is probably shared by the majority of lawyers, who have never had occasion to look into the precedents on the subject.

Under the law of this Commonwealth it is, however,

clear that a contract is not deprived of legal validity simply because it is concluded and signed on April 15. In two cases decided about a century after the passage of the Act to Commemorate the Recovery of the Books it was held that the statute is exhortatory merely and does not invalidate contracts concluded on Book Day. See *Barden v. Seaforth* and *Stims v. Wilforce*. There is no intimation of a contrary view in any of our precedents or statutes.

But the case before us requires, of course, a determination of the law, not of this Commonwealth but of Outerclime. By the provisions of our C.S.N.A. (N.S.) §1578-B-1 (Section 10 of "An Act to Facilitate Commerce between Newgarth and Outerclime") we are obliged to give full effect to the stipulation in the contract by which its interpretation and legal efficacy are to be determined by the law of Outerclime.

If we ignore certain recent legal events in the Republic of Outerclime, it would be perfectly clear that the law of Outerclime and that of our own Commonwealth are in complete accord on the question before us. The Act Commemorating the Recovery of the Books was passed at a time when Outerclime was politically a part of this Commonwealth. The decisions interpreting that Act which we have recited above were also rendered before Outerclime achieved its independence. When, in consequence of the civil war known as the War of the Judges, Outerclime became a separate nation, Article XII of its Constitution provided: "All statutes and judicial precedents of the Commonwealth of Newgarth hitherto effective within the territory of this Republic shall remain in full force and effect until repealed or amended by laws duly enacted by the House of Delegates."

Since there is no enactment of the House of Delegates of Outerclime that has any bearing on the question before us, it would seem clear, on the basis of the considerations so far adduced, that the plaintiff had a valid contract and that judgment should have been entered for him.

The action of the lower court in rendering judgment against the plaintiff is, however, predicated on the following considerations. Three years ago the question of the validity of a contract signed on Book Day arose in the case of *Pressman v. Nolens* decided by the Court of Municipal Appeals of the Republic of Outerclime. (C.M.A. Docket No. 8947, Nov. 5, 4302.) The Court of Municipal Appeals is an appellate court hearing appeals from the Municipal Courts located in the various cities of Outerclime. Decisions of the Court of Municipal Appeals are subject to review by the Supreme Judicial Court of Outerclime.

In the case of *Pressman v. Nolens* the Magistrate of the Court of Municipal Appeals declared a contract signed on Book Day to be legally unenforceable under the law of Outerclime. He based this decision entirely on an independent interpretation of the Act Commemorating the Recovery of the Books. He reasoned that since this statute forbade the concluding of contracts on Book Day, and provided no other sanction to enforce its prohibition, it must have been intended to render such contracts legally unenforceable. He reached this conclusion in apparent ignorance of the precedents that had given a squarely contradictory interpretation to the statute. No appeal was, however, taken from his decision to the Supreme Judicial Court of Outerclime, and the time for taking such an appeal has now expired.

The decisions of the Court of Municipal Appeals are not

published in any form generally accessible to the public. The Republic of Outerclime has, however, established a governmental agency known as the Office of the Co-ordinator of Governmental Activities. This Office has no power to issue regulations and is, in fact, simply a clearing house for information concerning the activities of the various branches of the Outerclimerian government. By statute the Co-ordinator is directed to determine when the publication of a particular decree, decision or regulation will promote the objective of his Office, which is that of developing a more effective co-operation among the various branches of the government through an exchange of information. When he deems such a publication desirable, the Co-ordinator directs the printing of the decree, decision or regulation in question and copies are then distributed, without comment, to the various agencies of the government.

After the decision in the case of *Pressman v. Nolens* was rendered by the Court of Municipal Appeals, the Co-ordinator directed that copies of it be mimeographed and distributed to all the agencies of the Republic of Outerclime. On receiving copies of this decision, it appears that a considerable number of the governmental agencies added a provision to their regulations to the effect that henceforth no legal significance should be attributed to transactions (including contracts, applications and notices) executed on Book Day. Among the agencies that thus attempted to bring their practices into conformity with the decision in *Pressman v. Nolens* were the Post Office, the State Insurance Office, the Public Printer, the Department of Taxation, the Boating Authority, the State Direction of Railways and Telegraphs, and the State Tobacco Monopoly. Through a misunderstanding of the decision, the State Oleomargarine Monopoly inserted into its regulations a provision that henceforth applications and contracts executed on Book Day should be given full legal effect.

Counsel for the defendant successfully argued in the court below that on the basis of the events recited above the courts of our Commonwealth must assume that under the law of Outerclime as it exists today a contract executed on Book Day is unenforceable. I believe that this conclusion is sound.

It is not our function to pass judgment on the wisdom of the law of Outerclime. Our task is to determine, not what that law ought to be, but what it is. In passing on that question it is our duty to content ourselves with the evidence presented to us and to refrain from conjectures as to what the evidence would have been if events had taken a different course.

When we approach the case before us with these cautions and restraints in mind, it seems to me that its decision becomes clear. In the case of *Pressman v. Nolens* the Court of Municipal Appeals has declared the law of Outerclime to be that a contract executed on Book Day is legally unenforceable. Some of the most important agencies of the Republic have amended their regulations to incorporate that decision, so that the principle it contains has passed over into the structure of the government of Outerclime. I therefore conclude that the Court of General Instances was entirely right in the action it took in the case before us and that its judgment should be affirmed.

TATTING, J. I concur in the conclusion reached by the Chief Justice. His opinion seems to me, however, to overlook a consideration that should be determinative of this case.

It has always been a cardinal principle of our jurisprudence that foreign law is to be regarded as a fact. This principle regulates the manner in which our courts ascertain the rules of a foreign legal system. When questions involving the law of another jurisdiction become relevant in the decision of cases arising in this Commonwealth, our courts are not at liberty to have direct recourse to the statutes and precedents of the foreign jurisdiction. Instead, they proceed by receiving the testimony of experts on the legal system in question. Foreign law is, in other words, proved just as any other fact is proved.

If foreign law is a fact, it follows that the decision of the Court of Municipal Appeals in *Pressman v. Nolens* must be considered by us as a determination of fact. Now nothing is more elementary than that we are not at liberty to question determinations of fact by a court having jurisdiction over the persons and the subject matter. Suppose, for example, that we had examined the evidence introduced in *Pressman v. Nolens* and concluded that the contract there involved was actually executed on April 16, rather than on April 15, as the Magistrate found. Obviously, this would give us no warrant for disregarding his decision. For our purposes, his determination of the facts of the case before him would have to be treated as conclusive. But if foreign law is to be deemed a fact, it must follow that his determination of the law of Outerclime is equally conclusive upon us.

This conclusion renders completely irrelevant any conjecture as to what would have occurred had the Magistrate's decision been appealed to the Supreme Judicial Court of Outerclime. This appeal did not in fact occur, and cannot now take place because of the expiration of time. We are not authorized to sit as a court of appeals reviewing the decisions of the courts of Outerclime. Yet if we were to decide that the contract before us was enforceable under the law of Outerclime we would, in effect, be arrogating this power to ourselves.

There is a second point on which I diverge from the Chief Justice. I cannot join him in attributing any significance to the fact that certain agencies of the Republic of Outerclime have amended their regulations in order to incorporate into them the decision in *Pressman v. Nolens*. The regulations of such agencies can no more be considered as having the force of law than, let us say, the regulations concerning quiet hours of a hospital operated by the state. This does not mean that these regulations are wholly without legal significance. Just as a nurse might be held to have been properly discharged who had violated the regulations of a hospital, so these administrative regulations might be given an indirect significance in certain kinds of litigation. If they remained long in effect, a course of practice might be established which might influence the decision of the Supreme Judicial Court if the question of the validity of a contract executed on Book Day were to come before it at a later time. But this kind of significance is something quite different from saying that these regulations constitute themselves a part of the law of Outerclime.

HANDY, J. The pronouncements just rendered show how if man permits his mind to become a playground for legal spooks for a sufficient length of time he will come in the end to believe these things really exist. Over the years my brothers and I have waltzed about with a great many minor shades and spectres from the world of legal theory, but in this case we are brought face to face with the greatest spook of them all, "The Law."

Now it is quite excusable for the unsophisticated layman to think that there is an abstract something called "The Law," that "exists," and is capable of answering all questions put to it. Certainly no lawyer and no judge of the Supreme Court of Newgarth has any warrant to indulge himself in a similar illusion.

What is this "law" that adjudicates controversies and answers inquiries? The veriest novice in our profession knows that a case is decided not by one thing, but by a lot of things. Among these are usually some words on paper. These words may have been written by delegates to a constitutional convention, by legislators, judges, or professors. The words may be printed and bound in buckram or mimeographed and stapled in loose pamphlets. There are, furthermore, many ways in which these words may be strung together. They can be slogans or catch-phrases; sententious pronouncements, or pained, analytical expositions like those that delight the heart of my brother Tatting. Much more important than the words are the people who will decide the case or who may affect its decision. These are witnesses, commissioners, judges, clerks, advocates, office lawyers and various kinds of lay bystanders. Some of these people are going to be perceptive, some obtuse; some kindly, some vindictive; some bold and persuasive, some timid and ineffective. All of these people are going partly to run themselves and partly to be run by habits of thought they have picked up here and there. The more esoteric of these habits of thought are the pride of the profession and go by the name of legal theory. Other habits of thought are shared by the profession with the populace,

149

though every effort is made to conceal that fact in the decisions of this court.

The client who asks his lawyer, "What does the law say about my case?" probably thinks there is some kind of legal spectre waiting out in the library to give the answer. When the lawyer tries to deal with his client's question, however, he has to translate it into something sensible before he can even go to work on it. The question he really puts to himself is phrased in some such terms as these: "When this case has run through the maze of all the things that may affect its decision — these things including words on paper, an assortment of people and a variety of different habits of thought —what is the likely outcome?" Having answered the question in these terms, the lawyer translates his answer back into the form the client expects. He expresses his guess as to the outcome of the case by saying, "The law says so and so about your case." Of course, sometimes he can't arrive at any prediction that is worth anything, but even in that case instead of saying, "I can't make a dependable guess as to how your case would come out if it were tried," he says, "The law in your case is uncertain." This gives the client the comfortable feeling that the spectre is still out there in the library, though temporarily in an uncommunicative mood.

To make my rather obvious point a little more obvious, I should like to relate an experience drawn from my own practice. In my firm one of the partners happened to be a very able advocate by the name of William Pebble. His peculiar talent consisted in an unusual ability to convey to juries and courts an understanding of the background of the cases he argued. It often happens that a case looks one way when it is lifted up into a realm of legal abstractions and has an entirely different complexion when it is placed down among the facts out of which it grew. The difficulty is, of course, to get those facts into the heads of the judge and jury and in that my partner William Pebble was, as I say, a master.

When clients came to us for advice we were often confronted with this sort of question: "If this case went to litigation, would the courts stick a legal label on it and proceed to give it the treatment called for by the label, or would they really be capable of seeing it as it looked in its whole setting, as it appeared to people like our clients who were a part of that setting?" This kind of question could arise, for example, in connection with the allegedly restrictive practices of the Fishing Co-operatives. If you draw a legal blueprint of these things, they are apt to look one way. If you throw the blueprint away, and get some sense of the whole situation, then they have an entirely different appearance.

Now so long as we had Pebble with us, when a client brought a case like that to us and asked, "What is the law on this point?" we tended to ask ourselves how the case would look to the judge and jury after Pebble had tried and argued it. Of course, this involved some risk because we could never be sure that Pebble would be there to try the case, and the client might not choose to have Pebble represent him in the event of litigation. Still, Pebble's influence so pervaded the office that we could not avoid taking his presence into account, and if some risk was involved, why of course some risk is always involved in advising a client of his rights.

When Pebble was gone we realized how much our advice on questions of law had been influenced by his presence. After his death when clients asked us to tell them what the law on a particular point was we had to acquire new habits of thought and we began to ask ourselves, "If this case goes to litigation, how will it look to a judge who sees it as an abstraction and who cannot be brought to understand its whole factual setting?" — for we knew that no one could take Pebble's place in the art of conveying that setting. The result was that " the law" on which our office advised its clients underwent a considerable change when one of our partners died, though he held no commission from the state, had written no treatises and was not, in fact, particularly learned in the law himself.

Now I should like to apply the same matter-of-fact analysis to the problem presented in this case, and I want to begin with the effect of the amendments introduced into the regulations of the governmental agencies in Outerclime after *Pressman v. Nolens* was decided. The Chief Justice begins by stating that the decision in *Pressman v. Nolens* established "the law" of Outerclime. He then proceeds to say that this conclusion is reinforced by the fact that the principle of that decision "passed over into the governmental structure" of Outerclime by virtue of the amendments introduced into the various administrative regulations. This seems to imply that even though the principle was "law" so soon as the Magistrate spoke in *Pressman v. Nolens,* it became "law" even more when it was injected into the administrative blood stream of the Republic. My brother Tatting, on the other hand, admits, in effect, that the injection took place, but contends that the administrative amendments did not put the principle within the main blood stream of "the law," but left it out among the capillaries, where it was a kind of near-law or almost-law. Neither of my brothers is indulgent enough toward the rest of us to inform us of the premises on the basis of which these conclusions are reached.

Now let us test this matter of the rule "passing over into the governmental structure" of Outerclime against some facts. What is the actual situation of the agencies of the Republic? Are they in such a state that a thing as intangible as a rule of law could "pass over" into them?

Here a little history is in order. In the War of the Judges the inhabitants of Outerclime were, of course, adherents of the judiciary. Accordingly, when they achieved their independence they set up a lawyer-ridden kind of government that approached a theocracy, with judges and lawyers in the place of priests. This worked so badly that it was quickly overthrown, substantial amendments were introduced into the Constitution and the whole organization of government was changed. The result of the experience was, however, to leave with the inhabitants of Outerclime an abiding distrust of lawyers.

This distrust is so strong today that not a single governmental agency in Outerclime has a legal staff. They are all dependent upon a pitiful little office connected with the Ministry of Justice. Without proper legal guidance, the whole administrative structure of the Republic has for years been on the verge of a complete breakdown. Every condition that can contribute to chaos obtains: overlapping jurisdictions, contradictory regulations, important regulations that are not published and practices that contradict the regulations that are published.

In an effort to remedy this situation (still without hiring lawyers) the House of Deputies hit on the device of the Office of the Co-ordinator of Governmental Activities. The

Chief Justice has described the theory of that Office. Far from curing the existing evils, the Office has compounded chaos. Every agency copies into its own regulations nearly every decree and regulation of every other agency. Lay clerks place these under the most bizarre headings, and when they are indexed at all, the index entries can be described only as the expression of personal whimsey. The loose-leaf binders of the agencies are running over, their filing cabinets have been expanded into the corridors, and every week a new Supplement to the last Supplement appears. No lawyer could possibly advise any client about the simplest matter coming before these agencies.

Against this background I may be forgiven if I say that I am unable to take seriously the Chief Justice's statement that the principle of *Pressman v. Nolens* has, by the confused scribblings and mimeographings of these lay clerks, "passed over into the governmental structure" of Outerclime. Placing anything as fragile as a rule of law within the maw of that sprawling monster is like dropping an orchid into a cement mixer.

I turn now to *Pressman v. Nolens*. I could ask for no better example of the fatuity of trying to derive "the law" directly from words on paper than the treatment my two brothers give to that case. We are told that *Pressman v. Nolens* (which for us is simply a set of words on paper) has established that under the law of Outerclime a contract executed on Book Day is void. But my brothers say nothing about another set of words on paper, those contained in Article XII of the Constitution of Outerclime. If these words are given an ordinary meaning they seem to me to say that a contract executed on Book Day is valid under the law of Outerclime. Why, then, do my brothers prefer the words of the Magistrate to the words of the Constitution? Some undisclosed premise must underlie that preference. Until that premise has been brought out into the open where we can see it and examine it, I think we may be forgiven for not being unduly cowed by the tone of inevitability that my brothers attach to their conclusions.

Now I should like to approach this question of determining "the law" of Outerclime in the same realistic way that we dealt with similar questions in advising clients when I was in practice. If we approach the thing in that spirit, it is apparent at once that we are not concerned with what happened to the defendant Nolens in *Pressman v. Nolens*. We may assume that he escaped the obligations of his contract, though as I shall show in a moment even that is not so. Our case, however, involves another plaintiff and another defendant. If the question, 'What is the law of *this* case in Outerclime?' is to have any meaning at all, it must mean, 'How would this case be decided if it had arisen in Outerclime instead of Newgarth?' The answer to that is very simple. It would take no William Pebble to convince the Supreme Judicial Court of Outerclime that *Pressman v. Nolens* was wrongly and even ignorantly decided. Any reasonably competent journeyman in the profession could accomplish that after about twenty minutes' study and with one hand strapped to his back.

This sufficiently demolishes *Pressman v. Nolens*. I should like to add a fact, however, of which my brothers are probably ignorant. It happens that my wife's cousin was attorney for Pressman in that litigation, and I have learned through him that the case was argued before the Magistrate on grounds that had nothing to do with the contract's having been signed on April 15. Though Nolens' attorney had entered a more or less perfunctory plea of the statute, he realized that a defense on that ground would avail him nothing and did not argue the point at the trial. The case as argued was a little complicated, and the Magistrate thought he saw a way out of his difficulties by seizing on the fact that the contract was entered on Book Day. When his decision was rendered it was so palpably mistaken that it was not even necessary for the plaintiff to take an appeal; the defendant settled out of court for the full amount of the claim. In a conversation with the Magistrate later my wife's cousin joked with him a little about the case, and the Magistrate, taking no offence, said that next time he would read the annotations first before he undertook to interpret a statute.

THE CHIEF JUSTICE. If Justice Handy does not desist at once from his persistent habit of bringing into our discussions matters outside the record, on which no proof properly cognizable by this court has been presented, I shall have to inquire what disciplinary steps are open to me to put an end to this practice.

HANDY, J. I withdraw the objectionable remarks. I realize that this habit of mine is offensive and is perhaps made doubly so by the fact that a certain prankishness enters into it. I should like to observe, however, that my indulgence can cause no possible harm. I have the only mind on this court impure enough to be influenced by the legally irrelevant. Since I already know the facts I so impiously blurt out, I am certainly not seducing myself. I am sure that my brothers have legal wills strong enough to put to one side the irrelevancies that drop from my lips. At least I am sure this is true of Justices Tatting and Keen.

On reflection I am not so sure of my brother Foster, and

perhaps for his sake I ought to desist. It may startle my hearers for me to say so, but in many ways I feel myself closer to Foster than to anyone else on this court. If he could only rip off that metaphysical jacket he has put on himself, and gain a little more freedom of action, I think we might get along very well indeed. Perhaps in some future incarnation he will finally leave his chrysalis behind him and he and I will fly about together with the freedom he now denies himself. But, of course, I shall meanwhile have been evolving myself in some direction or other, so that this happy reunion will probably never take place after all.

But I must break off this day-dreaming, which is as impertinent and irrelevant as the remarks that just incurred the censure of the Chief Justice. Summing up my views of this case, I should say that the essence of "the law" in terms of reality is prediction, but prediction based, not on a few words on paper, but on all the circumstances likely to influence the decision of a case. On that basis, I have no hesitancy in saying that under "the law" of Outerclime as it "exists" today a contract made on Book Day is enforceable. For that reason I conclude that the judgment of the Court of General Instances should be reversed.

FOSTER, J. I agree with the conclusion reached by my brother Handy, and I accept many of the premises on which that conclusion is based. In particular, I accept the premise that "the law" is not something lying inert in statutes and precedents, but is instead a process, an activity of men's minds projected upon things that merely "are." The ancient American philosopher Cardozo expressed the same truth (though without the air of rattling skeletons which my brother affects) when he said, "The law never is, but is always about to be."

Yet, though I accept my brother's premises, I insist that those premises be given a footing and an underpinning which I am sure my brother would describe as "metaphysical."

My brother finds the essence of law in prediction, but he fails to inquire into the conditions that make prediction feasible. Now it seems perfectly clear that prediction, or predictability, is the product of order. In the absence of some kind of order or structure, prediction is impossible. If I dissolve a quantity of salt in a cup of water, it is impossible to predict in what manner the molecules of salt will arrange themselves. Indeed, it is only with considerable license that we can speak of an "arrangement" at all, since all we have, or at least all that is accessible to our senses, is a random, formless dissolution of the salt into a fluid state. But so soon as a sufficient quantity of water has evaporated, and crystals begin to appear, there emerges, for the first time, order, and with it, a certain degree of predictability. In place of a random turbulence, patterns and regularities begin to assert themselves. Limits begin to be imposed on the things that can happen and it becomes possible to anticipate the future course of events.

My brother inclines by temperament to emphasize, on all occasions, the personal and contingent elements in legal questions, and he sometimes talks as if the whole field of law and morality were a kind of formless stew in which almost anything could happen. Of course he does not really mean what he says, as his own treatment of the case before us abundantly demonstrates. He asserts with great confidence that if this case were before the Supreme Judicial Court of Outerclime, that Court would hold the contract to be enforceable. He says, in effect, that this is a prediction not based on fortuitous personal factors — no William Pebble would have to argue the plaintiff's cause. My brother's demonstrations therefore necessarily assume that a certain ordering underlies human affairs, including legal events in Outerclime. For reasons of personal predilection he chooses not to inquire into the nature of that ordering, but instead simply asserts dogmatically a prediction which assumes its existence.

Where my brother is content to stop with the bare fact of prediction, I would go beyond that fact and inquire into the nature of the order or structure which makes it possible. In my opinion that order must be founded on justice, it must express in some measure a striving toward justice.

When I say that the order of human relations which we call law must express a striving toward justice, I do not pretend to be able to give an exact definition of the goal indicated by the word justice. Such a definition is not possible because the quest is not merely for a realization of so much of justice as is understood and articulated, but for a deeper understanding of the ideal of justice itself. No really vital impulse of human nature can be assigned an exact and unchanging goal. If you ask a scientist the true meaning of science he will tell you that it lies, not in the dead acquisitions of today, but in a method of revising and enriching those acquisitions. If you ask what that method is, you will be told that it cannot be defined with exactitude since it must always be adjusted to the task at hand, and no one can predict what tasks science will set itself tomorrow. We can say no more and no less of justice.

If I were asked to define what I mean by justice as I understand it today, I should say that it is an ordering of men's relations to one another within a group in such a way that the following ends will be advanced: 1) The members of the group are enabled to satisfy their common and separate wants with a minimum of conflict and waste; 2) Goods, burdens and functions are distributed so that each man is treated in a way that bears a rational relationship to his needs, capacities and services; 3) The individual is protected against the interference of others (whether acting corporately or not) where that interference is not justified by the ends just described and would restrict the freedom of the individual to develop himself in the directions to which he is prompted by his own nature.

This is vague, and necessarily so. It can gain meaning only within a context of institutions and other limiting conditions. The quest for justice must always be conducted with some sense of the proportion of means to end; it may be better to do without roast pig for a while than to burn down the house in order to have it at once. The problems of justice faced by each society are to some degree peculiar to that society. The Speluncean explorers were confronted with a problem virtually unique in human experience, that of finding some rational and just method of determining whose body should furnish the means of life for the others. There are solutions that might be imagined for this problem about which reasonable men would differ. Solutions can also be conceived that would obviously be irrational and unjust. At the other extreme was the solution actually adopted by the explorers, which was, in my opinion, clearly reasonable and fair. So it is with our own more complex societies; our solutions must be adapted to the problems we face and they must be as reasonable and just as we can make them.

Unless the order we call law expresses a striving toward

justice, the desideratum of order itself will not be achieved effectively. There is a natural impulse in men toward justice. An order that satisfies this impulse is an order supported by the native bent of men's minds. An order that violates justice is an insecure order, for its girders are vulnerable to the pull of human nature itself.

Skeptics who deny the truths I have just asserted are fond of adducing illustrations drawn from history and ethnology for the purpose of showing that in the realm of human organization all is relative and contingent. Societies have in fact been organized on the most fantastic principles — principles that seem to us to violate the most elementary demands of justice and rationality. Hereditary castes and totemic clans are beyond the pale of reason for us because we do not share the beliefs on which they are founded. But if men mistakenly believe, or have been brought by the fraud of their rulers to believe, that every human must pass through a hierarchy of castes in successive reincarnations, then an organization of society in hereditary castes may, for men entertaining such beliefs, be eminently fair and reasonable. The quest for justice in any society reflects not only the external conditions under which the society lives, but the state of knowledge and belief within the society. If the Speluncean explorers had believed in the efficacy of auguries, it might have been a rational procedure for them to ask their rescuers above ground to watch the flight of birds for guidance in their predicament. The fact is that they did not believe in auguries, and the resort to this method of resolving their problem would, for them, have been an irrational one. The citizens of our Commonwealth do not believe that they are the blood cousins of bears and owls, or that they are destined to become mosquitos in some future existence. Our citizens must seek justice in the light of their own knowledge. They should not be deterred from their quest by proof that other men in other ages and other places have entertained very different beliefs and have, in the light of their beliefs, tolerated or encouraged social organizations that seem to us clearly irrational and unjust.

If, as I have asserted, the order of law is an order that seeks justice, it follows that when we come to predict how a particular case will be decided under the law we must base our prediction on an understanding of the demands of justice as they affect the case before us. Unless we have good grounds for assuming that some irrational or personal consideration will intrude itself upon the case, we should entertain the presumption that the demands of justice will be met. This presumption is essential to assure the dependability of our prediction.

There is, however, another reason why we should presume in our predictions that the demands of justice will be met —a reason that cuts deeper than that just suggested. In the realm of human affairs it is impossible to effect a complete separation of prediction from prescription. If enough people believe that an event lying within their control will occur, it is virtually certain that it will occur. The politician who warns that a revolution will break out if he is not elected, is usually correctly understood to threaten a revolution. If the legal profession generally predicts that the Supreme Court will overrule a decision, this prediction is itself a factor tending to bring about the predicted event. Within the limits of their control over their own destinies, men tend to become what they believe they will become, and my neighbor's anticipations of me help to make me what I am.

Nowhere are the truths I have just expressed better exemplified than in the relation of judges to the lawyers who practice before them. Every judge of any experience on the bench knows how difficult it is to rise above the anticipations attorneys entertain of him. If those who appear before him argue the case on the assumption that he will follow mechanically the demands of abstract verbal symbols — like an unintelligent cook measuring out the misprints of a recipe — then the judge may be forced to decide the controversy in that manner, simply because he lacks the guidance necessary for a more reasoned treatment of it. If advocates assume that the judge will be motivated by personal biases, and allow this assumption to shine through their arguments, a moral environment of decision may be created in which it is impossible for the judge to recapture any degree of objectivity. It has been truly said that the judges are the mirrors of the lawyers who practice before them, and this is but a special illustration of the general truth that we all tend to mirror the expectations of our fellows.

From these considerations flows the moral necessity that, wherever possible, we base our predictions of the way the law will function on the assumption that it will act reasonably to meet the demands of justice. If the lawyers of a nation cease to consider this the normal assumption, to be entertained in the absence of convincing proof to the contrary, then the collective quest for justice is at an end, and law becomes what men expect it to be, a brute, contingent datum.

Now it is true that in the case before us the considerations I have been describing are at a minimum. The degree to which men are in fact shaped by the expectations of their fellows depends, of course, upon the closeness of the community in which they live and work as members. Within the family or the village the interaction that pulls men toward conformity with the anticipations entertained of them is direct and immediate. Between sovereign nations this interaction reaches its most attenuated form. Yet even when we are determining the law of a foreign nation, the moral need remains to base prediction on an assumption that justice and rationality will be sought by others as well as ourselves. If each nation of the world assumes in the administration of its own affairs that the law of other nations is reasonable and fair, this assumption will tend to bring into existence the condition accepted as most probable. If each nation treats the law of other nations as a brute fact, divorced from reason and fairness, a continued adherence to this assumption may bring about the very condition assumed.

By this lengthy but, I think, essential route I am finally brought to the issue directly before us. That issue is, 'How would the courts of Outerclime decide the question of the enforceability of a contract made on Book Day if that question were presented to them today?' I answer that question as my brother Handy does; they would decide in favor of enforceability. I am led to that conclusion by assuming that the law of Outerclime is, like ours, not an inert fact, but a process of reason, directed toward achieving order and justice. As my brother says, the way in which that law will be applied to a particular situation cannot be derived from some single fact or from a few words on paper. It is to be discovered by assuming that the process of decision will function rationally, that it contains within itself the capacity to restrict the fortuitous and personal, and that it possesses the means for correcting errors. If I do not make these assumptions, then I am utterly incapable of deciding the case before me. Without these assumptions I could neither predict that *Pressman v. Nolens* would be followed or that it would not. I should simply have to say that I have no idea what the course of legal events in Outerclime would be.

It should be observed that the case before us is not one tinged by any strong issue of public policy. Whether a contract made on Book Day is or is not enforceable is not something vital to the maintenance of commerce in either of the nations involved in this litigation, and it is one of those questions where the primary desideratum is to have a fixed rule. While adherence to precedent is often opposed in men's minds to justice, it is apparent that in cases like the present one justice itself is advanced by remaining within accustomed ways. The ends of justice that I have previously described can be realized only within a framework of rules that gives some stability to men's relations. A purely gratuitous change in existing rules, serving no definable end of justice, is itself an affront to justice.

My brother Tatting has already condemned the view just expressed as an "arrogation" of powers not possessed by this court. My brother Keen will no doubt echo this censure when his turn comes to speak. I am quite aware that the view of my brother Handy and myself can be regarded as presumptuous, since we are in effect telling the Magistrate of the Court of Municipal Appeals that he is wrong about the law of his own Republic. I am also quite aware that there is a certain risk in the determination we are making.

If we disregard the familial sources of information possessed by my brother, I believe we must confess we only *think* the Magistrate was wrong in *Pressman v. Nolens*. It may be that there lies hidden in our reports, misindexed and overlooked by the commentators, a precedent that overrules those on which we have relied as establishing that a contract made on Book Day is enforceable. If this should turn out to be true, then my brother Handy and I will cut a sorry figure indeed with future legal scholars. One can almost hear the professors of a later age exulting in the classroom over our presumptuous blunder, extracting from it for the delight of their students every bit of irony it contains, explaining how we declared the Magistrate wrong about his own law when he was not only right about his law but ours as well. Lessons of judicial humility will be drawn from our example. For myself, however, I would rather be wrong trying to do right than accept a conclusion that seems plainly wrong because by doing so I might delude myself into thinking I had no responsibility for the decision reached.

It is true that there is nothing so ludicrous as an act of unreason committed in an effort to act reasonably. Much of the highest and lowest comedy of literature is based on an exploitation of this fact. The caged ape who seizes the hat of a bystander and tears it to bits in blind fury arouses admiration for the sheer animal force of his rage. The ape who takes a proffered hat and solemnly attempts to feed it to a hungry brother in the mistaken belief that it is an edible excites only a pitying amusement. In modern times men in an effort to avoid placing themselves in the position of the second ape, are inclined to emulate the first. For my own part, I cast my lot with the ape who at least tries to act rationally. I believe that, despite setbacks and misunderstandings, he will live a longer life and be a happier ape than his more forceful and awe-inspiring fellow. If there is a pathos in reason stumbling, it is at least the pathos of life striving to live.

My brother Keen will castigate all I have said on the ground that my philosophy blurs the distinction between law and morality and threatens the established boundaries of the legal order. I assert in answer that nothing which lives has fixed boundaries; a stone can be measured and assigned definite dimensions, an amoeba cannot. I would rather have a system of law that was quick with the impulse toward justice than a system limited by a fixed course of metes and bounds, with the tombstones of dead aspirations marking every corner.

I comprehend thoroughly the qualms of those who fear "judicial usurpation" and who dread, as a moral cancer, any tendency on the part of officials charged with enforcing and applying the law to read into the law their own personal philosophies and predilections. There is a perfectly sound instinct back of this fear. The quest for order and justice must be a co-operative quest; it must proceed, so far as is humanly possible, in ways quest that are impersonal and predictable.

But any fear, however well founded, can assume morbid and destructive forms. An anxiety so intense that it prevents men from seeing the reality with which they must deal is a dangerous anxiety. I believe that the theories which attempt to rack the judge against the dead fact of law are based on a distorted view of the function of law and a perverted conception of the ways in which men's minds must necessarily work in deciding controversies.

In dealing with questions of legal philosophy I find it useful, before attempting to solve problems about the nature of the law in general, to ask myself how the same questions would be answered if they had been raised concerning some particular rule of law. "The law" is a forbidding abstraction, that presents no handles our minds can readily take hold of. On the other hand, we have daily occasion to interpret and apply rules of law. Now since the law is simply an aggregate of particular rules, the most profitable avenue of intellectual attack is plainly indicated. Let us take some of the issues that are mooted about the nature of law in general and see in what light they appear when they have been raised about particular rules of law.

When we speak of "the law" of a nation, two things are frequently assumed or asserted: 1) this law is something entirely distinct from morality and its limits are marked by the line at which the coercive sanction of the state ends; 2) this law can only be created and interpreted by certain official agencies of the state. Let us ask ourselves whether these assertions can be applied to a particular rule of law.

Now I take it to be a truism that no rule or principle of law that relates to a matter of any complexity ever has exact boundaries, so that one can say, "At this point the legal rule itself ends and men's conceptions of what it ought to be, or might be, commence." The meaning of a rule is always a complex thing, fusing moral and legal conceptions. Every rule of law represents the projection of a purpose, a purpose that changes imperceptibly with experience and increased insight. Often we can trace the history of a rule across time, marking how this decision restricted it, this line of authorities extended it, this economic development gave it a new direction, this scholarly article placed it in a larger context where it acquired a new significance. Throughout this development no one could deny two plain facts: 1) the rule never has at any point of time exactly fixed boundaries; 2) the rule changes not in response to a single force, but in response to many forces. Some of these are "official," like statutes and decisions; others are not, like the views of scholarly commentators.

Now if these things are true of a rule of law, it seems to me plain that they must equally be true of that aggregate of rules we call "the law". So long as that system of rules is stirred by a yearning for justice, it will be a system that blends with graying shades into the field of morality, and a system subject to the diverse influences of legislators, judges, scholars and laymen. It will be, and should be, a system that excludes from participation in its building no man who can contribute fresh insight and wisdom toward the achievement of its goals.

These considerations arm me with a tolerably complete indifference to the shafts my brother Keen will shortly dispatch in my direction. I am quite aware that I hold no commission from the Republic of Outerclime to interpret its laws. I am also quite aware that, according to the views of my colleague, the most off-hand indication of the meaning of a law has more weight, provided only it proceeds from "official" sources, than the considered judgement of scholars and philosophers. I have, I hope, sufficiently revealed my reasons for refusing to join my brother in this narrow conception of law and the judicial office.

It is my conclusion that the judgment of the Court of General Instances was erroneous and should be reversed.

KEEN, J. The opinions just rendered illustrate two of

the most baneful confusions that can be imported into legal thought. If some means cannot be found to stop the spread of these confusions, it will become impossible for this court to discharge its constitutional functions and we shall have to reconcile ourselves to an abandonment of man's effort to establish an order of society founded on law.

I refer, of course, to my brother Handy's propensity for confusing fact with law, and to the now inveterate inclination of my brother Foster to confuse his notions of what the law ought to be with the law itself. It is small wonder that my brother Handy should acknowledge a kind of covert sympathy for the views of his colleague, for the loose ways of thought that both embrace are equally at odds with any proper conception of the judicial office.

Though a certain indiscriminate blurring of law and fact permeates his whole opinion in this case (as it does everything he writes), the confusion of my brother Handy comes most plainly to the surface in his treatment of the amendments introduced into the administrative regulations in Outerclime following the decision in *Pressman v. Nolens*. The issue before us being one of the law of Outerclime, the Chief Justice proceeds to decide that issue as would any judge who brings to his task a correct understanding of the judicial function under our system of government, that is to say, he turns to official sources in Outerclime for indications concerning the state of the law in that Republic. One of these indications, itself sufficient, he finds in the decision of the Court of Municipal Appeals in *Pressman v. Nolens*. Another and confirmatory indication he finds in the fact that certain administrative agencies in Outerclime have amended their regulations to incorporate the rule of that case, so that its principle has, in his words, "passed over into the structure of the government of Outerclime."

A proper treatment of this last issue requires certain analytical discriminations that are not to be found in any of the opinions so far rendered. I shall have occasion shortly to make some attempt to supply this deficiency. The point I wish to make at this juncture is that the considerations which my brother Handy brings to bear on that issue are utterly without legal relevance.

With his usual penchant for going beyond the record of the case before him, my brother asserts that the administration of government in Outerclime is in a very confused state. Denied the assistance of lawyers, the lay bureaucracy of that Republic drafts and indexes its regulations badly, administers rules that differ from those it announces, and generally has difficulty in achieving any degree of coherence or regularity in its actions. In legal terms that he would not himself deign to employ, my brother in effect suggests that we take Judicial notice that the administrative agencies of Outerclime are in such a state that they have no rules or regulations.

Now if I thought it proper or relevant to do so, I might observe that I have myself a considerable first-hand acquaintance with affairs in Outerclime and I find my brother's account somewhat exaggerated. However, I do not propose any excursus into that question, for even if governmental administration in the Republic were in a much worse state than my brother describes, this fact would still be completely without legal bearing on our decision.

My brother's treatment of this issue gains a certain surface plausibility because he happens to be dealing with administrative regulations rather than statutes. The principle is, however, exactly the same. Does a statute lose its legal force because those charged with applying it have difficulty in understanding it? Are we to measure the statute, not by its words, but by the action taken under it? Or again, does a statute forfeit its validity because it is drawn by laymen who express their intention inartificially? Are we to review the proceedings of every legislature to determine how orderly they were before we grant the force of law to their enactments?

When viewed in its full implications the proposition of my brother is truly a monstrous one. It would suggest that statutes could be repealed through the mistaken indexing of a clerk in the Office of the Public Printer, that gambling houses could be legalized by the inertia of prosecutors, and that law itself should cease to tell people what they ought to do and instead merely describe what they choose to do.

No system of human order founded on law is possible if the question, 'What is law?' is allowed to be affected by considerations of the type my brother adduces. If the administrative agencies of Outerclime are confused about their own regulations, the way to remedy this situation is not to disregard those regulations, but to give them the full effect ascribed to them under the statutes of the Republic. The former course will only serve to compound the confusion and give it deeper roots; the latter may produce some temporary disruption, but in the long run is the only procedure by which the situation can be remedied.

No rule of any kind can achieve its purpose unless a force is attributed to it that goes beyond its immediate realization in practical affairs. There is a vital difference between prescription and description; to confuse the two is to lose the very ends of law. Some twenty-four hundred years ago an American jurist, Zechariah Chafee, compared the formal element in legal rules to the precepts of a railway time-table. He observed that if railway employees habitually start trains late in order to pick up stragglers, more people will in the end miss trains than if the time-table is strictly observed. If a time-table is to serve its purpose it must be taken seriously, and we must continue to aim at the ideal it embodies even though we know that three times out of four the 12:01 really leaves at 12:04. My brother, on the other hand, proposes that we throw away the timetable so soon as the trains begin to run behind time.

If a sense of respect for the enacted ideal is essential in running a railway, how much more essential it is in that highest of secular undertakings we call the law. Here a confusion of the rule with the fact of its realization threatens something more sinister than a disruption of plans and some disappointment of expectancies. If my brother Handy's views were ever to become generally accepted we should lose all those guarantees we have so painfully built up through the ages against caprice and arbitrary power. We should then have indeed, in the terms of an ancient comparison, a government of men and not of laws.

The true bent of my brother's philosophy can be revealed even in the analogy of the time-table. When men give up the effort to make the trains run on published schedules, we find not only that departures are late by varying and unpredictable degrees, but that trains are held for the families and friends of railway employees and for those with the power to dispense favors. It is no accident that my brother not only wants to be "realistic" about legal rules, but also proposes that the fate of defendants accused of murder be determined in private conversations with the Chief Executive and that the outcome of lawsuits tried before him shall depend on information derived through his wife's relatives. His proudly professed taste for earthy realities is in fact simply the expression of an unacknowledged penchant for personal rule.

In his efforts to remove all form and structure from the legal order, my brother is powerfully abetted by his colleague, Mr. Justice Foster. Now one cannot deny to the latter's conceptions a certain idyllic charm. He pictures the law as if it were a garden of peripatetic philosophers. A group of friends, of indefinite and varying composition, gathers in this garden to engage in the pursuit of a kind of poetic truth. The group so engaged changes from time to time, one man drops out and another comes in, visitors are occasionally invited to participate, and the whole work goes forward unevenly, sporadically and delightfully.

This is a very pleasing picture, but completely foreign to the realities of law and government. Law is in fact an apparatus of coercion applied by men to men and capable of depriving a man of his property, his freedom and his life. It is of the utmost importance that we give a clear-cut and unevasive answer to the question, 'Who can coerce whom?' 'Who can command with the power of the state back of him, and who cannot?'

It is significant that though my brother is fond of the somewhat vague expression "order," he never uses the more descriptive and appropriate term "organization." Law is an organization by which men are authorized to command others and by which men are obligated, under threat of the application of physical force, to obey certain kinds of commands. If my brother would keep this simple truth before him he would never fall into the confusion that vitiates the whole last part of his opinion.

174

In the closing paragraphs of his opinion he develops an argument that runs in some such terms as these: The precise scope of any particular rule of law is always to some extent indefinite. "The law" is simply an aggregate of rules. Therefore the scope of the law as a whole must be indefinite. Those of us who pretend we can draw a sharp line between law and morality are simply deluding ourselves.

The fallacy of this argument becomes immediately apparent when we inquire what is meant by law when a distinction is drawn between law and morality. Law in this context does not mean, as my brother assumes, a mere collection of abstract principles. It means rather a definite, human hierarchy of command.

The point I am making will be apparent if we consider the principles that must underlie the organization of any human enterprise, such as a hospital or a public dining hall. No such enterprise can be conducted in all of its details by fixed rules, mechanically applied. Some judgment and discretion must be exercised by cooks and waiters, physicians and nurses. Though there will be many clear-cut regulations, directing precisely what shall be done in particular instances, there will also inevitably be other regulations that leave room, and sometimes a wide room, for individual judgment. These are the rules of indefinite scope of which my brother speaks. But the discretion that is here not only permitted but perhaps even encouraged, cannot carry over to the basic organization of the enterprise itself. We intentionally refrain from telling our cooks how much pepper to add to the stew, but this does not mean that we are willing to have the waiters and dishwashers have a hand in the seasoning, or worse still, as my brother would like, any casual bystander who happens to talk glibly of his culinary skill.

Law in the sense that is sharply distinguished from morality consists of that body of principles which define who are agents of the state and what their authority to act in the name of the state is. In this matter there can be no tolerance for obscurity. The state may on occasion permit its agents to join Mr. Justice Foster in consulting the Muses in order to decide what they should do in a particular case. It cannot permit the appointment of its agents, or the scope of their authority when appointed, to be controlled by the same process.

The truths I am here enunciating are at least as ancient as the twentieth century, when O. W. Holmes uttered an aphorism that achieved great popularity among the Americans: "The . . . law is not a brooding omnipresence in the sky, but the articulate voice of some sovereign or quasi-sovereign that can be identified." When we remember that this sovereign possesses over us the power of life and death, we shall insist, I believe, that it be identified clearly and unambiguously.

These simple observations should, I think, enable us to penetrate behind the paradox that so enraptures my brother, namely, that although particular legal rules may be indefinite in scope, the legal order as a whole must have and does have exact boundaries. In fact we are talking about two different things. The legal order marks the limits of state power and tells us what particular human beings have authority to speak in the name of the state. Legal rules constitute the principles upon which these persons proceed in deciding cases and issuing orders.

The importance of the distinction I am taking is

nowhere better exemplified than in the field of international relations. Within our Commonwealth we have not had, since the War of the Judges, any major disorders, any irregular or challenged successions, any disputes that have threatened the essential stability of men's lives. This condition of tranquillity has obtained despite the fact that our citizens are sharply divided on matters of religion, politics and economics. During the same period we have seen in the relations of nations to one another every imaginable perfidy and disorder: broken treaties, undeclared wars, secret alliances, and the ruthless conquest of helpless peoples.

Why is it that we have harmony within nations and a savage anarchy among nations? Is it because my colleague's "quest for order and justice" is more vigorously pursued in municipal affairs than it is in the relations of one nation to another? Of course not. One might almost assert the contrary. Seeing that the essential ingredients of an effective legal order are lacking in the international field, men have sought to make up for that lack by an attempt to found international law directly on considerations of justice and morality. Learned treatises expound legal principles for the governance of international affairs that purport to be derived directly from the nature of man and the common need for peace and harmony. It is no accident that among the ancients speculation about a mythical "law of nature" had its chief vogue with writers on international law. Down through the centuries, both before and after the Great Spiral, these efforts to conjure into existence an international social order have failed. What has been lacking is not an indefinite thing called "the quest for justice," but a very definite and sometimes harsh and unpleasant thing known as "organization." Until we have an international organization which assigns to men a clearly defined power to command other men we may write a mountain of treatises and we shall still not bring about the condition of peace that we desire. What is needed in this field is not philosophers but policemen.

Against the background of these observations I should like now to turn to the immediate issues of the case before us. All of the court are agreed that the task with which we are confronted is that of answering a specific question (Is a contract executed on Book Day enforceable?) by an application of the law of Outerclime.

To me it seems perfectly clear that this question is answered for us by the decision in *Pressman v. Nolens*. My brother Handy attempts to make it out that we are confronted with two conflicting indications concerning the law of Outerclime, the case of *Pressman v. Nolens*, on the one hand, and the Constitution of the Republic, on the other. The short answer to this is that the Magistrate of the Court of Municipal Appeals in Outerclime is the duly authorized agent of that Republic, empowered to interpret and apply its Constitution. We hold no similar commission.

To my mind nothing at all hinges on the circumstances that the case of *Pressman v. Nolens* was decided by an intermediate appellate court rather than by a court of last resort. For proof that this is so, I refer to the opinion just rendered by my brother Foster. Not a word of his argument would have to be changed if *Pressman v. Nolens* had been decided by the Supreme Judicial Court of the Republic. He speaks of an assumption that the law of Outerclime is "a process of reason, directed toward achieving order and justice," that it has "the capacity to restrict the fortuitous and personal," and possesses "the means for correcting errors." These are the words he uses to build a ladder by which he can surmount the wall around the Outerclimerian garden of law. Once he is inside that enclosure I have great confidence that he would be as capable of correcting the errors of the Supreme Judicial Court as he was of a Magistrate hearing municipal appeals.

Despite my brother's glib conversance with ultimates, his opinions always reveal sooner or later that his proud declamations serve merely to cover his personal views of the controversy before him. The present case gives abundant proof of this. After declaring the law of Outerclime to be the opposite of what the agencies of that Republic declare it to be, my brother continues, "... the case before us is not one tinged by any strong issue of public policy. Whether a contract made on Book Day is or is not enforceable is not something vital to the maintenance of commerce ..." *etc.* By virtue of what eternal verity is this determination made? I should think it quite possible that the Supreme Judicial Court of Outerclime might regard our precedents enforcing contracts signed on Book Day as the profanation of an ancient symbol. They might decide it was time to remind a light-hearted generation that it must not trifle with the memories of an heroic past. They might regard my brother's remarks about the maintenance of commerce as sordid and irrelevant, and his inability to see that the case is affected by an issue of policy as the symptom of an atrophy of the moral faculties.

But I shall not press these remonstrances further, since I should like in the short time left to me to deal with the one point of difficulty in the case — a point not only neglected by my brothers but one that they could not, I fear, treat adequately simply because the premises from which they depart do not permit the proper analysis. I refer to the effect of the amendments introduced into the administrative regulations in Outerclime after the decision in *Pressman v. Nolens*. In order to test this matter thoroughly I shall proceed in the remainder of my discussion on the assumption that *Pressman v. Nolens* has itself no bearing on our case and that we must test the law of Outerclime solely by the administrative regulations now in force in that Republic.

Now since the general issue before us is that of determining the law of Outerclime on the question of the enforceability of a contract executed on Book Day, and since these regulations declare such a contract to be unenforceable, the sole question we have to decide is: Do these administrative regulations have the force of law in Outerclime?

In dealing with this kind of question one of the commonest errors is to allow oneself to be misled by the accidents of linguistic usage. My brother Tatting's opinion furnishes a neat illustration of this error. He seems to assume that only certain bodies known as "courts" and "legislatures" can make law. Anything that emanates from something called a "commission" or a "board" must have a force or significance less than that of law. This way of treating the question simply defaults before the task of analysis, and substitutes the prejudices of the lexicographer for the discriminations of the legal analysis. There is no magic in a word, and if a body of men called a "board" has the power to make a final determination of the rights of citizens it has by that token the right to make law. Deciding where sewer pipes shall be laid may not be the highest form of human endeavor, but if the Sanitary Commissioner can make a final determination of that issue which the police will enforce, then he makes law within the area of his competence, and there is analytically no distinction between his law and that of the Supreme Court or the Chamber of Representatives.

In determining what orders or regulations have the force of law we must proceed, therefore, by setting to one side the more or less fortuitous distinctions of linguistic usage, and ask ourselves, 'Does the rule in question effectively direct the application of the coercive power of the state?' Emphasis must be placed on the words "effectively direct," for we cannot include under the heading of law those standards or principles that merely influence in some measure the application of the state's power. Suppose, for example, that the Chief Executive gives a general order, as he did last March, directing all state agencies "to economize." No doubt such an order would have a very considerable influence on the actions of legislators, courts, commissions and boards. Yet no one would think that it had on that account become a part of the law of the land. The distinction becomes apparent if we set off against the pervasive but indefinite principle contained in that order the immediate and compelling direction conveyed in the statutory rule, "No suit on an oral contract shall be permitted four years after the cause of action first accrued." Here is a rule that acts as a kind of valve directly controlling the flow of state power; here are no questions of more or less — that valve is either open or it is shut, and when it is shut the state will lend no aid whatever to the enforcement of the barred debt.

As a second step in our analysis, after having

determined whether the rule effectively directs the application of the state's coercive power, we must ask the further question, 'Does the rule emanate from some person or persons acting in the name of the State?' For the coercive power of the state may be directed or controlled by standards that are not properly considered to form a part of the law. The most obvious example is the private contract. Here a set of rules, established by agreement, determine the rights of the parties and therefore control the application of the state's coercive power. For example, the direction "The Seller must deliver one third of the wheat before March 1", may just as effectively shape the actions of judge and sheriff as a statute would. Yet such a rule is properly not considered to be a rule of law for the simple reason that it is established by parties who do not purport to act in the name of the state and who have in fact no authority to act in the name of the state.

A humorist might interject the observation that on this basis the decisions of my brother Foster are not law since, so far as is known, he has never yet acknowledged that he acts on behalf of the state. Though presumably like the rest of us he draws his salary from the Commonwealth, his commission would seem to run directly from Universal Reason. I suppose the answer is that an element of agency is inherent in the very office my brother holds, and that he cannot by his communion with the eternal verities change the legal nature of his determinations. It would be artificial, to say the least, to apply a similar interpretation to the act of entering a contract and to say that the contracting parties act on behalf of the state whether they realize it or not.

It is of course true that there are instances where a contract may be regarded as having the force of law. This interpretation is properly applied to agreements executed pursuant to a recited statutory authority. The most notable illustration is to be found in contracts entered pursuant to the Act to Permit Certain Beneficial Measures of Self-Regulation among Competing Industrial Units. See C.S.N.A. (N.S.) §2348-B-10-22. Here, by an exception to our anti-monopoly laws, certain trade associations are authorized to enter contracts establishing conditions of fair competition over a specified area of an industry. It has been generally conceded that these contracts have the force of law, since they establish rules that control the application of the state's coercive power and they are executed pursuant to a specially conferred statutory authority.

The question immediately before me fortunately does not present difficulties of the type just discussed, since I take it there is no question that the various administrative agencies of Outerclime purport to act in the name of the Republic and in fact have the authority, within specific limits, so to act. A proper analysis of the effect of the regulations of these agencies is, however, beset by other difficulties — difficulties which cannot be resolved by anything contained in the record before us. We do not have before us the statutory authority under which these agencies act, nor do we have any means of knowing to what extent their regulations are subject to judicial review. Without a more precise knowledge of those subjects, it is impossible to give a wholly adequate answer to the question, 'Do these regulations have the force of law?' I shall have to content myself therefore with certain simplifying assumptions which can serve no further purpose than to indicate the lines of a correct analysis.

Let us assume in the first place that the regulations in

question are subject to a complete judicial review by which the courts of Outerclime would determine the propriety of the rules they contain without giving any persuasive force to the determinations already made by the agencies themselves. In that event clearly these regulations would not have the force of law. It could not be said that they cut fixed channels for the flow of state power. It is true of course that a citizen dealing with one of the agencies might through ignorance or inertia accept its ruling as final and neglect his opportunities for an appeal to the courts. This circumstance, even if repeated in hundreds of instances, could not give these regulations the force of law. The situation would be essentially the same as that of a man who might decide not to bring a lawsuit because he was advised by his attorney, perhaps erroneously, that he had no cause of action. Certainly no one would contend that such a determination had the force of law.

Nor would regulations thus subject to a complete and unrestricted judicial review gain the force of law merely because the courts might be inclined to attribute a certain weight to the determinations previously made by the agencies. Here the analogy most apt is that of a scholarly article or treatise, which may well influence the court toward a particular decision, but which does not, on that account, gain the force of law.

Let us now, pursuing our analysis in bold outlines, make an assumption exactly the opposite of that with which we started, that is, let us assume that the regulations in question are not subject to any degree of judicial review but are final and conclusive. In that event it is perfectly clear that they would have the force of law. They would effectively determine the rights of parties dealing with the agency; they would serve as an index directly controlling the application of state power.

Now it is unlikely that either of these extreme conditions actually obtains in Outerclime, that is, that these regulations are subject to a complete and unrestricted judicial review or that they are completely immune from control by the courts. In all likelihood the legal situation falls between these extremes, and complexities probably exist by virtue of the fact that the scope of judicial review varies with the different agencies. Nevertheless, I believe that I have correctly stated the lines along which the analysis should in any event proceed; I have sufficiently developed the principles that would have to be applied in the more complex situation that probably exists in fact.

A conversation I have just had with my brother on my right (which will not appear in the printed report of this case) leads me to the conclusion that the analysis I have just presented is incorrect. Though I do not agree with the form of my brother's objection to that analysis, I see on reflection that my reasoning does in fact contain a serious fallacy.

I have said that if the regulations were completely immune from judicial review they would have the force of law within the Republic of Outerclime. This is correct so far as the question is that of determining the rights of those who have occasion to deal with the agencies issuing those regulations. But that is not our question. We are dealing with a suit brought in a law court to enforce an ordinary private contract, and we have therefore to inquire what law would be applied in Outerclime to such a suit. Now I take it that on that question the regulations of the various administrative agencies in Outerclime are without significance, since they relate merely to the rights of citizens with respect to matters falling within the jurisdiction of those agencies and those agencies have no competence with respect to a suit of the type now before us.

One might argue, of course, that these regulations tend toward the establishment of a general principle and might therefore be expected to have some influence on the decision by a court of this question of the validity of a legal transaction executed on Book Day. But as I have already shown, a bare influence of this sort is not of itself enough; the effect of a rule must be directive and not merely persuasive before the rule can be said to have the force of law. Furthermore, though we are accustomed to extend judicial precedents by analogy, and almost every precedent has a legal force somewhat wider than the immediate case decided, we are not in the habit of giving a similar treatment to administrative regulations in deciding lawsuits that fall outside the area of activities toward which those regulations are directed. I do not believe that this attitude derives from the accident of linguistic usage by which we apply the term "law" to judicial precedents and commonly deny it to the rules and orders of boards and commissions. Rather I think it rests on a tacit premise of our legal order that it is not proper to reason by analogy so as to extend an administrative regulation beyond the area falling within the jurisdiction of the agency that issued it. Some of the most important premises of legal reasoning rest unfortunately not upon express enactments but upon general acceptance. The subservience of the courts to the legislature is such a premise. I believe the premise that denies an analogical extension to administrative rules has a similar footing.

It may be advisable at this point to recapitulate the

steps in my reasoning. I at first said that if no judicial review were permitted, this would give the force of law to the administrative regulations in question. I now see that though this may be so for those dealing with the agencies issuing these regulations, it is not so for purposes of this case. Immunity from judicial review simply gives these regulations the effect of law in the area of activities falling within the jurisdiction of the agencies, and this effect remains bottled-up within that area, as it were, by virtue of a predisposition of legal reasoning against an analogical extension of administrative regulations.

I had previously said, on the other hand, that if the regulations in question were subject to a full and unrestricted judicial review they would be without the force of law and without significance in this case. I now believe that I must reverse this judgment. I now see that the existence of an unlimited judicial review might actually increase the significance of the regulations for the case before us. I mean to say this: If these regulations are subject to judicial review this fact itself tends to show that they are not to be taken to imply principles peculiarly applicable to the work of the agencies issuing them, but are deemed to incorporate legal principles of general significance in the formation of which the courts should be given a hand. If therefore in spite of an unrestricted opportunity to appeal to the courts parties dealing with the administrative agencies have acquiesced in these regulations, this would tend to show an assumption that the rule contained in them had become a general principle of Outerclimerian law.

I must, on reflection, withdraw my last remarks. An uncharitable critic might point out that these remarks involve the very confusion for which I have censured my brother Handy, that is, the confusion between law and fact, or between the rule and the action that men see fit to take under the rule. The argument I have just advanced seems to assert, in effect, that the law can be established through the inaction of litigants and that the existence of a general assumption that an appeal would be unavailing may have the same effect as an appeal actually taken and adjudicated adversely. Of course these premises are wholly unacceptable.

It was perhaps unfortunate that I should have embarked on this thorny subject when the time at my disposal does not permit an opportunity to give to it the thorough analysis it deserves. My attempts to deal with the question (and no one realizes more than I their inadequacy) serve at least to confirm the judgment I originally expressed, that we do not have before us sufficient information to decide the question of the precise legal effect of these administrative amendments. The scanty outlines of the analysis I have presented would, I believe, serve as a useful guide if we were forced to determine that question. Fortunately, we are relieved of that task by the decision in *Pressman v. Nolens* which, for present purposes, sufficiently answers the question before us without involving us in any of the difficulties that might be presented if we had to rest on the administrative amendments alone.

Those who have followed the decisions of this court, and have witnessed my efforts to deal single-handedly with complex issues like that I have just discussed, will not have to be told that mine is not an easy position on this bench. With all the forces that surround me pulling in the opposite direction, it is no light undertaking to strive toward a clear conception of law and, with it, a clear and correct conception of the judicial office. It is with a sense of weariness that I review the attempt I have made in years gone by to enlist my brothers' aid in this undertaking. But I have resigned all hope of achieving that end. I know that my brother Tatting will continue to weave about every case presented to him an encircling filigree of irrelevant distinctions, my brother Foster will continue to make my task harder by doing everything he can to blur the distinction between law and morals, and my brother Handy — well, the least that can be said of him is that one who does not believe in law can scarcely be expected to lend aid in arriving at a clear definition of law.

On the basis of the decision in *Pressman v. Nolens*, I conclude that the judgment of the lower court was in accordance with the applicable law of Outerclime.

A majority of the court being of opinion that the judgment entered below for the defendant was proper, that judgment should be, and is hereby, AFFIRMED.

Note: This mythical hypothetical case was suggested by *Fidelity Union Trust Co. v. Field*, 1940, 311 U.S. 169. Holmes' famous aphorism about the "brooding omnipresence" is found in his dissenting opinion in *Southern Pacific Ry. v. Jensen*, 1917, 244 U.S. 205, 218, 222. The passage from Cardozo will be found in "The Nature of the Judicial Process," 1921, 126. Professor Chafee's comparison of legal forms with a railway time-table occurs in "Acceleration Provisions in Time Paper," 1919, 37 *Harvard Law Review* 747, 750.

The Inarticulate Premiss
Robert Seidman

What follows purports to give the opinions of three judges of the highest court of appeal in Newstate, Africa. The title is taken from a pregnant phrase of O.W. Holmes, an American writer on jurisprudence. He held that the result of a case depended upon 'the inarticulate major premiss' of the judge (or the unstated assumption which most influenced his judgment), at least in matters of first impression — i.e. cases in which the judges must determine for the first time what is the operative rule ('norm') of law. He urged this proposition in sharp opposition to the popular notion that a judge merely applied to the ascertained facts clear rules of law, which he found in earlier cases or in statutes.

In an appellate court in anglophonic Africa, each judge reads (or recites orally) his opinion. Frequently, these have been circulated beforehand, so that each judge knows what his brethren propose to say. Facts are never at issue in such appellant proceedings. The judges in the appellate court are required to accept as true the facts found by the trial judge. The only issues before the appeals court are legal: What is the true rule of law? How does it apply to the facts of the case at hand?

On the day of judgment, counsel are present, all in black gowns and short curled wigs. The court bailiff pounds his mace: everybody stands; the three judges walk solemnly to their high-backed seats behind the raised bench. They are dressed in brilliant crimson robes, with black cuffs and black sashes, and long wigs whose curls brush their shoulders. Solemnly, counsel bow from the waist; solemnly the judges acknowledge the courtesy. The judges take their seats, and a rustling fills the courtroom as spectators and counsel in turn sit down. Then all is silent. The bailiff calls out the name of the case, and the Chief Justice begins to read his opinion

IN THE SUPREME COURT OF NEWSTATE: DECEMBER 1965
The Republic v. Kwame s/o Nighihili[1]

MUGHIRI, C.J.: This is a novel case, the first of its sort since our recent independence from the British Crown. It raises the question of the approach to law and to legal problems which will best serve our new country.

My position is quite clear. The basic law of Newstate is still English law.[2] I am sworn to apply the law. I do not see how I can do anything except apply English law. My brother Ekpe says that he too is sworn to uphold the law; that he too wants to apply the common law; but he wants

---

1. The facts of this case are invented but there are many similar cases which have arisen in the courts of anglophonic Africa. In East Africa cases, the letters "s/o" and "d/o" mean "son of" and "daughter of" respectively.
2. All the anglophonic African states look to English law as the basic law. Several Nigerian statutes, for example, enjoin the courts to apply "the common law of England". See, e.g. Law of England (Application) Law, W.R. No.9 of 1958 s.3; and Interpretation Ordinance, Law of the Federation of Nigeria and Lagos, 1958, cap.89, s.45(1). The Ghanaian Courts Act 1960 is somewhat broader. It declares that the basic law is the common law, but states explicitly that the courts may look for precedent in any common law jurisdiction: Constitution (1960), s.40(e); Interpretation Act 1960, s.19(1); Court Act, 1960, C.A. 9, s.154(4).

to shape the common law to express our African instead of its British background. How he manages this, I cannot say, although I have read his opinion carefully. And my brother Mensah says that our theories of jurisprudence are destructive of the aims of a socialist independent African state. He claims that he can as a judge warp the law to fit what he conceives to be the demands of the new state.

This is all very interesting, but in the event we are at such loggerheads that we have been unable to agree upon the disposition of a very simple case. In my opinion, this demonstrates what happens when judges start trying to adjust what the law is to fit what they think the law ought to be. At any rate, in our judicial bankruptcy, we end by praying the executive to rescue us from the pit we have dug. This is regrettable, and in my opinion entirely because my brethren have wandered from the tried, tested, and true common law paths.

I turn now to the case at hand. This comes before us on appeal from a conviction for murder before a magistrate sitting with three assessors. Such a situation is, lamentably, all too common despite the remarkable advances made by Newstate since our independence only a few short years ago. The appellant lives in a primitive tribal community not far from the shores of Lake Swahili, in a compound with his three wives and nine children. His is a simple pastoral tribe, who have been tending their herds in conditions of relative peace and penury for centuries. A school has only recently begun to be built in his village; the appellant is, of course, illiterate.

In October last year, one of the wives of the accused's deceased father, a very old woman, named Chichumbi, came to live with the appellant. Chichumbi was apparently a quarrelsome old lady, and friction quickly developed between her and the appellant. In the course of their many quarrels, Chichumbi frequently claimed to possess powers of witchcraft; and she threatened to use these dark powers to injure the appellant and his family.

In January of this year, the accused's eldest son, a promising lad of some 12 years, became ill of a malady that seemed inexplicable to him and to the other members of his family and tribe. His right leg slowly seemed to atrophy, so that in a matter of a few months the boy lost all use of it; shortly thereafter his other leg became paralysed. His speech became thick and confused, and towards the end he had apparently lost all his senses, being little more than a vegetable. He died in a convulsion in July.

After his son lost the use of his legs, appellant took counsel with the elders of his tribe. They advised him to visit a famous seer, whom the magistrate called a 'witch-doctor', some three days distant from appellant's village. This witch-doctor, after performing a complicated customary ritual that lasted two days and a night, told the appellant that Chichumbi was a witch, and that she was causing the death of his son by occult power.

The appellant returned to his village and accused Chichumbi of being a witch. She at first denied the charge. Later, however, in the course of one of the frequent quarrels that marked the unhappy household, she claimed that in fact she was a witch, that she was slowly gnawing away at the boy's legs, and that she would attack each of accused's children and wives in turn.

Shortly after his eldest son died, accused's next eldest son fell ill of what was apparently the same malady, and Chichumbi again gloated over the illness, claiming to be the cause. As the magistrate and the assessors all found as a fact, the appellant genuinely believed that Chichumbi had killed his son by witchcraft, and was now killing his next eldest son as surely as if he had actually seen her attacking the children with spear or panga.[3] In the custom of his tribe, at least formerly, the killing of witches was not only permitted, but considered a meritorious deed. In former times, appellant might have appealed to the Kiama, or tribal council, who would have tried Chichumbi on the charge of witchcraft; but the Kiama has long since ceased to function. The appellant was thus faced with what seemed to him certain destruction from Chichumbi's witchcraft, and could see no institution to which he could appeal for relief. His tribal custom sanctioned self-help in such a case.

His youngest and favourite wife also fell ill of the same mysterious malady in July of this year. Three days later, the appellant returned late to his compound. He went to his hut and remained there for an hour, drinking beer and brooding. Suddenly, he grabbed his panga, ran to Chichumbi's hut where she lay sleeping, and attacked her in a savage frenzy, inflicting upon her wounds from which she died in a few minutes. Afterwards he appeared quite calm, and voluntarily walked to the headman's hut, where he quietly told the headman what had happened. The headman had him confined and reported the matter the next day to the police. In due course appellant was tried

---

3. Judges in witchcraft cases have frequently affirmed the reality of the defendant's fear of destruction by the witch. See, e.g. *Kanwaka Wa Malumbi & 69 Others*, 14 K.L.R. 137 (1932); *Galikuwa*, 18 E.A.C.A. 175 (Uganda, 1951); and *Konomba* 14 W.A.C.A. 236 (Gold Coast, 1952).

and convicted of murder, and sentenced to death.

The Penal Code of Newstate was enacted in 1930, when this Republic was a British colony. It was modelled, like the Penal Codes of Kenya, Tanzania, Uganda, Zambia, Malawi, Nigeria, and the Gambia, upon the Penal Code of Queensland, Australia, which in its main outlines and indeed most of its details restated the common law of crimes.[4] In this respect it does not differ from the penal codes of Ghana, Northern Nigeria, and the Sudan, although these Codes derive from different models than the Queensland Code.[5] Our task is to apply the Penal Code, expressing as it does in the main the common law of crimes, to the facts of this case. My brethren have invoked many large philosophical concepts to obscure this simple task. But I have taken an oath to uphold the law as it is, and there my function begins and ends. My personal philosophy cannot affect this task, because otherwise ours would become a government of men, not of law.

Appellant has advanced four defences before us. In the first place, he claims that under native custom he was entitled to kill Chichumbi as a witch. He tried to prove this

---

4.   See J. Read, "Criminal Law in the Africa of Today and Tomorrow", in *Journal of African Law* (London), Spring 1963, p.5.
5.   The Penal Code of Ghana was introduced in 1893. It was modelled upon the St. Lucia Code, which in turn was modelled upon the Jamaica Draft Code. The Northern Nigerian Penal Code and the Sudanese Penal Code were almost identical. They were both modelled upon Macaulay's Indian Penal Code of 1839. All (including the Queensland Code), except the Northern Nigerian and Sudanese Codes, were ultimately derived from Sir James Stephen's Draft Code of 1878, which was an attempt to codify the existing common law. It was never introduced in England.

native custom at the trial, by calling two of the village elders to testify. It may be that that was indeed the custom some years ago, but the elders could not cite a specific case occurring within the last decade. No doubt, they said, witches had been killed in that period; but because of the threat of penal sanctions such killings nowadays would be concealed. It is always very difficult to discover what is in fact the native custom obtaining at the time of the events in question. Native custom is changing very rapidly in these revolutionary times, as Newstate moves towards the new society which we all want to see. The assessors, who were familiar with appellant's tribe, were divided about the existence of this particular custom, although they all agreed that it had been prevalent in the past.

But even if the custom had been proved, it is an accepted principle of our law that native custom will not be enforced if it is repugnant to justice, equity, and good conscience. This rule was embedded in our law from the earliest days of the British over-rule. That rule, we are now taught, was in its central motivation an avaricious attempt to exploit our people to satisfy the greed of British entrepreneurs. That may well be; but one of its concomitants was a well-meant attempt to rescue our people from the sinks of superstition, ignorance, and paganism in which we then were, and to some extent still are. The British judges in colonial days were quite willing to invoke native custom in civil cases, where it did not violate the standard of justice, equity, and good conscience.[6] But they rarely, if ever, applied it in criminal cases, and, so far as I can discover, never to excuse murder.

Now by what standard ought one to measure justice, equity, and good conscience? To measure a native custom by the standard of indigenous justice would mean that every native custom would have to be sustained. That would deny the civilising mission of the English law. Obviously, therefore, the colonial judges adopted the standard of Englishmen. Since our law today is the same as it was before independence,[7] I conceive that I must apply the same standard.

My brother Ekpe makes a feeble attempt to show that the African personality is expressed in native custom. He claims that justice, equity, and good conscience is to be measured in terms of something he calls the African personality. How he can claim that his personality, educated at a British-run Christian secondary school, at Oxford, and the Inns of Court, bears any relationship to the personality of this appellant, still steeped in the ignorance and superstition of the bush, I find impossible to understand. At any rate, as I have said, our job is to apply the law. The

---

6. See, e.g. *Balogun v. Amodu Balogun*, 2 W.A.C.A. 290, 306 (Nigeria, 1935); *Cole v. Cole*, 1 N.L.R. 15, 21 (1898); and *Lukwago v. Bawa Singh* [1959] E.A.C.A. 282.

7. The typical constitution of an independent African state includes a proviso that all the laws in force immediately before the adoption of the constitution remain in force thereafter. See, e.g. Constitution, Ghana (1957), art.40; and Constitution, Nigeria (1960), art.154(4) - maintaining in force the Interpretation Act of 1889 (which made English law the rule in the Colony and Protectorates).

law today with regard to native custom in Newstate, as in all the anglophonic African states, is exactly the same as it was under the British. If there is such a native custom as the killing of witches, it plainly violates every English notion of justice. My brother Ekpe can if he likes, I suppose, disregard the law which he is sworn to uphold. I cannot. I therefore have no hesitation in declaring absolutely void the supposed native custom upon which appellant relies.

Even if I did not, however, I could not allow the defence. Our Penal Code states that defences to charges of criminal harm are to be interpreted in accordance with English law. Even if it did not so state, I should have so to interpret it, in light of the Code's origins, except in the rare case where the Code plainly departs from the common law.[8] What the appellant is really asserting is that he made a mistake of law. He thought that he was entitled by law to kill Chichumbi as a witch. In this he was mistaken. But

---

8. In *Wallace-Johnson*, 5 W.A.C.A. 56 (Gold Coast, 1941), the Privy Council said, in an oft-quoted dictum, that where a Colonial Code is "exhaustive", it must be read without glosses derived from English or Scots Law. However, African courts almost invariably cite English precedents as authoritative in interpreting the Codes, not infrequently even when the Codes are in terms to the contrary. In *Tene Dagarti* [1961] January-June Judgments (mimeographed) 48, for example, the Supreme Court of Ghana followed *D.P.P. v. Smith* [1960] 3 All E.R. 161 (House of Lords), in refusing to permit a defendant to advance a claim that although death was the reasonable and probable consequence of his act, he subjectively did not intend death and hence was guilty only of manslaughter. Cf. Criminal Code, 1960 (Ghana), s.11(3): defendant presumed to intend reasonable and probable consequences of his acts unless he proves to the contrary.

mistake of law has never been a defence in British law, except in very exceptional cases, of which this is not one. Indeed, our Penal Code says in explicit terms that mistake of law shall not be a defence to a criminal charge. I must, therefore, disallow the defence.

The second principal defence asserted by defendant is that of mistake of fact. He claims that he mistakenly believed Chichumbi to be a witch who was threatening the lives of everybody in his family, so that the only defence was to kill her; and that he killed her in self-defence and in defence of his family. Now it is an accepted principle of the Penal Code, and indeed of the common law, that where a criminal harm is done under mistake of fact, the guilt of the defendant must be measured by the state of affairs which he imagined to be true, not the state of affairs which was in fact true.[9] If a man threatens me with a water pistol which looks like, and which I believe to be, a real pistol, and I kill him because I believe that my life is threatened and there is no other way for me to save my life, I am not guilty of criminal homicide.

But there is a limit to the defence of mistake. The common law and our Penal Code declare that a mistake, to excuse a criminal harm, must be 'reasonable'. If I see my

---

9.   See, e.g. Criminal Code, Nigeria, s.25: Penal Code, Tanganyika, s.11; and Criminal Code, 1960 (Ghana), s.29(1). For the Common Law, see *Levett,* Crown Cases 538 (England, 1638). *Cf.* J. Hall, *General Principles of Criminal Law* (Indianapolis, 1960 edn.), p.363: "To understand the rationale of *ignorantia facti excuasat*, it is necessary to recognise and take into account the relevant ethical principle, namely, moral obligation is determined not by the actual facts but by the actor's opinion concerning them."

wife's car in front of my home, and I know that she almost never leaves the house unless she drives herself, I may say to myself, 'My wife is at home'. If she is not at home, then my mistake is a reasonable one; it is a mistake which the average person in my shoes would have made. But if I do not see my wife's car, and I still say to myself, 'My wife is at home', then my mistake is unreasonable, for the average man in my shoes would not have made that mistake. If the limitation of reasonableness did not exist in the penal law, then every defendant could claim that he acted under mistake, and nobody would ever be convicted of crime.

It thus falls to be considered whether it was a reasonable mistake for the appellant to believe that Chichumbi so threatened his life and the lives of his family by her witchcraft that his only recourse was to slay her. In interpreting any statute, the primary consideration is to give effect to the intent of the legislature; our job is to apply the law, not to make the law. This Code was enacted in colonial days by a colonial Council, and introduced by the colonial governor on the orders of the British Colonial Office. It was modelled upon the English common law. The legislature must therefore have intended that the test of reasonableness would therefore be that of the English common law—i.e. that of the reasonable Englishman, not the reasonable African. A few years ago the celebrated Chief Justice of the unlamented Federation, Sir Robert Tredgold, said exactly that.

"The test of reasonableness [in assessing mistake of fact as a defence] in itself implies an objective standard ... In applying it, the standard is what would appear

200

reasonable to the ordinary man in the street in England. The lives of considerable numbers of people are profoundly influenced by strange beliefs and phobias. But the existence of these peculiarities and the reactions that eventuate from them cannot be taken into account. It is the normal and average that must be the guide ...

On this basis, and bearing in mind that the law of England is still the law of England even when it is extended to Nyasaland, I do not see how any court, applying the proper test, could hold that a belief in witchcraft was reasonable so as to form the foundation for a defence that the law could recognize."[10]

Applying this standard to the facts of this case, it would seem plain that a belief that one's family is being destroyed by a witch, and that the only recourse in the circumstances is to kill her, is an unreasonable mistake. No doubt, Englishmen believed such nonsense hundreds of years ago.[11] But the law cannot serve its educative and civilising function unless we insist that the norms to be followed are

---

10. *Attorney-General of Nyasaland v. Frank* [1957] R. & N.L.R. 443.
11. Lord Hale is reported to have once charged a jury: "That there were such creatures as witches he has no doubt at all; for first, the Scriptures affirmed as much; secondly, the wisdom of all nations had provided laws against such persons, which is an argument of their confidence of such a crime. And such hath been the confidence of this Kingdom, as appears by the Act of Parliament which hath provided punishments proportionable to the guilty of the offence;" *A Trial of the Suffolk Witches* (1695) 6 St. Tr. 687, 700-1. See also W. Blackstone, *Commentaries* (London, 1781), vol.IV, pp.60-1.

those of civilised people of the twentieth century. Our law enjoins us that the model to be followed to achieve that objective is that of the reasonable Englishman. My brother Ekpe would use a different, African standard. My brother Mensah would not use any standard at all except his own subjective notion of what is beneficial to society. Presumably, if he happened to believe that the slaying of witches was to be desired, he would sanction homicides of this sort. Neither of them, it seems to me, can square their result with the plain fact that the Penal Code was intended by its authors to enforce civilising, *English* standards. Since that was the intent of the legislators, we have no choice but to carry it out.

There is another deep fallacy within the claim of mistake in this case. If we were to try to deal with the appellant on the basis that he thought that he was being threatened by Chichumbi's witchcraft, how ought we decide? English criminal law is based, in the main, upon a rational, scientific world. It deals with real, physical threats. It does not comprehend threats from occult powers. As has been often said in cases of this sort, the threat must be physical, not metaphysical. This is part of the civilising function of the law. If we are ever to lift our people from the slough of superstition in which they now lie, we cannot tolerate a system of law that accommodates witchcraft.

The third defence asserted by appellant is that of insanity. He claims that the very fact that he believed in witchcraft proves that he was insane. After all, he says, you measure my mistake by the reasonable Englishman, and then you say that the mistake is not reasonable. But is there any doubt that any Englishman who believed in witchcraft would be deemed insane? Therefore, he says, the proper verdict here ought to be 'guilty but insane'.

The argument, despite its seeming force, is thoroughly specious. The Penal Code, like the common law, is built upon the assumption that man has free will. In the words of an American court, it imagines that there are, as it were, two little men, labelled 'reason' and 'emotion' or 'instinct', wrestling for control of the individual's will.[12] The defence of insanity, like the defence of infancy, is available only when reason is incapacitated by disease or physical incapacity.[13] Apart from such incapacity, the law insists that the defendant must be judged by objective standards applicable to all reasonable men. This appellant had no mental disease; many normal Africans believe in witchcraft. And this is how it must be. The purpose of the criminal law is to protect society. It protects society in the main by punishing criminals as examples to the rest of the community. Except for a very few defences, like insanity, it disregards the personal idiosyncrasies of the individual defendant. It sets up a norm for all normal men to follow.

---

12. *Holloway v. United States*, 148 F. 2nd 665, 667 (App. D.C. [U.S.] 1945).
13. In the M'Naughten Rules, the defect had to be caused by mental disease. *Kemp* [1957] 1 Q.B. 399 (Queen's Bench, England). Compare *Tadee Oyee s/o Durur* [1959] E.A.C.A. 407 (Uganda): a high-grade mental defective not suffering from any specific disease of the mind permitted to plead insanity. In *Hotema v. United States*, 186 U.S. 413, 22 S. Ct. 895, 46 L.ed. 1225 (Supreme Court, U.S., 1901), the defendant killed a person he thought to be a witch, believing he was thereby obeying the Biblical injunction. Held, that if the defendant had formed an erroneous opinion regarding witches, although sane, he was liable; but otherwise, if suffering from mental disease.

That norm is expressed by the law which we are sworn to uphold. It may well be that the individual cannot control himself, as apparently this appellant could not. But if he is not severely punished for this crime, we shall be giving the green light to commit murder to everybody with a real or fancied grievance against any old or eccentric man or woman.

Thus the punishment of this appellant will serve as a deterrent to others in his community. His life is available to the state as a means to the greater safety of the whole community. In the words of Mr. Justice Holmes, a distinguished American judge upon whom my brother Mensah so heavily relies,

> "If I were having a philosophical talk with a man I was going to have hanged (or electrocuted), I should say, 'I don't doubt that your act was inevitable for you but to make it more avoidable by others we propose to sacrifice you to the common good. You may regard yourself as a soldier dying for your country if you like. But the law must keep its promises."[14]

The appellant's final claim is that he is entitled to the protection of the partial defence of provocation. It is our law, as it is the common law, that a man who kills as the result of the sort of provocation which would have aroused the passions of a reasonable man from the community from which the defendant comes, who actually kills while under the sway of that passion, before sufficient time has elapsed

---

14.   O.W. Holmes, *Holmes-Laski Letters* (Cambridge, Mass., 1953), p.806.

for a reasonable man's passion to cool, and who uses no more force than appropriate to the provocation, will be guilty not of murder but of manslaughter — a lesser crime, for which there is no death penalty. It is a concession which our law makes to the frailty of the common clay. But that defence must fail here, as there was a very long time indeed between the provocation and the deed; there was ample time for passion to have cooled. The courts have never permitted the defence of provocation in witchcraft cases, save in the very narrow situation where the deceased is surprised in the very act of juju, as a result of which the defendant loses his temper and kills the apparent witch then and there. Since none of these conditions applies to this appellant, I am constrained by authority to deny the defence of provocation.

This is a case of first impression in our recently independent Newstate. Our task as judges is to uphold the law. That law, in this case and in most cases that arise, is either the common law of England, or statutory law with some accommodation to customary law in limited situations. In either case, our job is to look to the language of the legal norm, and apply it to the facts. My brother Mensah urges that we are entitled to make choices based upon our notions of what is best for the community in determining what the law ought to be in cases where it is ambiguous; and so he proposes to change the provocation rule for purposes of this case. But judges do not legislate; yet brother Mensah says that we should act like legislators. Indeed, he does not like any part of the criminal law; he says so. Not liking it, he proposes to change it.

Nor can I blithely overrule precedent as does my brother Mensah. As I have said, I am sworn to uphold the law. The law is expressed by statue and by the cases interpreting it. My oath does not bind me to uphold only statute law; it binds me to uphold all the law. I cannot amend my oath at will; and I fail to see how brother Mensah manages to square his light dismissal of the doctrine of *stare decisis* with this judicial oath.[15] Obviously, if a decision be taken *per incuriam*, that is one thing;[16] but how can the law lay any claim to even-handed justice when one rule will be applied today, and another tomorrow, depending upon what the individual judge conceives to be best for society?

I say that that is nonsense, and dangerous nonsense at that. A prominent Ghanaian writer on legal subjects, Dr Ekow Daniels, has defined the common law as 'unchanging principles distilled from the sayings of sages and wise judges over the centuries'. He says, 'the more the common law changes (or seems to change), the more it remains the same.'[17] I agree. Our job is simply to announce what the law is. When new situations arise, all that we must do is to apply these unchanging principles to them. That does not call for us to determine what the sociological effect of our judgement could be. The law demands stability. We cannot give it stability by manipulating it to match our personal

---

15. The doctrine of *stare decisis* requires a judge, save in exceptional circumstances, to follow a rule of law established in a precedent case.
16. A decision given *per incuriam* is a decision which inadvertently overlooks controlling case or statutory authority. If the earlier precedent decision was given *per incuriam*, the doctrine of *stare decisis* does not require the judge in the later case to follow it.
17. E. Daniels, *The Common Law in West Africa* (London, 1964), p.169.

notions of what is 'just' or 'proper' or even what we may personally think desirable for Newstate. We are only jurisprudential slot-machines; insert the facts, and we are supposed to grind out a decision in accordance with the immutable principles of the common law.

We are, no doubt, Africans by heritage. But we are also trained in the English cultural tradition. There is not one of our leaders, nor one of our lawyers or judges, who has not been trained in that tradition. If our new fatherland is ever to advance to the levels of culture and civilisation of the modern, western world, we must adhere to the time-tested, eternal principles of the common law. Dr Daniels concludes his excellent book on *The Common Law in West Africa* by saying, 'Whatever declaration is made in the future [about the content of the law of the West African Anglophonic states], English law will certainly remain its basis.'[18] I fervently hope and trust that that prediction will remain true of Newstate as of West Africa. I would dismiss the appeal.

EKPE, J.: My learned brother the Chief Justice says that this is a simple case, and then writes twelve pages of philosophy, jurisprudence, penology, and criminology to show us how simple it all is. Obviously the result in this case depends upon one's philosophical approach to the problem.

I refuse to yield one inch to the Chief Justice in my devotion to the common law, nor in my belief that as judges we must apply the law that is, not the law that ought to be. But I disagree with him sharply about the defence of native

---

18. *Ibid.,* p.396.

custom.

Customary law—the law that governed the African people before the advent of colonialism, and that still governs most of the day-to-day legal relationships of most Africans—expresses the spirit of the African people, just as every system of law expresses the spirit of the community from which it springs. Nobody could be more dismayed than I at the chaotic condition of our present law, where every tribe and indeed every clan has its own system of customary law. Some day, we must have a single, unified, state-wide system of law. I would endorse the following statement by the distinguished Professor of African Law at the School of Oriental and African Studies of the University of London:

> "If the uniform legal system which I have referred to is to evolve in a satisfactory manner, one which expresses the characteristic ethos and way of life of the people, it is essential that immediate attention be paid to the present customary law, which reflects, *par excellence*, the people's own choice of legal system."[19]

My learned brother disposes of the defence of custom on three different grounds. In the first place, he says that it does not exist; in the second, he says that it violates English notions of justice, equity, and good conscience; and in the third place, he says that it is not a defence under the Penal Code. I disagree on all three counts.

There is no doubt that the custom which appellant

---

19.   A.N. Allott, "The Study of African Law", in S.J.L.R., 1958, p.257.

claims exists did exist not so many years ago. That custom, therefore, expressed the choice of law made by the people of whom appellant is one. The fact that the British imperial masters in the years before independence did not allow it as a defence is simply another indication of the blind refusal of the British to let Africans be Africans. I take it that the custom was adequately proven by proof of its existence before the British destroyed it.

But then it is urged that the custom denies justice, equity, and good conscience, as measured by British standards. To justify this claim, the Chief Justice insists that he is merely interpreting the intention of the legislature. He says that since the same statute is now in force as in colonial days, the legislature must have intended it to be interpreted in the same way. By what crystal ball my brother peeps into the brains of all our legislators he does not reveal.

We all know, however, that one or the great motivating forces for our African revolution is that expressed by the concept of the African personality. Every people has certain characteristics which are uniquely theirs — their language, their history, their customs, in short their very genius. The phrase 'African personality' sums up all that is distinctively African about us — everything that makes us what we are. Our African personality was submerged during the days of Empire, and today remains submerged in those territories regrettably still under foreign overlordship. If the African revolution has any meaning, it must be a vehicle in which we can express ourselves. It must express, therefore, the African personality.

What better expresses our African personality than the law which, as Professor Allott puts it, we voluntarily chose when we had the choice available? To insist, as does my brother, that we must follow English standards denies the historical meaning of the stirring times through which we have all lived. Is it for this that the martyrs who died before the bullets of the white-supremacist police gave their lives? Did the brave thousands who demonstrated in the face of terror do so in order to be told by this court of an independent African state that their long-standing tribal customs are to be void because the average Englishman thinks them wrong?

My brother reaches his conclusion because he places English law on a higher plane than African. In the light of modern anthropological notions of the relativistic nature of all culture, this is plain nonsense. Our African law is neither better nor worse than that of England; it is only different. It does express our ethos, our *Volksgeist*, in a way that no English law can. I deny that we need the so-called civilising influence of England, either in law or elsewhere.

Our indigenous customs need no defence from me. Witchcraft belief starts from fundamentally different premisses from those of English scientific thought. It assumes that man is divided into three parts: a personality soul, a mystical soul, and a physical shell. A mysterious, other-worldly entity — call it a god, if you will — is believed to seize control of the personality soul of the witch, which can then travel forth from its physical shell to attack the physical shell of its victims. Now I personally do not believe this, but how can I say that one who does believe it is fundamentally wrong? How different is this belief from any mystical belief in another world? And if, in defence against such dread forces as these, African custom deems it proper to take up arms in self-help, I fail to see that the custom denies justice, equity, and good conscience. All our concepts of justice are relative. I for one cannot see that this custom is any more barbarous than the gentle art of modern warfare, for example, or the notion that a policeman may kill a prisoner who is guilty of the most petty offence while attempting to escape. In short, the concept of justice, equity, and good conscience must be measured by African, not English standards.

My brother's assertion that the Penal Code does not admit of the defence of custom is merely a function of his exaggerated deference to the common law. I agree with him that the common law expresses the distilled essence of unchanging principles. But those principles infuse its spirit, not its particular form.

Perhaps the most important of those principles in the criminal law is that no man may be convicted, at least of serious crime, unless he has a guilty mind—a *mens rea*, to use the familiar Latin term. The essence of this doctrine is that every crime demands a sense of guilt on the part of the defendant. Here, this appellant acted according to the custom which he believed to apply to him. He believed that he acted under overwhelming necessity to defend the very lives of his children, his wife, and himself. How can my brother say that he had *mens rea*? And without this, no man ought to be convicted of serious crime.

My brother the Chief Justice keeps insisting that he is only applying the law which he is sworn to uphold. I think that he was sworn to uphold the law of Newstate, not the law of England. That law, like all law, must reflect the ethos of our own people. He denies the whole meaning of African independence by his slavish devotion to the narrowest interpretation of the common law. The function of the

African judge is to mould and adapt the received common law, faithful to its basic and unchanging principles, to its new setting. Anything less will be a betrayal of the revolution and of the African personality.

Nor can I agree with my brother Mensah that he has a right to mould the law to meet his own idiosyncratic notions of what is best for society. I agree with the Chief Justice that such a notion changes the law, from the rules by which the game is to be played, to a mere device by which society can be manipulated to reach ends that may be thought desirable.

The very essence of justice is predictability. The subjects of the law are treated fairly when the law is applied with absolute, even-handed precision; not for nothing is Justice invariably portrayed as the blind goddess. To adopt the view that law is merely a technique of social engineering, and the judges merely social engineers, negates the whole notion that ours is indeed a government of law, not of men.

I would allow the appeal and discharge the appellant.

MENSAH, J.: I had thought that I was sitting on a bench with fellow judges. Instead, I find myself in the company of two mystics. One adheres to the *mystique* of the common law, and the other to the *mystique* of the African personality, and together they try to dispose of a practical, rather simple problem in government. I cannot seem to make my colleagues understand that as judges we participate in the process of government. We participate in a special, indeed a unique way. Our task, however, is not to apply immutable principles, but rather to solve practical problems.

Before I can answer the problems posed by this murder case, I must examine briefly how judges in fact solve problems. A few problems that judges face are simple; the rule of law applicable clearly covers the case. In such a situation, I agree with the Chief Justice that we are merely judicial slot-machines, so to speak. But those situations only come to this court because some lawyer is either too avaricious or too stupid to tell his client that he is wasting his time and money. Every case that comes to an appeals court (where we can consider, of course, only points of law) almost always involves situations where the applicable rule is vague as applied to the facts in question.

So judges are mainly concerned with trying to solve questions where the law is vague or ambiguous. The question that we must always resolve is, by what rule or test are we to resolve the ambiguous? My brethren find the answer in some transcendental principle. The Chief Justice finds it in the immutable principles of the common law.[20] Brother Ekpe finds it in the ethos of the African personality, which he holds is expressed in the rule of customary law. Like the Chief Justice, he believes in immutable principles. Why the one chooses the common law as his principle, and the other the African personality, I do not know. I search the stars, but can find no clue which will identify for me the great Immutable Principle which ought to control our decision.

Now it seems to me that the only intelligible way to resolve the pervasive ambiguities in the law is by reference to the social effect of the decision.[21] My brethren charge

---

20. *Cf.* Blackstone, *op. cit.* fn.11, *passim.*
21. See, e.g. B. Cardozo, *The Nature of the Judicial Process* (New York, 1921), *passim.*

me with being a sociologist-cum-legislator. But a legislator can select any rule which he wants to solve a problem. Our job is much narrower. We can only select a rule which is tenable within the ambiguities of the authoritative statute. And in deciding what will be the most desirable rule, it seems to me that we should make use of all the material available from the social scientists — the sociologists, the economists, the political scientists. We should make our choice in the light of Newstate's declared national objective of socialism.

No doubt my brethren will charge me, as my brother Ekpe already has, with believing in a government of men and not of law. To a degree, of course, this is true. But it is true of their decisions also. The only difference is that I look for the test in the pragmatic results of the rule upon society. They look for guidance in what they call an immutable principle. I suggest that the real source of any immutable principle lies locked in the personal prejudice of the individual judge. So theirs is a government of men and not of law just as much as mine, except that they will not admit it, nor will they expose their inner processes of reasoning to the light of discussion, as I feel I do.

Law has a dual function. It must give stability to social relationships, and at the same time admit of social change. So long as we abide within the limits set by statute or common law rule, I submit that we are giving the law as much stability as is possible. At the same time, because I would adapt it to new situations as they arise by frankly shaping it to social ends, it is continuously reshaped according to the demands of our emerging, socialist society.

Now all law developed in just this way; as Holmes has

said, 'The life of the law has not been logic, but experience'.[22] In every case, judges have interpreted the existing law in light of social demands as they viewed them. Since judges in the past have come mainly from the exploiting classes in society, in general their decisions have tended to reflect their class interests. But not invariably; sometimes judges have given expression to interests far wider and more democratic than their class position might indicate, with the result that there exist in the common law, of both England and the United States, many very democratic elements.

Sometimes a whole area of law which was developed in an earlier period becomes irrelevant in a later one; or sometimes, as here, a foreign import simply does not meet the local situation. The common law of crimes was developed to meet the emergent demands of England, mainly in the nineteenth century. When it is applied to twentieth-century Africa, it creaks at the joints, for it is based upon values and concepts which were apt to meet the demands of nineteenth-century England, but not necessarily apt to meet present-day African requirements. It can be applied here, today, only by wrenching our society, our values, or the law, into weird and unseemly forms. Fundamental reform, of course, is for the legislature, not for us; but where we can reach a more defensible result within the scope of the Code, we ought to feel free to do so.

By the same token, customary law was developed to meet the demands of a subsistence economy, based upon

---

22. O.W. Holmes, *The Common Law* (Boston, 1881), p.1.

a culture that was mainly pre-scientific. Laws developed for that society are, like the common law, largely irrelevant to the modern, industrialised, African society which is our common aim. To impose a rigid system of law, drawn from another society or another time, upon modern Africa is to condemn us to the same system of domestic backwardness and foreign domination as existed in the imperial era. Brother Ekpe's invocation of customary law has an attractive revolutionary air. But it is only pseudo-revolutionary, for it condemns us to stagnation.

Turning now to the facts of this case, what result ought to obtain? In the first place, we are faced with the problem of native custom. Obviously, many native customs are simply inappropriate to a modern, industrialised, socialised economy. One such custom that we can do without is the slaying of supposed witches, not to speak of the whole pre-scientific superstition of witchcraft itself. I suggest that a custom of that sort ought to be outlawed, not because it violates English notions of justice, but because it violates sensible rules for our new country.

We can dispose of the defences of mistake of law, and of insanity, with equal celerity. No country has ever admitted the defence of mistake of law. To do so makes the defendant, and not the judge, the person who determines the applicable law; and that would be an impossible result. The defence of insanity, as my brother has said, is limited to physical infirmities; and this defendant is perfectly sane.

The defence of reasonable mistake is rather more tricky, but on the whole I reach the same conclusion as the Chief Justice. Recently, an African in London was charged with practising medicine without a licence.[23] He had received a bogus certificate as a doctor in 'naturopathy', and supposed that he was entitled to call himself doctor by reason of that certificate. The Court found that it was not unreasonable for him so to believe considering his recent arrival in England (he had been there but two years). If we stand that case against *Frank*,[24] cited by the Chief Justice, we reach the amazing result that an African in England is judged by the standard of a reasonable African, but in Africa, by that of a reasonable Englishman!

The answer, of course, revolves around the devilish little word 'reasonable'. The Chief Justice says that the reasonable man means the average man. That is not exactly true. Judges decide what is a reasonable man. They determine this not on the basis of a statistical average, but rather on the basis of what they think is a proper standard for the community. They set this standard in terms not of the ideal, but not necessarily of the average either. Rather, it is a statement of what is, in their belief, an attainable standard for the average citizen. Obviously, it must be set a little higher than the statistical average, or else there would never be any improvement in society. When we set a standard as 'reasonable', therefore, we are setting a norm of conduct. The proper way to set a norm of conduct is to look at the results desired.

The Chief Justice does exactly that when he says that, without the limit of reasonableness, every defendant could plead mistake as a defence. I believe that if we do not

---

23. See *Wilson v. Inyang* [1951] 2 All E.R. 237 (King's Bench).
24. See fn.10 above and the accompaning text.

exclude the defence of witchcraft in cases like this, every rogue who wants to kill an enemy will claim witchcraft as a defence. I would therefore say that mistake of fact in this case fails as a defence, because it is not reasonable.

There remains the defence of provocation. Now I am quite prepared to say that a reasonable man in the defendant's position, with his background and in the circumstances, would have been provoked to kill. The nature of the threat of witchcraft is that the passage of time serves only to inflame the passions, not to cool them, as the facts here demonstrate. The operative result of admitting provocation as a defence here is consonant with the demands of society. The appellant will remain under judicial control, since he will receive an appropriate jail sentence. Realistically, his crime is not that he killed, but that he believed in witches. In jail — assuming that we have a modern penal system, which is probably illusory — he could be educated out of his superstitions, thus saving society the threat of a repetition of his crime.

This seems to me the best practical solution of the problem available within the scope of the Code. To reach this decision requires that we overrule a number of cases in which it has been held that provocation is not available in witchcraft cases unless the act of witchcraft takes place in the immediate presence of the accused. But far better to overrule authority which no longer accords with present notions of justice, than to do injustice!

I cannot help but point out that if I were free to decide this case as a legislator I would unload as excess baggage the whole conceptual framework of British criminal law. That law is based almost entirely upon the notion of deterrence as the principal objective of punishment, and hence of the criminal law. It assumes that, once a man has committed a crime, he may be used by society as a means of social control. I deny that this postulate is compatible with the African revolution, which ought above all else to base itself on humanitarian considerations. Our President has publicly endorsed the view of President Nkrumah of Ghana, that a central assumption of our Government is that no man shall be a means, but only an end.[25] In the criminal law, that means to me that we may not use him as an instrument of deterrence, but only treat him with a view to reformation. To achieve such a goal would require the complete reworking of our penal codes. That project ought to have high legislative priority throughout Africa.

In the event I would reduce the crime to manslaughter. The Chief Justice would affirm the conviction for murder; and my brother Ekpe would acquit. Since there is no majority in this court in favour of any course, the conviction below must stand.

I am, however, authorised by my brethren to state that, in the unusual circumstances of this case, we all join in petitioning the President to exercise his powers of clemency to reach a result which accords with justice. What that result may be, he will have to say. Obviously, we judges, who are supposedly experts on the subject, have been unable to agree on this, being unable to find a common jurisprudential basis on which to reach a decision.

---

25. Kwame Nkrumah, *Consciencism* (London, 1964), p.95.

Derek and Charles v.
Anne and Martin
Allan Hutchinson and Derek Morgan

THE SUPREME COURT OF CANENGAUSTRUS[1]
Judgment September 31, 1986

DOCTRIN, C.J.: This appeal arises from a road traffic accident near Ottloncanwash on April 31, 1980 in the late evening. The accident has given rise to several causes of action that have been consolidated for the purposes of this appeal. There are four central issues to be decided: whether Derek can recover damages for Anne's negligence; whether Derek was contributorily negligent; whether Martin was responsible for his failure to rescue Derek; and whether Charles can recover damages for emotional distress, and if so, against whom.

The facts of the case are relatively clear and are not in dispute. Derek was driving home along a quiet, narrow and winding country road that was unpaved, unmarked and unlit. As he rounded a sweeping bend, he saw a single headlight approaching close to the other side of the road; he assumed this to be a motorcyclist. Unfortunately, the

---

1. Canengaustrus is a small, little-known island in the mid-Atlantic. Something of a geographical enigma, its capital, Ottloncanwash, is equidistant from Ottawa, London, Canberra and Washington. Coincidentally, it is a common law jurisdiction and its law is a unique blend of Canadian, English, Australian and American sources.

light was that of a sports car driven by Anne: the off-side headlight was not working. At the last minute, Derek realized his mistake and applied his brakes. Regrettably, his braking system did not function properly. The car swerved, left the road, and came to rest in a shallow ditch at the side of the road. Anne, who had also taken avoidance action, was unaware that a serious accident had occurred and continued on her journey home.

The accident occurred near the isolated farm of Martin. At the time of the accident, he was standing on his front porch, calling in his dog for the night. Although he saw and heard the accident, he did nothing to ascertain whether anyone was injured or in need of help. For reasons best known to himself, he closed the door and retired to bed. Derek was trapped in his car. His right leg, stuck under the dashboard, was broken in two places. Reliable medical evidence indicated that if Derek had received immediate assistance, for example, by having the pressure on his leg relieved, the further complications which arose could have been averted. Sadly, he remained trapped for over half an hour and the blood flow to his leg was irreversibly impaired. As a result, his leg has been amputated.

Approximately thirty-five minutes after the accident, Jane came upon the scene. She was driving from Ottloncanwash to her home in the village of Tormanyork. She immediately went to Derek's aid, dragging him from the wreckage after levering away the dashboard. She administered artificial respiration; this probably saved his life. Jane then ran to Martin's farm and persuaded Martin to telephone for an ambulance. Derek was rushed to hospital where an emergency operation was carried out. His life was in the balance. A telephone call was made by the police to Charles, who lived with and apparently enjoyed a homosexual relationship with Derek. Charles' answering service advised them that Charles was away on business. The police succeeded in locating Charles and left a message for him. Charles telephoned the hospital and was told by the staff that it would be some time before there would be any definite news, but that Derek was presently in the intensive care unit. Fortunately, through the skill of the hospital staff, Derek's life was saved. But this experience has left its tragic mark on Charles. The psychiatric evidence establishes that Charles has suffered severe shock, organic depression and a change of personality as a direct result of the injury suffered by his friend. Also, the relationship between Charles and Derek has ended. After spending three months in hospital, Derek moved back to his parents' home. He is confined to a wheelchair.

The trial judge held that, as Derek was fifty percent to blame, his damages should be reduced accordingly. The third party proceedings brought by Anne against Martin was dismissed. The judge concluded that there was no legal duty to rescue. Charles' claim against Anne for compensation for his emotional distress was allowed. Anne's application to the Court of Appeal was dismissed and Derek's cross-appeal on the question of duty to rescue was also dismissed. Anne now appeals to this court and Derek cross-appeals.

The case raises a number of moral issues. However, I should make it clear from the outset that my concern is with the legal aspects of this case alone. Of course, the law, as a social force, overlaps with religion and morality, but it is incumbent upon me to resolve the issues presented in accordance with the law as it is, and not as some would like it to be. Like Sir George Baker, "my task is to apply the law free of emotion and predilection"; see *Paton v. Trustees of British Pregnancy Advisory Services,* [1978] 2 All E.R. 987 at 989. In blunt terms, "with purely moral obligation the law does not deal"; see *Buch v. Amory Manufacturing Co.,* 69 N.H. 257 (1897). Furthermore, as has been constantly emphasized, the desirability and continued existence of any particular law is for the legislature and not for the judiciary to decide. There is a clear separation of governmental powers in Canengaustrus. The legislature has the constitutional responsibility to enact laws designed to achieve substantively just results; the judiciary has the task of interpreting, applying and dispensing this received wisdom. As Kitto, J. said, to discuss cases "in terms of 'judicial policy' and 'social expediency' is to introduce deleterious foreign matter into the water of the common law—in which, after all, we have no more than riparian rights"; see *Rootes v. Shelton,* 116 C.L.R. 383 at 387 (1967). In this way, the fundamental democratic demands of consensus, as sought in the political process, and rationality, as embodied in the legal process, are met. The formal and neutral application of the rules infuses the law with a central integrity and ensures that the law is insulated from political or moral controversy; see *Duport Steel Ltd. v. Sirs,* [1980] All E.R. 529 at 551.

Was Anne Negligent?

The issue of negligence can be dealt with expeditiously. The task for the Court is to determine whether Anne owed Derek a duty of care, whether that duty was breached and whether the breach led to cognizable damages; see *Donoghue v. Stevenson,* [1932] A.C. 526. There is, of course, no general duty of care. In order to be successful, a plaintiff must show that he was a foreseeable plaintiff; see *Palsgraf v. Long Island Railroad Co.,* 162 N.E. 99 (1928). The court must be persuaded that there are no considerations of policy which dictate that this *prima facie* duty of care be circumscribed so as to deny the liability of the defendant; see *Anne's v. Merton London Borough Council,* [1978] A.C. 728 at 751-752. The essence of the law has been succinctly captured by Macdonald, J. in *Nova Mink v. Trans Canada Airlines* (1951), 2 D.L.R 241:

> "The common law yields the conclusion that there is a duty only where the circumstances of time, place and person would create in the mind of a reasonable man in those circumstances such a probability of harm resulting to other persons as to require him to take care to avert the probable result."

That a road user owes a duty of care to other road users is without question. The issue is whether Anne, in failing to have her car in proper working order, breached the standard of care to which a reasonable man would adhere.

It is well established that a breach of a statutory duty, while not conclusive evidence of liability, raises a *prima facie* case that the standard has been breached; see, for example, *Queen v. Saskatchewan Wheat Pool* (1983), 143 D.L.R. (3d) 9 and *Clinkscales v. Carver,* 22 Cal. 2d 72 (1943). It was argued by counsel for the respondent that the *Highway Traffic Act,* R.S.C.E.S., c.198, being a regulatory statute and carrying its own penalties for violations, was not designed to determine the standard of care in civil suits. It seems to me that if the legislature, in its wisdom, has seen fit to enact legislation to ensure safety on our nation's highways, this Court ought not to treat such a pronouncement lightly. The legislature is in the best position to decide what the appropriate standards should be. Though let it be clear that, by accepting such a definition, this Court is in no way fettering its judicial discretion.

In *Sterling Trusts Corp. v. Postma*, [1965] S.C.R. 324, Cartwright, J. considered the effect of a statutory duty in the context of a civil action for negligence. He settled on the following rule (at 329):

> "I think it is plain that once it has been found (i) that the respondents committed a breach of the statutory duty ... and, (ii) that the breach was an effective cause of appellants' injuries, the respondents were *prima facie* liable for the damages suffered by the appellants."

In the present case, the evidence satisfied this two-fold test. A defendant can rebut the *prima facie* case by showing that the statutory breach occurred without any negligence on his part. I agree with the trial judge that the malfunctioning headlights could reasonably have been discovered. Accordingly negligence on Anne's part has been established.

Was Derek Contributorily Negligent?

The more contentious question is whether Derek was also negligent and, if so, to what extent his negligence reduces Anne's liability. Although Anne's negligence may have increased the likelihood of an accident, the realization of

225

that risk was in large part the responsibility of Derek who was also in breach of the relevant statutory provisions. The duty on Derek is aptly summed up by Lord Justice Buckley in *Lee v. Lever*, [1974] R.T.R. 35 at 39:

> "It is not the law that a driver is entitled to assume that all other users of the road will in all respects and at all other times obey the Highway Code or otherwise drive with all due care and circumspection or use the road in every way in which it should be used. It is incumbent upon any driver to be prepared for foreseeable hazards, including hazards resulting from the foreseeable bad driving of other drivers or a foreseeable breach ... [I]t is incumbent upon every user of such a roadway to drive in a way which enables him to meet an emergency or a hazard presented [by other drivers]."

The failure of Derek to ensure that his car was maintained in a roadworthy condition, such that it would be able to negotiate the normal hazards of night driving in the countryside, is strong evidence of his contributory negligence; see *Parish v. Judd*, [1960] 3 All E.R. 33. Accordingly, the Court of Appeal was quite correct in refusing to disturb the trial judge's reduction in damages by fifty percent under the *Negligence Act*, R.S.C.E.S., c.315, ss.2 and 5.

Did Martin Have A Legal Duty To Rescue?

The issue of whether there is a legal duty to rescue Derek raises one of the most sensitive and heated academic debates in tort law. Indeed, counsel for the appellant presented a most able and humanistic argument that this Court should give legal effect to what all agree is a clear moral obligation to one's fellow citizen. Appellant's counsel went on to argue that the law of tort itself was based on society's conception of right and wrong. In fact, the "neighbour principle" itself was said to stem from the biblical duty to love one's neighbour; see Luke, ch.10, v.29.

I am not persuaded, however, that we should vest this moral duty with legal sanction. The opinion of the court in *Union Pacific Co. v. Cappier*, 72 P. 282 at 282-83 (1903), is as relevant today as it was at the turn of the century:

"With the humane side of the question courts are not concerned. It is the omission or negligent discharge of legal duties only which come within the sphere of judicial cognizance. For withholding relief from the suffering, for failure to respond to the calls of worthy charity, or for faltering in the bestowment of brotherly love on the unfortunate, penalties are found not in the laws of men, but in that higher law, the violation of which is condemned by the voice of conscience, whose sentence of punishment for the recreant act is swift and sure."

A survey of early cases reveals no legal duty to rescue, even where the litigants had a particular relationship such as a business association or the like; *Osterlind v. Hill*, 160 N.E. 301 (1920) and *Yania v. Bigan*, 155 A. 2d 343 (1959). In *Yania*, the plaintiff was the widow of a business visitor, who had jumped into the water to aid the defendant. The plaintiff's husband subsequently drowned when the defendant refused to come to his aid. The court held that there was no legal duty unless the defendant places the plaintiff in peril. Likewise, in *Osterlind,* the defendant rented a canoe to the plaintiff which, in full view of the defendant, capsized and the plaintiff drowned. Once again, the court held no legal duty to effect a rescue.

Appellant's counsel pointed to a more recent decision which held that a ship's captain has a duty to rescue a passenger who falls overboard; see *Horsley v. Maclaren,* [1969] 2 O.R. 137. Counsel argued that the courts are expanding the duty to rescue and urged this court to do so in this case. It is true that there are now several specific relationships that will give rise to a duty to rescue. However, most of these are founded upon statutory duties, such as the obligations of parent to child, or upon some implicit agreement, such as between members of a social outing; see *Farwell v. Keaton,* 396 Mich. 281 (1976). This court is bound by a long line of eminent authority. Until the legislature deems it appropriate to introduce a general duty to rescue, we ought not to upset the delicate balance the common law has developed. Aside from the moral dimension, there exist very real technical and administrative difficulties associated with the introduction of such a general duty. What would be the extent of Martin's liability? And to whom would he be liable? Would Anne benefit from Martin's misfeasance? These problems combine to support the existing rules. Consequently, Martin cannot be found legally liable for his failure to rescue Derek.

Can Charles Recover For Emotional Distress?

Recovery for nervous shock caused by negligence is a relatively recent arrival on the tort scene. Prior to 1925 and the decision of *Hambrook v. Stokes Bros.*, [1925] 1 K.B. 141, courts were most reluctant to allow plaintiffs to recover for nervous shock without any bodily injury to themselves. This reluctance was founded upon the view that such awards were difficult, if not impossible, to determine, and that nervous disorder and emotional upset was easy to feign. The remarks of Mitchell, C.J. in *Huston v. Borough of Fremansburg*, 61 A. 1022 at 1023 (1905), are pertinent:

"It requires but brief judicial experience to be convinced of the large proportion of exaggeration and even of actual fraud in the ordinary action for physical injuries from negligence; and if we opened the door to this new invention the result would be great danger, if not disaster to the cause of practical justice."

Since the turn of this century, the marvels and advances of medical science have come upon us with great speed. The field of psychiatry has grown to a point where diseases of the mind can be diagnosed and treated with a confidence that approaches certainty. And it is with matters of certainty that the courts of justice deal. As a result, courts have now begun to award redress to plaintiffs who have suffered recognizable psychiatric illness as a result of the defendants' negligence; see *Hinz v. Berry*, [1970] 2 Q.B. 40 and *Brown v. Brice*, [1984] 1 All E.R. 997. Initially, it was only admitted in cases where the plaintiff personally was in peril of physical harm; see *Dulieu v. White and Sons*, [1901] 2 K.B.

669. But the *Hambrook* case *(supra)* recognized that in certain specific relationships, such as between a mother and child, serious injury to another could be the basis for recovery; see *King v. Phillips,* [1953] 1 Q.B. 429.

There has been a gradual widening of liability. The general trend has been to allow recovery where the plaintiff has come upon the immediate aftermath of an accident; see *Marshall v. Lionel Enterprises,* [1972] 2 O.R. 177. Perhaps the best test is the one laid down by Torbriner, J. in *Dillon v. Legg,* 29 A.L.R. 3d 1316 at 1326 - 27 (1968):

"In determining, in such a case, whether defendant should reasonably foresee the injury to plaintiff, or, in other terminology, whether defendant owes plaintiff a duty of due care, the courts will take into account such factors as the following. (1) Whether plaintiff was located near the scene of the accident as contrasted with one who was a distance away from it. (2) Whether the shock resulted from a direct emotional impact upon plaintiff from the sensory and contemporaneous observance of the accident, as contrasted with learning of the accident from them after the occurrence. (3) Whether plaintiff and the victim were closely related, as contrasted with an absence of any relationship or the presence of only a distant relationship. The evaluation of these factors will indicate the degree of the defendant's foreseeability."

In the present case, Charles was nowhere near the scene of the accident and did not even come upon the aftermath. He was some 250 miles from the scene. Secondly, while he may well have experienced true emotional disturbance rather than mere grief (which is not recoverable; see *Duwyn v. Kaprielian* (1978), 2 O.R. (2d) 736), it was not from the "sensory and contemporaneous observance of the accident" as is required; see, for example, *Hathaway v. Supreme Court*, 112 Cal. App. 3d 728 (1980). Furthermore, I am not persuaded that there existed the necessary relationship between Derek and Charles to warrant an extension of the rule. In *McLoughlin v. O'Brian*, [1983] A.C. 410, where a mother was two miles away from the accident and only heard of it two hours later, the lack of immediate physical proximity was counter-balanced by the fundamental nature of their relationship as mother and family and her arrival at what amounted to the "immediate aftermath" of the accident when she visited the hospital. Notwithstanding this, it was argued that the facts of the present case were sufficiently analogous to existing doctrine to warrant recovery. Although it is true that the law must develop from case to case, we must also strive to maintain certainty and generality so as to avoid a doctrinal wilderness of single instances. As Lord Wilberforce said, "there remains a ... real need for the law to place some limitations on the extent of admissible claims"; *id.* at 423. That limitation must be drawn where "the good sense of the judges decides"; see *Bourhill v. Young*, [1943] A.C. 92 at 110 per Lord Wright. In *Spade v. Lynn & B.R. Co.*, 47 N.E. 497 (1897), Allan, J. offered an appropriate warning:

> "The law must be administered in the courts according to general rules. Courts will aim to make these rules as just as possible, bearing in mind that they are to be of general application. But as the law is a practical science, having to do with the affairs of life, any rule is unwise

231

if, in its general application, it will not, as a usual result, serve the purposes of justice. A new rule cannot be made for each case ... One may be held bound to anticipate and guard against the probable consequences to ordinary people, but to carry the rule of damages further imposes an undue measure of responsibility upon those who are guilty only of unintentional negligence.

In conclusion, therefore, I hold that, although Derek is entitled to recover from Anne, his damages will be reduced by fifty percent as a result of his own contributory negligence. Further, Charles has no claim against Anne or Martin for his emotional distress and Martin, while worthy of our moral opprobrium, is not liable to anyone for his failure to rescue Derek.

MILL, J.: This appeal requires this Court to decide the proper basis of liability for physical harm, whether the law of civil wrongs should be extended to impose legal liability for nonfeasance (the so-called "duty to rescue") and, finally, the extent of liability for negligently inflicted emotional distress.

Reading the judgment of Doctrin, C.J., it readily becomes apparent that her conception of the judicial role is confused, schizophrenic, and altogether too restricted. It involves an ineffectual sleight of hand which a moment's mature reflection reveals as self-contradictory. I say this more by way of clarification and introduction to my own judgment than as vindictive criticism of much of the doctrinal substance of her view of the common law. Indeed, I hope that it will become clear that I am in broad agreement with some of her conclusions. My concern here, however, is to clear away the rhetoric behind which her cloak-and-dagger approach to public policy lurks.

Concepts such as duty, reasonable foreseeability and causation are veiled terms through which the courts formally express the choices they have made. They operate as a convenient screen behind which the real social drama is played out. As Lord Denning bluntly noted, "common law adjudication is ... at bottom a matter of public policy which we, as judges, must resolve"; see *Home Office v. Dorset Yacht Co. Ltd.*, [1969] 2 Q.B. 412 at 426. This sentiment gained the express approval of Lords Dilhorne and Diplock; see [1970] A.C. 1004 at 1051 and 1058 respectively. The common law is a vast and intricate doctrinal edifice, but its chief architect has been policy and not logic. In practice, judges have been reluctant to expand the ambit of liability other than by analogical reasoning; see *McLoughlin v. O'Brian* [1982] 2 W.L.R. 982 at 988-89. Whenever a court decides that compensation is payable only for loss that was "reasonably foreseeable", it *reaffirms* a policy decision taken years or decades ago. The appeal to "policy" is unavoidable and judges ought now to acknowledge this. There is obviously potential danger in this course of action. What strikes one judge as a suitable "policy risk" may appear to another to be the height of folly. But the threat of such idiosyncratic appeals can be diminished by a systematic theory of civil liability.

For too long we have lacked an adequate theory to explain the social function of negligence liability and of the fault system of liability that is built upon it. The true test of any theory, of course, is its ability to predict or account for the full diversity and complexity of life. Without the capacity to formulate some general hypothesis, we cannot have a system of law which people can confidently base their expectations on and plan their behaviour. To reply with Aristotle, as my colleague Justice Wright is wont to do, that the real purpose and only proper effect of tortious liability is to restore to a person what has been wrongfully appropriated — the concept of "corrective justice" — offers no insights into the source of the norms by which the conduct was judged wrongful. Thus, the experiential basis of my proposed theory confounds any critics who suggest that the theory rests on unrealistic behavioural assumptions. It is open to criticism only insofar as its postulates seek to explain the totality of those conditions. The behavioural consequences of the tort rules which this theory produces are beyond the scope of this Court to examine, beyond even the bounds of the theory to predict *in the individual case.*

My model is premised on the fact that the world is finite, an aggregate of scarce resources. Choices must be made, for example, as to the use, conservation and distribution of fossil fuel. So too must difficult choices be countenanced everywhere in our society. In torts, we must recognize the continuing force of Lord Atkin's dictum that "acts or omissions which any moral code would censure cannot, in a practical world, be treated so as to give a right to every person injured by them to demand relief"; see *Donoghue v. Stevenson*, [1932] A.C. 562 at 580. Ours is a practical world and "the law aims at practical justice rather than logical consistency"; see *Caltex Oil v. The Dredge "Willemstad"* (1976), 135 C.L.R. 529 at 545 per Gibbs, J. It is for this reason that I find Justice Lefft's abdication of the judicial task so distasteful and unjustified.

This concentration on the practical world, with its scarce resources, further leads me to reject the constitutional separation of powers doctrine so rigidly adhered to by Chief Justice Doctrin. To believe that the legislature, with its tightly constrained timetable, can accommodate law reform at the drop of this Court's hat is to live in some other world. Political indifference and its legislative ally, inertia, are facts of life. Unless we properly appreciate the effects of these forces, we close our eyes to the distributive consequences of the law and fail in our political and social duty to ensure that the law meets the demands of contemporary society. The true measure of common law adjudication is the extent to which it can resolve today's problems in a fashion that will allow for both the predictive certainty of the law and the optimalization of accident costs and resources.

In order to keep the law in step with the march of modern society, judges must look beyond the letter of the law to its motive force and spirit. Unlike Doctrin, C.J., we must not remain "timorous souls", but become "bold spirits"; see *Candler v. Crane, Christmas and Co.,* [1951] 2 K.B. 164 per Lord Denning. It is my honest and firm conviction that the notion of "allocative efficiency" is the golden thread which weaves together into a fine garment the seemingly disparate strands of the common law. Hitherto, this has only been vaguely glimpsed and partially grasped. Accordingly, although the theory of tort law suggested here has a clear political dimension, it does not represent a naked and personal political choice on my part. Indeed, a judge who follows and substantiates the logic of "allocative efficiency" more closely satisfies the democratic ideal of adjudication than the unthinking formalist.

As in life, two unavoidable facts dominate the law of tort: risk and uncertainty. As agents of the law, the courts must select doctrines that minimize both. By creating precedents, the courts promote efficient resource allocation by optimizing these two related concepts. It is not without significance that the response to uncertainty has occupied the forefront of human endeavour. Many of the distinctive institutions of primitive society, like polygamy and extended family groups, can be understood as such a response. With the recognition of the institution of private property came the related doctrine of contract. Of course, all contracting is risk-shifting; see *Photoproductions Ltd. v. Securicor,* [1980] 1 All E.R. 556 and *Globe Refining Co. v. Landa Cotton Oil Co.,* 190 U.S. 540 (1903). As a society develops, its wealth increases. Moreover, as the opportunity for interaction expands, there will be a corresponding rise in the probability of interfering with or harming others' interests. More state-imposed control is demanded. But, unless we are watchful, this increased protection could interfere with the market's ability to ensure that voluntary exchanges result in resources gravitating toward their most valuable uses. The goals of private and social allocative efficiency may be lost.

Undoubtedly, the desirability of social efficiency as a goal requires a value judgment as to the justness of the underlying distribution of income and property rights. But the modest ambition of my proposal is to optimize the use and exchange of whatever rights people start out with; this respects the proper bounds of political and judicial action. There is no longer general optimism concerning governmental intervention in the economic system. Tort law, dealing as it does mainly with accidents, does not lend itself well to state intervention to redistribute wealth. It is unrealistic to think that interest groups will overly concern themselves with redistribution through the tort system or will place accident compensation reform on their agenda for legislative action anyway. This point is perhaps not fully grasped by Justice Prudential, whose well intentioned, but misguided energies may now become a real cost in the world of imperfect information. My judgment attempts to come to terms with this precise problem.

Rules of tort law must be designed and implemented so as to facilitate and simulate the operation of a free and competitive market. If there were no barriers to effective bargaining, the assignment of legal rights would not affect the social efficiency of the final outcome. For example, Dexter lives next to a cricket ground, owned by Cowdrey, and is frequently assailed by hard-hit balls. Dexter could take adequate precautions at $500, but it would cost Cowdrey $1,000. If Cowdrey were legally liable, he would bargain to pay Dexter $500 to take the necessary precautions. If Cowdrey were not legally liable, Dexter would have to spend $500 on precautions. Either way, the *socially* efficient level of precautions would be taken.

In a world in which bargaining is often prohibitively costly, the initial assignment of rights is of crucial importance and has a fundamental impact on the allocative efficiency of societal resources; see *Miller v. Jackson*, [1977] Q.B. 966. The practical implementation of my thesis must, and does, take account of this fact. The rule of liability is relevant and will determine whether resources are used in an economically efficient manner. In most accident situations, private bargaining is not feasible. The necessary information may be unavailable, imperfect or too expensive, there may be too many parties to the potential transaction or there may be the problem of excluding free riders —

those who do not pay for the benefits they receive — from the bargain. This, of course, is the case with Anne and Derek. Consequently, the rules of liability must as closely as possible approximate the apportionment of risk that would have been arrived at by the litigants *if they had been able to bargain.* Any dispute which reaches a court is, after all, only a case in which the bargaining process — settlement out of court — has broken down.

The economic logic of the competitive market must become the unifying force of the common law. The market and the legal system are similar operational institutions. Like the market, the legal system is a competitive process in which the pursuit of self-interest serves to promote an efficient allocation of resources. If the invisible hand of the market is replicated by the pen of the impartial judge, inefficient rules will be litigated out of the system. The adversary system would substitute for marketing strategies; the judge acting as a consumer in choosing between two fiercely promoted products. Legal rules could be cast as economic incentives to encourage individuals to maximise efficiency. Like the economic actor, the legal actor could be presented with the costs of any course of action in order to decide whether to incur those costs. The common law of tort, therefore, should ensure that the joint value of interacting activities is maximized and that joint cost is minimized. More particularly, the law must seek to encourage individuals to achieve a level of safety at which the value of the risks involved in an activity is equal to the cost of the precautions necessary to maintain that degree of safety. As Lord Macmillan said, "the law exacts a degree of care commensurate with the risk created"; see *Read v. J. Lyons Co. Ltd.,* [1947] A.C. 156. In short, individuals must be persuaded to "internalize" the costs of accidents in the cause of improved social justice. As such, the central task of tort law is to design rules of liability which will provide a sufficient incentive to achieve an efficient level of safety by deterring carelessness and rewarding care. As the Court summarized in *Losee v. Buchanan*, 51 N.Y. 476 at 484 (1873):

> "By becoming a member of civilized society, I am compelled to give up many of my natural rights, but I receive more than adequate compensation from the surrender by every other man of the same rights, and the security, advantage and protection which the laws give me ... We must have factories, machinery, dams, canals and railroads. They are demanded by the manifold wants of mankind, and lay at the basis of all our civilisation. If I have any of these upon my lands ... I am not responsible for any damage they accidentally and unavoidably do to my neighbour. He receives his compensation for such damage by the general good in which he shares and the right which he has to place the same things upon his lands. I hold my property subject to the risk that it may be unavoidably or accidentally injured by those who live near me; and as I move about upon the public highways and in all places where other persons may lawfully be, I take the risk of being accidentally injured in my person by them without fault on their part. Most of the rights of property, as well as of person, in the social state, are not absolute but relative, and they must be so arranged and modified, not unnecessarily infringing upon natural rights, as upon the whole to promote the general welfare.

The centerpiece of negligence law is the seminal judgment of Judge Learned Hand in *U.S. v. Carroll Towing*, 159 F. 2d 169 (1947). The test for liability developed by him has a long and impeccable pedigree; see, for example, *Mackintosh v. Mackintosh*, 36 Jur. 678 (1864), *Chicago, Burlington & Quincy Rly. Co. v. Krayenbuhl*, 65 Neb. 889 (1902) and *Conway v. O'Brien*, 111 F. 2d 611 (1940). The beauty of this test is its elegant simplicity and sweep. With subtle adjustments that remain loyal to Learned Hand's ambition, this algorithm can be made to resolve all the problems of accident liability, like causation, contributory negligence and rescue, that so vex Doctrin, C.J. and others.

In *U.S. v. Carroll Towing, supra*, an unattended barge had slipped its moorings and collided with another ship. In holding the barge owners liable, Judge Learned Hand stated that:

"[T]here is no general rule to determine when the absence of a bargee or other attendant will make the owner of the barge liable for injuries to other vessels if she breaks away from her moorings ... It becomes apparent why there can be no such general rule, when we consider the grounds for such a liability. Since there are occasions when every vessel will break from her moorings, and since, if she does, she becomes a menace to those about her, the owner's duty, as in other similar situations, to provide against resulting injuries is a function of three variables: (1) the probability that she will break away; (2) the gravity of the resulting injury, if she does; (3) the burden of adequate precautions. Possibly it serves to bring this notion into relief to state it in algebraic terms: if the probability be called P; the injury, L; and the burden B; liability depends upon whether B is less than L multiplied by P; i.e., whether B<PL ... In the case at bar the bargee left at five o'clock in the afternoon of January 3rd, and the flotilla broke away at about two o'clock in the afternoon of the following day, twenty-one hours afterwards. The bargee had been away all the time ... At the locus in quo ... barges were being constantly "drilled" in and out. Certainly it was not beyond reasonable expectation that, with the inevitable haste and bustle, the work might not be done with adequate care. In such circumstances, we hold—and it is all that we do hold—that it was a fair requirement that the [barge owners] should have a bargee aboard (unless he had some excuse for his absence), during the working hours of daylight.

Following from this, a basic presumption operates that losses will lie where they fall unless there are compelling reasons for their reallocation. This will only occur if it would have been cheaper for the defendant to have avoided the accident than to make good the expected losses. The accident cost is the magnitude of the loss if an accident occurs reduced by the probability of the accident occurring. If the defendant were to compensate the plaintiff under any other circumstances, it would lead to an economically inefficient result. It would be a waste of societal resources to require the defendant to spend a greater sum to avoid an accident which would result in losses of a lesser amount. The Learned Hand test encourages cost-rational actors to modify their behaviour by taking cost justified precautions to avoid liability; see *Watt v. Hertfordshire C.C.*, [1954] 1 W.L.R. 535 and *Wyong Shire Council v. Shire* (1980), 46 C.L.R.

40. As such, carelessness per se does not result in actionable negligence for "it is only the requirement that the care be commensurate with the risk and danger"; see *Nussbaum v. Lacapo*, 27 N.Y. 2d 311 at 319 (1970).

Two examples will suffice to illustrate the efficacy and desirability of this approach. In *Hedricks v. Peabody Coal Co.*, 115 Ill. App. 2d 35 (1969), a child was drowned and the negligence was the failure to prevent the use of an inherently dangerous waterhole by children known to play there. Damages to the child were assessed at $200,000, but the cost of fencing off the waterhole would have been between $12,000 and $14,000. The defendant was found liable as the prevention "cost was slight compared to the risk to the children involved"; *id.* at 45. Also, in *Bolton v. Stone*, [1951] A.C. 850, plaintiff was struck by a ball from the defendants' cricket ground. There was a twelve foot perimeter fence and a ball had only been hit out of the ground six times in about thirty years. The House of Lords refused to impose liability. The risk of injury was negligible and the cost of further precautions immense. As Lord Reid said:

> "In the crowded conditions of modern life even the most careful person cannot avoid creating some risks and accepting others. What a man must not do, and what I think a careful man tries not to do is to create a risk which is substantial ... In my judgment, the test to be applied here is whether the risk of damage to a person on the road was so small that a reasonable man in the position of the appellants, considering the matter from the point of view of safety, would have thought it right to refrain from taking steps to prevent the

danger.

An application of the Learned Hand test to the facts of the case at bar is instructive. Interestingly, Doctrin, C.J. failed to mention some of the more pertinent facts. As we know, the loss to Derek was estimated at $1 million, but we also know from the evidence that Anne could have repaired her headlight for $250 and that there was a relatively significant possibility that an accident would have occurred, say .001 or a one in a thousand chance. Translating these into "economic" terms, it means that, as the accident cost is $1,000 (.001 x $1 m.) and the avoidance costs were $250, Anne ought to be held liable. It would have been more efficient for Anne to take precautions than to have allowed the accident to occur. It is an economically efficient use of society's resources to require an expenditure of $250 to save a loss of $1,000. However, this finding does not conclusively dispose of Anne's liability. As the objective of the law is to maximize overall social welfare, it is important to consider Derek's actions.

In general terms, where the cost to the plaintiff of avoiding the accident is less than the cost to the defendant, the impetus for shifting the loss disappears. Indeed, it would be efficient to do so. Consequently, the loss should shift only where expected accident costs and the defendant's avoidance costs are less than the plaintiff's. Under such a straightforward regime, optimal safety would be achieved as each party would have a powerful incentive to minimize accident costs and maximize avoidance costs. In the present case, as Derek could have repaired his faulty brakes for $200 ($50 less than Anne's avoidance costs), the loss will remain with Derek. Anne will not be liable. Derek should have taken the safety measures as they cost less than the predictable accident costs.

To interpret the *Negligence Act* as requiring a distribution of loss based on the proportionate fault of the parties, as Doctrin, C.J. does, undermines the clarity and deterrent effect of that law. Such an apportionment of liability would be inefficient for the parties would be obliged to spend, jointly, more than an efficient amount on accident prevention. Where each party is liable for fifty percent of the loss, that is $500 each in this case, Anne would have an incentive to spend $250 to avoid the accident and Derek would have an incentive to spend $200. This means that either a total of $450 will be invested in accident avoidance (an increase of $250 over the cheaper avoidance cost) or nothing will be invested, on the basis that, knowing the other to have an incentive to prevent the accident, each might make no investment at all. This would result in an avoidable cost of $800; that is, the loss less the cheaper avoidance cost. The attempt to achieve an efficient level of accidents and safety can only be undermined by liability rules which enjoin the judge to assess the individual and relative culpability of the parties' conduct in each case.

Before leaving Derek's claim against Anne, a word ought to be said about causation. This issue has created considerable consternation for Doctrin C.J., if not in this particular case, certainly in other cases. Also, Justice Wright, by making causation the fulcrum of liability, has had to grapple continually and inconclusively with this traditionally perplexing problem. All of this is unnecessary. Once the Learned Hand test is accepted as the basis for liability, the puzzles of causation can be solved with confidence. As Lord Reid observed, causation exists when the defendant's act increases the risk of injury to the plaintiff; see *McGhee v. N.C.B.,* [1973] 1 W.L.R. 1 and *John Pfeiffer Pty. Ltd. v. Canny* (1981), 36 A.L.R. 466. In *McGhee,* the fact that an employer's failure to provide showers added to the risk that the plaintiff's dermatitis might develop was held to be a sufficient ground for liability. In strict terms, therefore, the probability of harm in the Learned Hand formula is the difference between the probability that the accident will occur if the defendant is negligent or not. For instance, in *Berry v. Sugar Notch Borough,* 191 Pa. 345 (1899), the fact that the plaintiff was speeding when his car was hit by a fallen tree during a violent windstorm was not a cause of the accident as the probability of the accident occurring was the same whether he drove slowly or speedily. In the present case, Anne's failure to repair her headlight undoubtedly increased the chance of an accident by at least .001, as did Derek's failure to fix his brakes. This latter fact seems to elude Wright, J. and undermine his whole fragile "background theory of rights."

Another dilemma for my judicial colleagues has been the duty to rescue. The "efficiency" account of the law offers a convincing and moral response. As the courts are slowly beginning to accept, there is no significant or meaningful difference between misfeasance and nonfeasance. Any set of circumstances can be so arranged and presented as to meet either definition; see *Rowland v. Christian,* 69 Cal. 2d 108 (1968) and *Spreacher v. Adamson Companies,* 30 Cal. 3d 358 (1981). Furthermore, the courts and legislatures seem to be committed to extending the liability of potential rescuers; see *Farwell v. Keaton,* 396 Mich. 281 (1976) and Utah Code Ann. § 41-29 to 31 (1953). The natural and obvious next stop is to establish a general duty to rescue. This advance will reflect and respect the moral and economic underpinnings of the common law. It is both inefficient and immoral for a good swimmer to be free to ignore the cries of a drowning person; see *Gautret v. Egerton* (1867), L.R. 2 C.P. 371. In such circumstances, the costs to the swimmer are slight compared to the tragic and high costs of the drowning person. Nevertheless, it would be counter-productive to impose an obligation to rescue in all circumstances. It might, for instance, discourage people from becoming good swimmers or visiting the beach. Also, the incidence of rescue might decrease as such acts would no longer be seen as motivated by heroic altruism, but by fear of legal liability. However, as Martin could have at least telephoned for an ambulance at little or no cost and certainly at less cost than Anne, Derek or Charles, he must assume liability.

Doctrin, C.J.'s refusal to establish such a duty of "easy rescue" is indicative of her pusillanimity. Legislative inaction does not necessarily mean a desire to retain the *status quo*, but can be interpreted as an indication that the legislature feels it is more appropriate for the courts to change the law; see *Alvis v. Ribar*, 85 Ill. 2d 1 (1981). As regards the administrative problems, while they do present difficulties, they are of no greater magnitude than the initial question of liability under Doctrin C.J.'s approach. The most sensible distribution of losses is to have the original tortfeasor pay for the damages as if an early rescue had been effected and the "rescuer" pay for the remainder. In the present case, therefore, Martin would be responsible for the payment of a large portion of Derek's and Charles' damages.

Finally, Charles' claim for emotional distress can be

easily and expeditiously disposed of. It is not so much a matter of liability as of proof; see *Molien v. Kaiser Foundation Hospitals*, 27 Cal. 3d 916 (1980). While it is difficult to imagine what cost-effective steps he could have taken to avoid injury, we can safely assume that they would outweigh the accident and avoidance costs of Anne, Derek or Martin. Liability, therefore, seems established. However, I do agree with Doctrin, C.J. that we must be careful not to encourage or facilitate bogus claims. It is desirable that the law should march with medicine, "but in the rear and limping a little"; see *Mount Isa Mines v. Pusey* (1970), 125 C.L.R. 383 at 395. Nonetheless, in line with increasing medical sophistication, the courts have recently begun to recognize and accept broader recovery for nervous shock; see *McLoughlin v. O'Brian, supra* and *Sinn v. Burd*, 486 Pa. 146 (1979). Accordingly, as cogent medical evidence was led, Charles ought to recover for his emotional distress. His sexual orientation is no concern of the courts.

In conclusion, therefore, I hold that Derek cannot recover against Anne, but that he ought to receive a significant amount of damages from Martin. Also Charles would be eligible for recovery of damages from Martin and Anne.

WRIGHT, J.: As is often the case, I have the dubious distinction of following Justice Mill. It will come as little surprise to those who follow the proceedings of this Court that Justice Mill and I do not see eye to eye on the proper basis for compensation for injuries. Our bone of contention is that compensation matters are intrinsically questions of the moral entitlement of individuals in particular circumstances and not impersonal measurements of social utility. As Cicero said, "the study of law must be derived from the depths of philosophy"; see *De Legibus* i., 5. The resort to economic calculations does not take individual liberty seriously. When one person harms another, the injured has a moral right to demand and the injurer a moral duty to pay compensation.

The utilitarian ethic, espoused by Mill, J., is incapable of furnishing sufficiently compelling reasons to deserve people's allegiance and support. It demands that individuals' wants, desires and projects be submerged or discarded in the interest of utility maximization; they are to be treated as mere entries on the debit side of society's moral accounts. Yet such tastes and preferences constitute an individual's moral integrity. Without these, individuals would cease to exist morally. Under such utilitarianism, individual projects are simply resources for use in the general welfare and are liable to be acquired by others. Utilitarianism seeks to maximize benefits, regardless of their distribution throughout society. Individuals are robbed of any intrinsic merit or importance. Indeed, the sacrifice of individuals is not only permissible, but is often demanded and sanctioned.

The recent Pinto affairs illustrate the callousness of life under such an "efficient" regime; see *Grimshaw v. Ford Motor Co.*, 174 Cal Rptr. 438 (1981). As a result of the explosion of Pinto fuel tanks in rear-end, low velocity collisions, people died or were injured. Ford carried out a cost benefit analysis of whether to recall and reinforce the cars:

BENEFIT

Savings -180 burn deaths, 180 serious burn injuries, 2,100 burned vehicles.
Unit Cost - $200,000 per death, $67,000 per injury, $700 per vehicle.
Total Benefit - 180 x ($200.000), 180 x ($67,000), 2100 x ($700) = $49.5 million.

COSTS

Sales- 11 million cars, 1.5 million light trucks.
Unit Cost - $11 per car, $11 per truck.
Total Cost - 11,000,000 x ($11) 1,500,000 x ($11) = $137.5 million.

Under Mill, J.'s theory of liability, Ford not only made a good commercial decision not to recall the cars, but adopted a morally commendable course of action. To have recalled the cars would have been to squander social resources. That corporations rest their business decisions and safety strategies on cost-benefit analyses is deplorable enough. For the courts to sanction and clothe such operations with moral legitimacy is intolerable.

Fortunately, the courts are not so irresponsible as Mill, J. would have them. In *Grimshaw,* the plaintiff received $3.5 million and $125 million in punitive damages. Unfortunately, the punitive damages were reduced to $3.5 million on appeal. Nonetheless, the courts openly condemned such reprehensible conduct. Importantly, the court applied the principles of strict liability rather than the negligence standard. This points up a fatal flaw in Mill J.'s arguments. Not only does his liability scheme lead to a perverse decision, but it confounds his central claims that "economic efficiency" is the structural framework of the common law. On the contrary, it is his own personal political preference and an unjust one at that.

Clearly, information costs undermine and reduce the potential internalization of accident costs. How are Derek and Anne to discover the avoidance costs of the other? His whole scheme assumes that everyone has information about everyone else's costs. Indeed, even Learned Hand, J. conceded that "care is the only one ever susceptible of quantitative estimate, and often that is not"; see *Moisan v. Loftus* 178 F. 2d 148 at 149 (1949). At best, all risk quantifications are more impressionistic than precise. Moreover, at least in a theoretical sense, all risk is necessarily foreseeable and, therefore, one can place no limits on liability. No greater a supporter of utilitarian arguments than Posner, J. has opined, while speaking of assessment of damages, that "the exactness which economic analysis rigorously pursued appears to offer is, at least in the litigation setting, somewhat delusive"; see *O'Shea v. Riverway Towing Co.*, 667 F. 2d 1194 at 1201 (1982). Indeed, the whole operation is artificial and counter-factual. The retrospective evaluation of the probability of something happening which has already happened is fanciful. The problem of applying the pseudo-scientific standard of "efficiency" to real-life problems is amply revealed in *Union Oil Co. v. Oppen*, 501 F. 2d 558 (1974). Furthermore, economic welfare is so protean a concept as to be able to justify as "efficient" a regime which determined beforehand the most likely cheapest cost avoider in particular activities and held them strictly liable whatever the actual costs.

Also, although attitudes to risk in our society are not uniform, Mill, J. seems to assume widespread risk-neutrality. But there exists an asymmetrical distribution of risk-aversion and risk-preference. For instance, large-scale manufacturers can afford to be relatively indifferent to risk as they can effectively spread and pass on anticipated losses. On the other hand, individuals tend to be risk-averse and are less able to calculate and off-set future losses. Mill, J. seems to overlook entirely the maldistribution of both attitudes and exposure to risk. At the very least, the Learned Hand test would need substantial adaption to affect these realities. The very act of allocating and settling risk favours the risk averse. For instance, he offers no account of why we ought not to have a reverse Learned Hand test in which loss would be carried by the person who caused it unless there are sufficient reasons to shift it. As the Pinto fiasco demonstrates, this would effect a complete change in patterns of compensation. Furthermore, according to Mill, J., the law provides incentives to individuals to organize their behaviour in accordance with the dictates of economic efficiency; they will be rational maximizers of their resources. In order to do this, of course, a necessary piece of information will be knowledge of what that law is. There is nothing to suggest that people do take the law into account in actually planning their daily lives. The available information suggests that individuals do not consult legal materials before planning their activities.

A case that Mill, J. relies on to support and substantiate his analysis, when read properly, exposes his disingenuousness. In *Bolton v. Stone*, [1951] A.C. 850, the plaintiff failed to recover after being hit by a cricket ball from the defendant's ground because the risk of such an accident was not sufficiently substantial. However, as the later case of *Miller v. Jackson*, [1977] Q.B. 966, makes clear, there is a hidden ordering of the social utility of the respective activities. Cricket occupies a special place in the hearts of Englishmen. It is not so clear that the courts would have reacted similarly if the cricket ground had been a water sports center; see *Kennaway v. Thompson*, [1981] Q.B. 88. Under Mill, J.'s scheme, all activities are accorded equal significance; the playing of cricket is considered at least as important as the right of individuals not to be injured.

These difficulties strike at the root of any utilitarian argument. Although its rationale is to enhance and promote individual freedom, its operation reduces and neglects that liberty; it forces individuals to concern themselves with the projects and plans of others. Individuals deserve and merit respect simply as individuals. They are autonomous: they possess certain rights that cannot be overridden by appeals to general utility. Rights are trumps over social welfare. Individuals are not to be conceived of as a means by which to maximize social utility, but instead are to be treated as ends in themselves. What is needed is not a maximizing and collective standard, but a distributive and individualizing principle. As Stephen, J. so well put it, "the task of the courts remains that of loss fixing rather than loss spreading"; see *Caltex Oil Pty. Ltd. v. The Dredge "Willemstad"* (1976), 136 C.L.R. 529 at 558. The law must control the market, not be controlled by it. Individuals count. Although rather overstated, Lord Scarman in *McLoughlin v. O'Brian*, [1982] 2 W.L.R. 982 at 987, emphasizes the priority of principle over policy:

> "The distinguishing feature of the common law is this judicial development and formation of principle. Policy considerations will have to be weighed: but the

objective of the judges is the formulation of principle. And, if principle inexorably requires a decision which entails a degree of policy risk, the court's function is to adjudicate according to principle, leaving policy curtailment to the judgment of Parliament. Here lies the true role of the two law-making institutions in our constitution. By concentrating on principle the judges can keep the common law alive, flexible and consistent; and can keep the legal system clear of policy problems which neither they, nor the forensic process which it is their duty to operate, are equipped to resolve. If principle leads to results which are thought to be socially unacceptable, Parliament can legislate to draw a line or map out a new path.

The imposition of legal liability ought to depend on moral entitlements as determined by causal enquiries. "Efficiency" is to be deplored for its casual nihilism. A deep sense of morality and rights pervades the common law. The Learned Hand test is, at best, a crude and misguided device to compromise and concretize individual rights. People are completely free to act, except when they cause harm to others; see *Beshada v. Johns-Manville Prods. Corp.*, 447 A. 2d 539 (1982). This moral principle is the driving force behind the common law: any system of tort must respect and implement such a moral notion. Tort law is a private ordering that articulates the immanent rationality of immediate personal interactions. Causa and culpa are intimately connected. As Lord Dunedin said, liability is "to be determined by common-sense principles. What is the cause of the loss?"; see *Leyland Shipping Co. v. Norwich Universal Insurance Co.*, [1918] A.C. 350.

It would, of course, be ridiculous to pretend that negligence did not once form the backbone of accident liability. Yet, over recent decades, there has been a gradual movement from negligence to strict liability. The negligence principle was firmly established in *MacPherson v. Buick Motor Co.*, 217 N.Y. 330 (1918), notwithstanding decisions like *Rylands v. Fletcher* (1868), L.R 3 H.L. 330. Strict liability began to reassert itself in *Escola v. Coca Cola Bottling Co.*, 150 P. 2d 436 (1944). On holding that a soda bottle manufacturer was absolutely liable for injury caused by a defective product, Traynor, J., *id.* at 440-441 articulated the rationale for strict liability:

> "Even if there is no negligence, however, public policy demands that responsibility be fixed wherever it will most effectively reduce the hazards to life and health inherent in defective products that reach the market. It is evident that the manufacturer can anticipate some hazards and guard against the recurrence of others as the public cannot. Those who suffer injury from defective products are unprepared to meet its consequences. The cost of an injury and the loss of time or health may be an overwhelming misfortune to the person injured, and a needless one, for the risk can be insured by the manufacturer and distributed among the public as a cost of doing business ... Against such a risk [of injury from defective products whether negligently manufactured or not] there should be general and constant protection and the manufacturer is best situated to afford such protection."

Since that seminal judgment, strict liability has begun to

colonize accident liability; see *Greenman v. Yuba Power Products*, 377 P. 2d 897 (1963) and *Shaffer v. Victoria Station Inc.*, 588 P. 2d 233 (1978). Those cases which speak in the rhetoric of negligence achieve results more consistent with the dictates of strict liability. For instance, in *Hughes v. Lord Advocate*, [1963] A.C. 837, the defendants were liable for injuries caused by an explosion which the court accepted to be "so unlikely as not to be foreseeable." Throughout the law of tort, there has been a subtle, but profound shift in the structural foundation of the law; see *Bankstown Founding Pty. Ltd. v. Breisting* (1986), 60 A.L.J.R. 362 at 364 per McHugh, J.A. and *Buchan v. Ortho Pharmaceutical (Canada) Ltd.* (1984) 8 D.L.R. (4th) 373. As early as 1936, in *Grant v. Australian Knitting Mills*, [1936] A.C. 85, a manufacturer was liable even though it had sold without complaint almost 5 million similar products over 6 years. To recognize the change from negligence to strict liability is to take a step much smaller and less controversial than that in *MacPherson, supra*, or *Donoghue v. Stevenson*, [1932] A.C. 562. As Murphy, J. concluded, "what is reasonable care often becomes such a high standard that it amounts virtually to strict liability. In one sense, strict liability is but another aspect of negligence, both being based on responsibility for the creation of an abnormal risk"; see *Cartwright v. McLaine* (1979), 143 C.L.R. 549.

All of this, of course, is as it should be. The common law must move forward, but in so doing it must retain a principled integrity with the past. So it is with the incremental progress in tort law. As Windeyer, J. in *Benning v. Wong* (1969), 122 C.C.R. 249 at 271 expressed it:

"We need not doubt, nor need we disguise, that this

movement and development of the law is the result of the creative work of courts making at times a conscious choice between allowing or disallowing a remedy and thus creating or denying a right. Nevertheless those who insist that the common law is still on the move should remember that it must always march in step. Decisions in cases passing at the moment must be in step with those which have just gone past, although not necessarily with those at the head of the column. Moving the metaphor from the parade ground to the field, it is as sound a maxim for law as for war that operations should be from a firm base. That an advance must be from a position which has been securely established ..."

The political morality that explains and shows the doctrinal materials in their best light is one founded upon the right of individuals to be secure against non-consensual invasions of their personal integrity. Fault amounts to an interference per se. The focus is rightly placed upon activity rather than the defendant's conduct: the *what* happened is more important than the *how* or *why*. Within such a regime, causation becomes not *a* basis for liability but *the* basis. It is the fulcrum of liability. Not only does it make strong ethical sense, but accords with common sense and intuitive notions of fairness. While this might give rise to the occasional penumbral puzzle, it is clear that Anne was the cause of the accident in the present case. But for Anne's failure to repair her headlight, the accident would not have occurred.

No doubt, Doctrin, C.J. and Mill, J. will complain that this ignores Derek's contribution to his own misfortune. Yet it is surely a foundational principle of the common law that defendants take their victims as they find them; see *Smith v. Leech Brian & Co.,* [1962] 2 Q.B. 405 and *Watts v. Rake* (1960), 108 C.L.R. 158. While the condition of Derek's car may well have extended the causal chain, it does not alter the primary fact that Anne was responsible for setting the chain in motion. Such a determination is as simple as it is fair. It also avoids another doctrinal swamp into which Doctrin, C.J. and Mill, J. have been lured; see *Daly v. General Motors Corp.,* 20 Cal. 3d 725 (1978) and *Overseas Tankship (U.K.) Ltd. v. Morts Dock and Eng. Co. (The Wagon Mound),* [1961] A.C. 388. Further, the acceptance of a defence of contributory negligence would admit through the back door the very same utilitarian constraints on individual rights that were refused entry at the front. To use Derek's conduct to reduce Anne's liability is to set in motion a process that would ultimately erode Derek's rights. Although a sleeping passenger is more susceptible to serious injury than an alert one, it is ludicrous to reduce the defendant's liability on this account; see *Sloan v. Flack,* 150 So. 2d 640 (1963) .

Both Derek's and Charles' injuries were caused by Anne's activities; if she had not acted as she did, there would have been no harm. The fact that Charles' injuries are emotional rather than physical is irrelevant. Once the court is satisfied, as Burke, J. in *Battalla v. State of New York,* 10 N.Y. 2d 237 (1960), put it, of "the quality and genuineness of proof," there need be no further argument. It is illogical and unfair to hinge liability, as Doctrin, C.J. seems to do, on whether the damage suffered is physical or emotional.

The wise refusal of the common law to recognize a general duty to rescue supports the arguments used to justify strict liability and illustrates the perversity and uncertainty of Mill, J.'s "efficiency thesis." Moreover, contrary to what Doctrin, C.J. states, it is because of the law's concern with morality not in spite of it. As Jessup, J. succinctly expressed it, "no principle is more deeply rooted in the common law than that there is no duty to take positive action in aid of another, no matter how helpless or perilous his position is"; see *Horsley v. MacLaren*, [1970] O.R. 487. The imposition of a duty of care rightly depends upon the existence of some special relationship or the creation of risk which amounts to a positive acceptance of responsibility; see *Racine v. C.N.R.*, [1923] 1 D.L.R. 924 and *South v. National Railroad Passenger Corp.*, 290 N.W. 2d 819 (1980). In other circumstances, there is no promise or commitment to act and, therefore, no positive expectation of rescue. To require gratuitous acts of rescue flaunts individual freedom. As Deane, J. noted, the common law has not "embraced the embarrassing moral perception that he who has failed to feed the man dying from hunger has truly killed him"; see *Jaensch v. Coffey* (1984), 54 A.L.R. 417 at 439. A similar principle animates other areas of the law. In contract, there is no general duty to co-operate, unless it is necessary in order to effectuate the exchange; see *Seaman's Direct Buying Service v. Standard Oil*, 181 Cal. Rptr. 126 (1981). In a very real sense, the "rescuer" ought not to be liable as she did not cause the plaintiff's dilemma or damages.

A glance at the solution offered by Mill, J. betrays the muddled and dangerous nature of his thinking. In general, the imposition of a duty to rescue underlines the fact that a person's own welfare is of no special interest; it must be discarded for the social good. The pauper might have to sacrifice his life to rescue the president, but the president might be acting irresponsibly to attempt a rescue of the pauper. Apart from its obvious iniquity, such a rule is unworkable as the rescuer must first ascertain the "worth" of the plaintiff before knowing whether there is a social obligation to perform or refrain from a rescue. Further, a rescue rule is a form of conscription into social service; the rescuer becomes an insurer for the fool-hardy, risk-preferring or powerful. An obliged rescue is tantamount to a tax, a forced exchange exacted by government. Whereas a rescue rule leads to unjust results and renders it uncertain where liberty ends and obligation begins, a no-rescue rule is consistent with both moral and economic principle; see *Hargrave v. Goldman* (1963), 110 C.L.R. 40 at 66. In the present case, Martin would be free to engage in any rescue attempt he chose, but he would not be obliged to attempt any rescue. At least in my conclusion, I fully agree with Doctrin, C.J. on this issue. However, I disassociate myself entirely from Mill, J.'s decision. He has sown the wind and, unless we respond promptly, we will reap the whirlwind. He has contrived a decision that places almost exclusive responsibility upon Martin for the losses to Derek and Charles. The logic or fairness of such a decision completely eludes me.

I would like to conclude my judgment with some general remarks on why strict liability is preferable to a no-fault compensation scheme, so ably and fondly espoused by Prudential, J. I believe that strict liability comes out on top in any comparison of the two major objectives of any scheme of compensation, its effectiveness in reducing accidents and its administrative costs. As Mill, J. states, any system of accident liability must create incentives that minimize the sum of accident costs and avoidance costs. In general, as everyone is a potential plaintiff or defendant, a move from one scheme to another will tend to shuffle incentives around rather than reduce the overall level of accidents. What a no-fault system loses in incentives can be made up for by the rigorous enforcement of a robust criminal law. But, and Mill, J. is at least right in this, the ideal world is not the practical world. Unless a change is made in the criminal law and its enforcement, the introduction of a no-fault system will actually reduce the incentives. Although other legal systems, like Sweden's, may manage to enforce vigorously and effectively the criminal law, Canengaustrus has neither the appropriate substantive criminal law nor, it seems, the will to enforce it fully. Accordingly, a decentralized system of private actions, based on strict liability, provides the most self-contained and realistic method to maintain and enforce the norms of optimal behaviour.

Prudential, J. astutely notes that the costs of administering any tort system are considerable. Certainly under a negligence regime as proposed by Doctrin, C.J. and Mill, J., the uncertainty of the standard generates immense costs; see, for example, *Hammontree v. Jenner*, 97 Cal. Rptr. 739 (1971). A scheme of strict liability is not so vulnerable. Its focus of inquiry is narrow and clear; therefore, the frequency of litigation and its cost will be reduced. If the litigation process is streamlined, the cost of the reduced litigation can be pared down. Finally, under any scheme, the cost of hiring a physician to determine the actual damages in each individual case remains uniformly high.

In conclusion, therefore, I hold that Anne is responsible to Derek and Charles for the full extent of their damages.

Martin is under no legal obligation at all.

PRUDENTIAL, J.: The late F.R. Leavis wrote in his *New English Poetry* (1932) at 17, that:

> "[P]oetry can communicate the actual quality of experience with a precision unapproachable by any other means. But if the poetry and the intelligence of the Age lose touch with each other, poetry will cease to matter much and the age will be lacking in finer awareness."

I have read in draft the opinions delivered by my colleagues. Whereas Mill, J., Doctrin, C.J. and Wright, J. allow intellect to operate unmitigated by poetry, Lefft, J. indulges in a poetry that drifts free from intellect. My own solution to this appeal lies in forging a rapprochement between the actual quality of experience (partially, but cynically demonstrated by Justice Lefft) and the intellectual fervour of Justice Wright. It will become clear that I reject the sentiments espoused by Doctrin, C.J. whose formalistic inquiry into the conduct of the parties is misplaced. It is the plight of the injured plaintiff and not the conduct of the defendant that deserves our attention. The pseudo-intellectual rigour of Mill, J. and his indifference to the fate of individuals in the march to improved social welfare fill me with despondency and horror.

The judgment of Wright, J. has intuitive appeal; it seems ethical, practical and efficient. Yet, his principle of "causative responsibility" is thoroughly unequal to the massive task he sets it. In practice, it amounts to a crude and cumbersome norm by which to allocate compensation. Justice Wright still lives in the Platonic cave of abstract justice. He is not only naive, but dangerous. Common sense is a notoriously unreliable source of guidance for practical affairs. In the pluralistic society of Canengaustrus, its identity is vague and indeterminate. Causation is a labyrinth for which Wright, J. offers no realistic through-route. At bottom, he has to smuggle in substantive value judgments as formal causal criteria. Recall the memorable words of Andrews, J. in *Palsgraf v. Long Island Rly. Co.*, 248 N.Y. 339 at 352 (1928):

"Any philosophical doctrine of causation does not help us. A boy throws a stone into a pond. The ripples spread. The water level rises. The history of that pond is altered to all eternity: it will be altered by other causes also. Yet it will be forever the result of all causes combined. Each one will have an influence. How great only omniscience can say. You may speak of a chain, or, if you please, a net. An analogy is of little aid. Each cause brings about future events. Without each the future would not be the same. Each is proximate in the sense it is essential. But that is not what we mean by the word. Nor on the other hand do we mean sole cause. There is no such thing ...

As we have said, we cannot trace the effect of an act to the end, if end there is. Again, however, we may trace it part of the way. A murder at Sarajevo may be the necessary antecedent to an assassination in London twenty years hence. An overturned lantern may burn all Chicago. We may follow the fire from the shed to the last building. We rightly say the fire started by the lantern caused its destruction.

262

A cause, but not the proximate cause. What we do mean by the word "proximate" is that, because of convenience, of public policy, of a rough sense of justice, the law arbitrarily declines to trace a series of events beyond a certain point. This is not logic. It is practical politics ..."

Causation is and must always remain a choice; see *Kinderavich v. Palmer*, 127 Conn. 85 (1940). If we are to abide by general rules, we must be prepared for arbitrary results. Each accident is unique and demands a unique causal inquiry—"cause and effect find their beginning and end in the limitless and unworkable ..., [h]ence arbitrary limits have been set"; see *Atlantic Coastline Rly Co. v. Daniels*, 8 Ga. App. 775 (1911). Indeed, in the present case, which Wright, J. labels simple and straightforward, it is unclear why "common sense" would burden Anne with the whole cost of the accident. Surely Derek was an "active" factor in the accident and Martin might have been. In any fault-based compensation scheme, the conundrum of causation represents an insuperable barrier to the achievement of personal or social justice. Only a shift to a no-fault regime can overcome this impasse.

As for a "negligence" regime, blindly adhered to by Doctrin, C.J. and zealously championed by Mill, J., it is unclear why rules laid down in the days of the horse and carriage should continue to govern us today. Having witnessed a phenomenal increase in the scale and gravity of destruction which modern technology can wreak, Baron Bramwell's decision "to put up with such mischief as reasonable care on the part of others cannot avoid" is no longer acceptable; see *Holmes v. Mather* (1875), L.R. 10 Ex.

261 at 267. As we enter the third millennium, the victims of society's collective progress deserve more protection. Our society is dominated by subservience to neither a thoroughgoing holistic nor an atomistic ideology. The law of torts may indeed be the paradigmatic law of the mixed society. It is our responsibility as Justices to ensure that the balance is the best we can make it. Unfortunately, the present mixture is in need of titration. We should add a hefty dose of concern and compassion for our fellow human beings to the tort system. The hotch-potch of add-on or modified plans used to bolster up the private tort action needs comprehensive reconsideration and amendment. The time for makeshift tactics is well passed. In the age of mass torts and toxic devastation, it is perverse to model accident compensation around "snails in ginger beer bottles" and "exploding parcels". My judgment today should be read as a set of guidelines for a long overdue experiment in social reform.

We now have an overwhelming body of data that catalogues in precise detail the litigation lottery. The cost of accidents is astronomical. In Canada, for instance, out of a population of 25 million, 3.5 million sustain product-related injuries annually, 4,000 are killed and 11,000 permanently disabled. Losses are over $2 billion in product-related injuries alone. Of these victims, forty-five percent never recover anything. Further, only one percent reach the courts and most of those are settled on the courthouse steps. Over fifty percent of the compensation ultimately paid out is lost in administering and financing its recovery, mainly to lawyers. These statistics are repeated in every common law jurisdiction. But, revealing as they are, they are even more disturbing when it is remembered that "negligence" is a feature endemic to modern life. For instance, strong evidence suggests that a "good driver" makes about nine mistakes every five minutes. Against such statistics, the efficacy of tort law as a compensatory or deterrent device is illusory.

Dissatisfaction with existing tort law is now a universal phenomenon. Committees, commissions, courts and commentators have railed for long enough. Unhappily, this court still does not speak with one voice. I refrain today from moving in advance of the legislature only after long, hard and sustained reflection. I have kept in mind what was said in the related context of vicarious liability by Lord Wilberforce in *Launchbury v. Morgans*, [1973] A.C. 127 at 136:

"I do not know on what principle our Lordships acting judicially can prefer one of these systems to the others or on what basis any one can be formulated with sufficient precision or its exceptions defined. The choice is one of social policy ... Whatever may have been the situation ... in the youth of the motor car, it is very different now, when millions of people drive for a vast variety of purposes and when there is in existence a complicated legislative structure as to insurance—who must take it out, what risks it must cover, who has the right to sue for the sum assured. Liability and insurance are so intermixed that judicially to alter the basis of liability without adequate knowledge (which we do not have the means to obtain) as to the impact this might make on the insurance system would be dangerous, and in my opinion, irresponsible."

Today, I hesitate to remind the legislature that we are all

better informed, the evidence is clear and overwhelming. Yet even some of my enlightened judicial colleagues, who recognise the thoroughly decrepit character of the common law of torts, still insist that only the legislature can step in. This is impractical and unnecessary. The difficulties of legislative action, of weighing and balancing competing political forces, is so great that even urgent law reform may be frustrated. Throughout our legal system, legislation overtakes and overwhelms the common law. The age of statutes is upon us. The judiciary must respond or, at least, belatedly acknowledge this shift. This does not mean an unthinking obeisance to legislative wisdom. Judges must become constitutional partners in keeping the law in tune with contemporary society; see *Jaensch v. Coffey* (1984), 54 A.L.R. 417 at 456 per Deane, J. The judicial timidity evidenced in cases like *Maki v. Frelk,* 40 Ill. 2d 193 (1968) does not befit our democratic responsibilities. The common law must grow and develop with society. As the court concluded in *Alvis v. Ribar,* 85 Ill. 2d 1 (1981):

"We believe that the proper relationship between the legislature and the court is one of cooperation and assistance in examining and changing the common law to conform with the ever-changing demands of the community. There are, however, times when there exists a mutual state of inaction in which the court awaits action by the legislature and the legislature awaits guidance from the court. Such a stalemate exists and the legislature has, for whatever reason, failed to act to remedy a gap in the common law that results in injustice. It is the imperative duty of the court to repair that injustice and reform the law to be responsive to the demands of society."

With their training and experience, the judiciary may properly be entrusted with this democratic responsibility to prompt and, ultimately, to cajole the legislature to action. While greater power correctly lies with the legislature, this does not mean that the judiciary is relegated to the role of constitutional ciphers. As such, my judgment today is a clarion call for action. It may give the legislature the opportunity for a second look, not a passive glance, but an active investigation. Canengaustrus must embrace and implement a thoroughgoing and comprehensive scheme of accident compensation.

The implementation of such a scheme is not a revolutionary move. It simply universalizes the relief that underpins the present world of accidents. Through a combination of compulsory and voluntary insurance schemes, society has generally considered it appropriate to spread the economic consequences of accidents over the whole community. The search for negligent or strictly liable defendants is fictional; a vain attempt to control the aggregate sum payable by society. If loss-distribution is our goal, the patchwork of tort actions, private insurance and public relief is a grossly inefficient way to proceed. They are fundamentally incompatible and hostile. Indeed, the resort to insurance undermines the "rationality" assumptions of Doctrin, C.J., Mill, J. and Wright, J. People lack sufficient ability to make rational judgments about accident prevention and, therefore, they insure. Behaviour in the face of danger is not motivated by concern for personal safety, but for its financial consequences. To seek, as Mill, J. might, to explain the distribution of accident insurance purchased as a function of individually optimal decisions is absurd: the demand for insurance refutes any assumption of risk neutrality. It reflects and corresponds to the maldistribution of information and resources. It is not enough to be "prudent", one must also be rich enough to carry insurance; see *Redding v. Lee*, [1983] 47 A.L.R. 241 at 284 per Mason and Dawson, J.J. My plea is to introduce minimal levels of compensation below which it is morally unjustifiable to allow anybody to fall. Private insurance can still exist and prosper: market forces can provide a cushion for the wealthy who fall heavily or awkwardly on the state safety-net.

To introduce such a scheme of comprehensive accident compensation is a tall order for the Exchequer. Candour obliges us to recognize, as Justice Lefft does, that the notion of communal responsibility is a two-edged sword. Not only does the community have a duty to safeguard its members, but it must do so in a way that best suits the community at large. If the population is daily subjected to the dangers of modern technological life, it follows that its productive capacity is constantly at risk. Any injury to a human being is a loss to society. The loss occasioned to the injured person cannot be recouped; it is a net social loss. Once it is conceded that this loss can never be made good, the question becomes whether any one person should be required to bear that loss. For instance, Doctrin, C.J. perceives the harm suffered one dimensionally; the harm inflicted is solely on Derek. But it seems to me that when a person suffers injury, so does the economy. There exists a *real* social cost. Moreover, by failing to recognise the full extent of these social costs by artificially transferring it to innocent victims, we reduce the demand for action to reduce injuries and avoidable causes; see *Todorovic v. Waller* (1981), 37 A.L.R. 481 at 563 per Murphy J.

Thus, the community has not only a clear duty, but a vested interest in hastening physical and fiscal rehabilitation. That is what maximizing social welfare truly means. It is not to be hedged with utilitarian calculations nor swamped by hedonistic fervour; it is a programme that eschews slogans and tokenism to encourage care and responsibility. If this proposal means some minor injuries go uncompensated so that the most serious, lasting and debilitating injuries are fully compensated, so be it. If it means that there are those whose pre-accident earnings cannot be fully reimbursed from the state fund and they must forego the last few drops in order to allow the blood to flow more freely to all parts of the body politic, so be it. There are no simple or perfect solutions, only difficult choices.

The most persistent argument made against "faultless" insurance schemes is that the deterrent effect of tort law is lost. I have never been persuaded that there is anything to be lost. For the law to act as an effective deterrent, there must exist a correlation between the sanction and an individual's behaviour. Yet, under the existing system, while there may be a massive award of damages based on a minor deviation from the behavioural norm, there will be no liability, no matter how heinous the breach, so long as no one is injured. The prevalence of insurance further diminishes the impact of tort law and the courts' failure to acknowledge this exacerbates the situation; see *Lamb v. Camden Council*, [1981] 2 W.L.R. 1038. Insurance, like an increase in oil prices, is merely another cost of doing business or owning a car. Anne knows this well.

Furthermore, the existence of criminal regulation undermines the deterrence argument. Why would overworked legislators deliberate over the introduction of manifold regulations to control careless conduct, if this merely duplicated results under the civil law? The probability of criminal sanction better encourages pre-accident safety measures and possible post-accident liability in tort.

The vision of social justice I have argued for will offend my colleagues. Mill, J. will recall those "eccentric principles of socialist philanthropy" which so fatally offended his judicial kin sixty years ago; *Roberts v. Hopwood* [1925] A.C. 578 at 594 and *Bromley L.B.C. v. G.L.C.*, [1982] 2 W.L.R. 62. Lefft, J. will be dismayed because an insurance scheme requires society, on behalf of injured persons, to enter the marketplace of compensation. But its strengths are that it makes some effort to recognize the levelling quality of injury and death. Within the structure of administrative bureaucracy, it seems to restore to the law of tort its paradigm nature in a mixed society and not, as would the despair of Justice Lefft and the agnosticism of Justice Mill, destroy it. They are equally in danger of losing sight of the mixed society which demands a mixed law. Our natural and proper feelings of compassion for injured persons must not bankrupt the strained resources of the Exchequer. Nor must our concern for fiscal logic eclipse our compassionate response to injury. We must take into the post-industrial age some incarnation of essential principles which have served us well, but whose present forms have now outlived their usefulness.

There must be an incentive to recover offered by effective rehabilitation. To encourage a return to productive and gainful employment, there must exist a fair margin of return on independent effort. This incentive must not be handicapped by the tendency for levelling state benefits or denying effective help for long-term incapacity. Real compensation must be the goal. Full and adequate financial assistance carefully tailored to the severity of injury and to the victim's financial status must be the aim. Such a system will provide a direction and an objective for individuals that will subvert charges of state paternalism. Redistribution is not a valid ambition in matters of accident compensation.

The coverage offered must be properly comprehensive. Injury, not cause, is at issue. I recognize that this raises in the most acute manner possible what is to be counted as an injury. Objectors will point to the potentially arbitrary lines which this formulation might require. While I am sensitive to such critics they do not carry the day. They are the intellectual Luddites of the litigation system. Their objections are based either, in good faith, on the redistributive anomalies which accident compensation throws up or, more mischievously, on a secret desire to return to the formalities of a system of pleading which operates to the satisfaction only of lawyers and to the glorification of none. Both are mistaken. A comprehensive accident insurance scheme is such an enormous leap forward from our present haphazard, arbitrary and capricious tort scheme that it cannot and ought not to be jeopardized by the sensibilities of radical reformers or conservative critics.

Why have such schemes not been introduced if they are so desirable and workable? The answer is simple: there are no votes in accident compensation. Legislators daily make rules with little expectation that they will have any substantial impact upon people's lives; they are directed towards future electoral prospects. Accident victims are a diffuse class and lack an effective lobbying voice. As has been astutely noted, "the average man is not greatly stimulated by potential difficulties: until they actually beset him he remains an optimist and a sturdy supporter of what is familiar"; see *Compensation for Personal Injury in New Zealand* (1967), s.14. Like the New Zealanders, I believe the people of Canengaustrus have begun to realize that accidents regularly befalling large numbers of their fellow citizens are not so much due to human error as to the complicated and uneasy environment in which we live. It is the risk of social progress; its cost ought to be shared among society. As Judge Fuchs said in *Montgomery v. Daniels, 38* N.Y. 41 (1975):

> "I believe that the concept that the individual is the basic and ultimate unit in society must be supported by recognition of the value of one's physical, mental and emotional integrity, including freedom from pain and suffering and the ability to live an uncrippled life. The automobile, a modern bane and boon, daily threatens that integrity for millions of people."

Finally, there is the moral and legal dilemma of the rescue situation. Although the introduction of the proposed scheme ameliorates the plight of the injured, our concern must be to reduce the incidence of injury. The attempt to increase safety and reinforce moral standards of care through the tort system has been an unmitigated disaster. The appropriate device for such control is the criminal law. It focuses on the punished behaviour that is morally culpable.

The offences of careless driving and unhygienic preparation of food are obvious illustrations. Similarly, the failure to effect an easy rescue can be dealt with in this way. As in Vermont and Czechoslovakia, it ought to be a criminal offence to fail to rescue someone who is in imminent and serious danger when there is no serious danger to the potential rescuer; see Vt. Stat. Anne. tit. 12, § 519 (supp. 1971) and C.S.R. 1964, Oblansky Zakonik, ss. 415-19.

Not only is criminal law a more efficacious deterrent than tort law, but it encourages us to take a more caring, less alienated attitude towards our fellow citizens. As such, it is a natural corollary to a comprehensive insurance scheme. Anyone who is injured in a rescue attempt will automatically be compensated. Also, it seems entirely proper, and accords with common law morality, that the "rescuer" ought to be criminally liable whether or not the victim is injured, if there existed a serious possibility of injury. Finally, we should not underestimate the moralizing power of the criminal law. Law must not only keep up with morality, but give moral guidance to the less sure or weaker among us.

My support for the early implementation of a new compensation scheme has created a dilemma for me in disposing of the present case. Do I act today as a legislator and introduce such a scheme or give the legislators one last chance? Reluctantly, I have decided to stay my hand. This is not for fear of upsetting the insurance markets or because all existing mechanisms for compensation would grind to a halt. Rather, out of deep respect for our constitutional traditions, I defer to the legislators this one last time. I will uphold the decision of the lower court. The patent absurdity and inequity of that result is not lost on me. I can only hope it is not lost on others too.

LEFFT, J.: The writing of this judgment has been an occasion of very mixed blessings. It is very sad in that it is the last judgment I ever intend to give. It concludes a legal career that I now view as being an embarrassing and inexcusable dissipation of energy and time. Yet it is an occasion of happiness for me as well. I have finally come to accept the true nature of the enterprise that I have participated in as lawyer and judge for the past forty years. I have moved from the shadows into the light. Stepping through the veil of my ideological ignorance, I see the existing world for what it is—horrible, depressing and unnerving. Yet this is not a harbinger of despair, but a case for some small hope. The circumstances of my "conversion" provide some explanation and offer some encouragement to others.

While strolling through Memorial Park recently, my attention was caught by a young group of demonstrators who were distributing leaflets. Out of idle curiosity, I went over to listen. The pamphlet contained a battery of staggering statistics and information: every minute the world spends $1.3 million on military objectives and thirty children die through lack of food or health care; one nuclear submarine costs more than the annual education budget of twenty-three developing countries with 160 million school children; the United States government paid farmers to take over forty million hectares of land out of production while 450 million people in the world starved. These figures went on ad nauseam. As I left the Park, I walked through a run-down part of Ottloncanwash. Ragged children played in the dirty streets and asked me for money as I passed. Families lived in dilapidated buildings. People lined up at hostels for food and shelter. Deprivation and degradation were everywhere. The contrast with my own pleasant neighbourhood was stark and sickening.

That night and over the following days, I agonized over that experience. Whichever way I looked at it, I could not avoid the conclusion that I had previously rejected, but always feared; that the judicial process is a major force in creating, sustaining and justifying our social situation. As organs of state power, the courts must accept their share of responsibility for the plight of the homeless and the poor. Judges hold in place the deep structure of society that sacrifices people for profits.

The vast paraphernalia of legal rights and entitlements amount to nothing more than a sugar coating on a bitter pill. Although suffering and domination are rife within society, the ideal of governance according to the Rule of Law masks these offensive facts. Far from being a vehicle for social justice, the law represents a formidable barrier to significant social change. Lord Scarman is correct in stating that "the law ... operates not in Utopia, but in the world as it is"; see *Sidaway v. Bethlehem Royal Hospital Governors*, [1985] 1 All E.R. 643 at 665. But more is the pity for that.

The ideological potency of the law is subtle and profound. It contrives to be both friend and enemy. It persuades us that contemporary life is almost rational and just. Although there are blemishes and sores, this is the best there is. Certainly better than the anarchy that would thrive in the absence of law. It is the natural and, therefore, inevitable form of an ordered social life. Distinct from the naked power play of party politics, the judicial process is a passive conduit of an elusive rationality. The law claims to be neutral between individuals who self-interestedly determine their own social universe. Yet this simplistic process hides substantial and manifest injustice. The legal process places society in a condition of bondage. A powerful instrument of mystification, it breeds a false sense of moral security and political resignation. Yet its continued success depends on our acquiescence. Like Canengaustrusian Railways, the legal and political process is sustained in bankruptcy by a sinister combination of naivety, self-interest and fear of alternatives; see, for example *Bromley L.B.C. v. Greater London Council*, [1982] 2 W.L.R. 92.

Of course, judges are not neutral or neutered political agents. Judgments are rationalizations of our ideological prejudices. The legal order is not a coherent moral scheme, but an elaborate shell to facilitate and protect concrete economic interests dressed up in doctrinal gibberish; see *Rondel v. Worsely*, [1969] A.C. 191. Accidental death and injury are not only individual psycho-medical problems, but are components of a pervasive socio-economic system. They are not conditions that can be isolated and cauterized, like non-malignant tumours, from the body politic. The problem is more rooted and bespeaks a cancerous society. It is the very structure of social relations that must be attacked, if we are to achieve any meaningful and effective change.

Although the judicial function is carried on in diverse, ingenious and sophisticated forms and often with genuine and well-intentioned sincerity, as the judgments of my former colleagues amply demonstrate, the judiciary cannot escape indictment in this grand affair. Doctrin, C.J., Mill and Wright, J.J. may be the chief culprits, but Prudential, J. is fully implicated. Her criticisms of the others are valid as far as they go, but she remains firmly within this unfortunate tradition. Although variously expressed and disguised, their judgments are nothing more than a crutch for a terminally ill society. Each one legitimates the tragic toll of human life in our industrialized society. They present accidents and injuries as an inescapable and natural feature of modern life. But I do not think that there can be any real improvement unless there is a crucial shift in the way people think about themselves as members of a community. Individuals must comprehend that life in a community entails mutual obligations and interdependence. The present attitude toward health and misfortune reveals its impoverished sense of community and its modern tendency to bureaucratic solutions. Society is institutionally incapable of imagining alternative modes of social life other than an anarchic individualism or a bureaucratic collectivism; organisational parasites locked in a destructive embrace that is crushing contemporary society. Although there has been a general movement from charity to citizen rights, from special to universal schemes, from minimal to optimal payments, from private to public sources, the efficiency dictates of a market economy have always constrained this progress. So profound is their commitment to the status quo that one judge has gone so far as to condemn enterprise liability as "socialistic"; see *Markle v. Mulholland Inc.*, 509 P. 2d 529 at 546 (1973).

While they disagree about the redistributive role of the state, all the judges envision a similar kind of just society. The basic dynamic is individualistic and competitive. The only shared experience is one of isolation and fragmentation. However, although feting the individual and celebrating personal freedom and action, the law recommends a set of social organizing principles that rest on a pessimistic notion of human personality. Individuals are, at best, ambivalent to others; at worst, they are distrustful of others. By expecting the worst of human nature, a collective lifestyle is entrenched that stifles the full potential of each person to care for others and instead treats others as foes, not friends.

The attitudes of all my colleagues toward compensation exemplify the full force of this wretched situation. The common law task is to restore individuals to the position they were in before the accident. In its more grandiloquent moments, tort insists on the "general underlying principle ... that whoever unlawfully injures another shall make him whole;" see *Bullerdick v. Pritchard*, 8 P. 2d 705 at 706 (1932). Prudential, J. does not object to this standard: he wants all of society to bear this burden and to make compensation available regardless of the injury's particular cause. Clearly, these proposals represent a substantial improvement over prevailing arrangements. Yet, they are much too limited in their remedial and distributive ambitions. Prudential, J. shares with his colleagues the same objective: to ensure through the payment of money and the provision of institutional health care that victims are reconstituted. Victims can then resume their roles as rugged operatives in the bruising market of individual competition. Where the misfortune is too great to allow such reconstruction, the aim is to ensure that the individual is able to live out her days in reduced physical discomfort, at a minimal level of material satisfaction; see *Sharman v. Evans*, [1977] 138 C.L.R. 563 and *Lim v. Camden H.A.*, [1980] A.C. 174. Economics and efficiency always temper care and concern. Health has been converted into another commodity to be traded for and traded off in the market. Human life and suffering represent just one more variable in the production-consumption equation. As the court put it in *Helene Curtis Inds. Inc. v. Pruitt*, 385 F. 2d 841 at 862 (1967), "the balancing [between the need for adequate recovery and viable enterprises] ... involves a determination of the most just allocation of the risk of loss *between members of the marketing chain*". The victim is reduced to a weak link.

This obscene reduction of people to a piece of property reaches its most egregious form in the arguments of Mill, J. His bottom line is that it does not pay to be too careful. Indeed, he seems committed to the view that the taking of certain safety precautions would be unjust as they will squander valuable social resources. Even if we took such ludicrous and despicable talk of a market in accidents seriously, the law is concerned with particular accidents and, if "efficiency" has any value, it is only over the totality of accidents; see *O'Shea v. Riverway Towing*, 677 F. 2d 1194 at 1201 (1982). Of course, the very notion of "efficiency" is anathema. We would not contemplate using "efficiency" to justify tortured confessions, slavery or baby markets, so why rely on it to determine the incidence of death and injury? While characteristically extreme, Mill J.'s supposedly rational scheme shows the political bias of his colleagues. Rationality is not a formal device, but embodies a deep structure of values. Although the courts would not enforce a $1 million bargain to undergo a .000001 chance of death, they would enforce the payment of a $1 bus ride which, statistically, offers a far higher risk of injury.

Nonetheless, the excesses of Mill, J. must not be allowed to deflect criticism from his colleagues. All combine in their treatment of injury and death as economic events. Each accident is considered remedial by the payment of money.

People are simply their property; their worth is measured by the value of that "capital asset"; see *Graham v. Baker* (1961), 106 C.L.R. 340. As Oscar Wilde might have said, "the law knows the price of everybody, but the value of nobody." For instance, the bulk of a damages award consists of a sum for discounted future earnings; see *Andrews v. Grand & Toy Alta. Ltd.*, [1978] 2 S.C.R. 229 and *Seffert v. Los Angeles Transit Lines*, 56 Cal. 2d 498 (1961). This means that, for exactly the same injuries, an infant may get $100,000, a young adult $250,000, and a senior citizen $30,000. A victim's worth is her or his income loss.

Indeed, the whole law of damages is not only based on "unprovable predictions, metaphysical assumptions and rationalized empiricism", but on a vicious conservatism; see *Skelton v. Collins* (1966), 115 C.L.R. 94 at 118 per Windeyer, J. With bare-faced condescension, the courts sanction the child of an unemployed plasterer receiving substantially less in damages than one similarly injured whose father owns a prosperous business. The reason is that the children will likely "follow in father's footsteps"; see *Connolly v. Camden & Islington A.H.A.*, [1981] 3 All E.R. 250 and *Arnold v. Teno*, [1978] 2 S.C.R. 287. Furthermore, not only does the law of damages, by preserving the income of claimants, perpetuate the existing maldistribution of wealth, the rules on collateral benefits extend the gap between rich and poor. For instance, whereas private insurance need not be brought into account, some public provisions, like unemployment benefits, reduce the plaintiff's recovery; see *Bradburn v. G.W. Rwy* (1874), L.R. 10 Ex. 1 and *Redding v. Lee* (1983), 47 A.L.R. 241. Mindful that it is the richer among us who carry private insurance and the poorer who depend on public benefits, the law manages to exacerbate economic inequality in even tragic circumstances.

In all its guises, the whole process of accident compensation serves to dehumanize. It encourages the maker of Pintos to act as it does and, more, to claim moral and political legitimacy for its economic endeavours. Compensation for injury simply pays off our collective conscience. We add insult to injury by offering cold cash instead of communal support. We can ignore the injured by pretending to have taken care of them. It escapes me why "the common law has ... not embraced the *embarrassing* moral perception that he who failed to feed the man dying from hunger has truly killed him"; see *Jaensch v. Coffey,* [1984] 54 A.L.R. 417 at 439 per Deane, J. If the judges identified more with the hungry than with the moralist, the law might become socially relevant. Accident victims must become moral subjects involved in their own rehabilitation and not administrative objects of state-enforced benevolence. Our law reflects a profound indifference to life and suffering: its crassness dents further the already battered self-esteem of the injured victim. The sentiments of Esher, M.R. in *Le Leivre v. Gould,* [1893] 1 Q.B.491 at 497 that "a man is entitled to be as negligent as he pleases towards the whole world if he owes no duty to them" still inform the law. In 1969, Breitel, J. in *Tobin v. Grossman,* 24 N.Y. 2d 609 (1969) held that a mother who did not see, but heard and came upon the aftermath of a bad accident to her son could not recover; "this is the risk of living and bearing children."

No matter how comprehensive or generous, compensation schemes only address part of the problem. They are all cure and no prevention. Compensation must be subordinated to safety and health. The overriding objective of the law must be to equalize risk throughout society and restore control of those risks to those who undergo the dangers flowing from such risks. Of course, it will never be possible to eliminate risk in our lives. But the second-best alternative is to ensure that all persons can decide the risks to which they are individually exposed. We must share risk collectively and equally. Achieving this objective demands a complete restructuring of all aspects of social life. The time to begin such an heroic effort is well past. As well-intended as they are, Prudential, J.'s proposals will function as much as a crutch for crippled society as a means for social improvement. Instead of simply treating individual symptoms, our response to injury must take in the total environment in which people live, work, play and die. The democratic control of risk must be of at least the same importance as the treatment of injury and misfortune.

The first step must be to redistribute knowledge and information. The corporate elite hold a monopoly on knowledge which comprises the foundation and guarantee of its power. Indeed, this very assumption of information-deprivation is the motive force of Mill, J.'s "efficiency" scheme. He treats transaction costs as a natural given rather than a political choice. The debacle of the Ford Pinto case illustrates the pernicious operation of a system based on an unequal distribution of knowledge. The possibility of bargaining with a manufacturer over the safety of a car you wish to buy is fanciful. What does a consumer know of a product compared to its manufacturer? For instance, the purchaser of the thalidomide drug lacked adequate resources to discover information about it in order to make a truly informed choice about using it. The fact that the manufacturer possessed, but concealed the available information compounds the injustice; see H. Teff and C.

Munro, *Thalidomide: The Legal Aftermath* (1976).

Throughout our lives we are constantly exposed to risk, but starved of proper information as to the extent of that risk. Moreover, exposure to risk is thoroughly maldistributed. White and blue collar workers do not face the same risk of injury. Whereas a manager of a quarrying company has a .004 chance of injury, a quarryman has a .098 chance; see 2 *Royal Commission on Civil Liability and Compensation for Personal Injury* (1978). Furthermore, the quarryman does not receive compensation for this exposure in his wages, but earns substantially less than the manager. The reliance on choice as a justification is, of course, hopelessly unrealistic. As the court in *Green v. Sterling Extruder Corp.*, 471 A. 2d. 15 at 21 (1984) said, "the practicalities of the workaday world are such that ... the employee works 'as is' or he is without a job." As regards domestic injuries, incidence of injury depends on the quality of the product bought which, of course, is a function of wealth. In the instant case, Derek is more exposed to injury in his old jalopy than is Anne in her expensive sports car. Also, the level of environmental pollution to be endured is higher in poorer residential areas than in richer ones; there is a strong inverse relationship between smog levels and property values.

Finally, the notion of risk-sharing proposed is neither novel nor radical. Although its pervasive implementation would revolutionize society, its general validity is recognized and upheld by existing doctrine. Only the English courts have refused to incorporate it into the law; see *Sidaway v. Bethlehem Royal Hospital Governors*, [1985] 1 All E.R. 643. Although artificially confined to medical situations, a clear feature of tort law is "informed consent";

see *Cobbs v. Grant,* 8 Cal. 3d 229 (1972) and *Reibl v. Hughes,* [1980] 2 S.C.R. 880. Doctors are required to supply their patients with all the necessary and available facts of the material risks of a procedure in order for there to be intelligent consent. As the court declared in *Canterbury v. Spence,* 474 F. 2d 772 at 780 (1972):

> "The root premise is the concept ... that 'every human being of adult years and of sound mind has a right to determine what shall be done with his own body ...' True consent to what happens to one's self is the informed exercise of a choice, and that entails an opportunity to evaluate knowledgeably the options available and the risk attendant upon each."

This requirement rests upon a person's right of self-determination. Founded on the need to promote individual responsibility and to encourage informed decision-making, it is impliedly defended and espoused by all of my former judicial colleagues. Yet it remains arbitrarily and illogically confined to peripheral situations. If it were not held in check, it would consume the whole of the tort law. Its present constriction highlights the arbitrary character and deep indeterminacy of the law and reveals the illegitimate hierarchy of power its confinement serves to sustain.

In taking my leave of this court, I implore you to follow my lead. I dedicate my remaining years to this struggle. Humanity stands on the edge of the abyss. We must re-group and make good on our commitment to ourselves. Love and power must converge. We must give voice to the inarticulate speech of the heart. Victims of the world unite. In the eternal words of John Donne:

No man is an Island, entire of itself;
Every man is a piece of the Continent, a part of the
main.
Any man's death diminishes me,
Because I am involved in Mankind;
And therefore never send to know for whom the bell
tolls;
It tolls for thee.